LANGUAGE HABITS
IN HUMAN AFFAIRS

Those who copy animals *must* behave as *dog*matists, *cat*egorists, absolutists, "know-alls"; they must become fanatical, intolerant; when they meet others of their kind, a fight must follow, etc. They do not want to think, they are not interested in investigating, for why should they? They "know it all," they are self-satisfied in their ignorance, they "know" that they "know all," which is all there is to know about it. They will persecute others who think. For them thinking and science are crimes, or, at best, an unnecessary waste of time; and, if forced to think, it is a serious pain to them. They take everything for granted. Critical thought and the spirit of inquiry are entirely foreign to their makeup.

(1924)

In the old days philosophers amused themselves with writing books on the art of controversy; it is equally amusing to study the reverse—the art of abolishing controversy. Which one is more useful, more *human*? Which more animalistic?

(1926)

To achieve adjustment and sanity and the conditions which follow from them, we must study structural characteristics of this world *first*, and, then only, build languages of similar structure, instead of habitually ascribing to the world the primitive structure of our language. All our doctrines, institutions, etc., depend on verbal arguments. If these arguments are conducted in a language of wrong and unnatural structure, our doctrines and institutions must reflect that linguistic structure and so become unnatural, and inevitably lead to disasters.

(1933)

ALFRED KORZYBSKI

Language Habits
in Human Affairs

An Introduction to General Semantics

WITH A FOREWORD BY
ALFRED KORZYBSKI

><><><><><><><><><><><><><><><><><><><><><><><

IRVING J. LEE, Ph.D.
School of Speech and University College
Northwestern University

><><><><><><><><><><><><><><><><><><><><><><><

HARPER & BROTHERS PUBLISHERS
New York   London

To my Mother and Father

CONTENTS

CONTENTS

FOREWORD

×××

Language Habits in Human Affairs by Dr. Irving J. Lee
appears to be a quite unique and most needed book in these
troubled years.

Language problems are extremely complex, perhaps comparable with the complexities of human life itself. A great
many learned treatises have been written throwing side-
lights on this important subject, but to my knowledge no
writer has analyzed language as an essential part of *human
living*. If we stop to reflect, we must face the fact that
every human being is born into a *neuro*-linguistic and
neuro-semantic environment from which there is no escape.
At present sciences are taking care of deadly environmental
dangers such as plagues, epidemics, factory conditions
where harmful chemicals are used which slowly kill off
the workers, etc. But the academic linguists in their de-
tachment and interest in abstract verbiage somehow disregard our *neuro*-linguistic and *neuro*-semantic environ-
ments as *environment*, and therefore do not (and, perhaps,
could not) produce any constructive practical results in
building up sanity in education, and so ultimately in human
living. It is true that these academicians and verbalists
would have to know more about *living* human reactions.
They would have to study not only neurology, psychiatry,
general semantics, verbalisms written or spoken in hospitals
for the "mentally" ill, etc., but also the pathological reactions found in politicians, journalists, etc., and even in
educators and scientists.

Dr. Lee has a significant title for a chapter, "Language
for the Living." I am sorry he has not yet written a whole
book on "Language and Human Destruction" in which the
language habits of such sick individuals as Hitler, Goeb-

bels, etc., are analyzed. Today the world at large has to consider a serious situation, unparalleled in history, where a few sick individuals, through verbal distortions, falsifications, identifications, etc., have trained a whole generation in a pathological use of our *neuro*-semantic and *neuro*-linguistic mechanisms, whereas one of the main assets of humanity is the constructive use of these mechanisms. This sick use of language affects, after all, the rest of mankind who read or even listen to gossip based on improper evaluation.

The issues ahead, extremely serious in their consequences, involve ultimately the sanity of the race, which unsound *neuro*-linguistic reactions will not solve.

No matter who wins this war, we will have to talk things over, which means the use of language. The future thus depends upon our ability to discover and use the methods of sanity in speech and action. Distorted *neuro*-linguistic performances by present-day abnormal "Führers" have already affected the linguistic habits of politicians, etc., who knew how to abuse language before, but not to such a pathological extent. Already endless harm has been done to the public and military morale, and special measures will have to be taken to prevent the contagious disease of the pathological use of language from being perpetuated indefinitely.

This book seems to be a sound attempt in the new and constructive direction. Its theoretical foundations are solid, presented in a common-sense practical language. Besides, from his long study the author gives a wealth of examples which are very illuminating and important. For years I have been hoping that a student of general semantics would write just such a book. I am satisfied that Dr. Lee has done it. In my own work I shall have to keep his book on my desk as a handbook that I may benefit from his erudition and examples.

The solution of human problems usually depends upon a consciousness of the difficulties. Even quicksand is not dangerous once we are forewarned. Up to now the quicksands and dangers inherent in the abuse of *neuro*-linguistic and *neuro*-semantic mechanisms have been entirely neglected; and so, not forewarned, we plunged blindly ahead into difficulties.

I do not see how any honest and intelligent person can claim honesty and intelligence if he is not aware through reading this book what language as a living issue can do.

It is a mistake to assume that "all" politicians, lawyers, newspapermen, etc., are corrupt; that most "educators" are uneducated misfits; that most scientists, physicians, etc., are unscientific, etc. It is enough to realize that willy-nilly they are caught in the deadly quicksands of *neuro*-linguistic issues, about which no one forewarned them, for the average linguists themselves do not know of these dangers. I hope Dr. Lee's book will be read widely and applied, so that some present and impending dangers to humanity and culture will be eliminated.

ALFRED KORZYBSKI

PREFACE

It is no accident that the role of language habits in human affairs should be studied today. As in that other time,

> . . . we are here as on a darkling plain
> Swept with confused alarms of struggle and flight,
> Where ignorant armies clash by night.

When the "confused alarms" become too piercing, when the old "certainties" have given way, and we grope for new orientations, it is almost inevitable that attention will center on our means of evaluation. And language, serving as the vehicle of our ways of thinking, becomes a matter of concern. As Kenneth Burke so acutely put it, "In periods of firmly established meanings, one does not *study* them, one *uses* them."

The history of these times will be written in words, but we here and now in 1941 know that there was fighting with them as well. The wielders of power realized too well that words could be used as weapons; and while the outward objectives may have been territories and supplies, the fastening and enchaining of men's minds came as deeper effects.

In quieter moments someone could have argued quite persuasively that "human nature doesn't change." Of course, the human class of life remains different from that of animals and plants, and in this sense only does "human nature" persist. But observe the behavior, the responses, the modes of interpretation of any living being, and there little permanence is to be found. We have come to know the influence of climate, temperature, pressure and humidity, the role of the surrounding physical and social conditions, the place of vitamins, the effects of new eyeglasses—and a thousand other factors which shape our reactions.

But somehow we have not been so sharp in our awareness of the *linguistic* and *evaluational* factors about us. We are born in and live in a language milieu that is tremendously influential in determining what we believe and how we act. We listen to and take over existing habits of speaking and thinking which profoundly affect our ways of doing things. And if by the vagaries of existence those habits lead to confusion, misunderstanding, and conflict, we become caught in a kind of system from which escape comes only by much effort.

An historian, someday, may call this the Era of the Organized Lie. He may be mindful of the legend-making of Alexander, the imposturings of Napoleon, the distortions of Bismarck. He may know, in the words of the Editor of *Decision,*

the coarse lies of ordinary bandits, the perfumed lies of courtesans, diplomats and priests; the ponderous lies of professors, the obvious lies of journalists, the innocent lies of children, the lies of generals, sailors, poets and lunatics.

The roster may be imposing and the pages full. But it remained for an Adolf Hitler to insist that "in the size of the lie there is always contained a certain factor of credibility," and since "the great masses of a people . . . more easily fall victims to a great lie than to a small one," he who would have power over them will exploit their credulity.

It helps little to condemn the brutishness and animalistic character of such a "psychology." It is enough if we never forget that this play with words on men's minds has brought with it consequences awful and terrible.

Organized lying, however, is by no means the only verbal problem with which we are faced today. There remains something even more fundamental—the necessity of knowing how to "talk sense," of knowing how to use the gift of speech intelligently, of being able to manipulate the language in our own daily living and in our affairs with others so as to avoid the blockages, misevaluations, and cross purposes that seem so much a part of the modern world. We have here no esoteric concern with the origin or magic of the speech process, but with the practical business of human existence in which words are used. It is our view that in the affairs of men it may be as important to understand what is involved in "talking sense" as to know how to increase one's bank balance.

Some of the issues may be discovered by starting with a paragraph Chief Justice Hughes once wrote.

The arch enemies of society are those who know better, but by indirection, misstatement, understatement and slander seek to accomplish their concealed purposes or to gain profit of some sort by misleading the public. Dishonesty in purveyors of opinion is the worst of civic vices. We shall have differences enough among the sincere. Then there will always be a multitude who are congenitally unable to think straight. Freedom of expression gives the essential democratic opportunity, but self-restraint is the essential civic discipline.

There can be no quarrel with such a diagnosis, but the medicine seems somehow inadequate. Of what use is self-restraint without the knowledge and means by which "to think straight"? Of what avail is freedom of expression with the obligations of honesty, but without the ability to avoid the snares and mistakes in language use which breed the misevaluations? What good is the will to good-will without the way?

This halfway attack is symptomatic of so much contemporary analysis. Too many of our scholars have become efficient diagnosticians. They have shown very carefully what the educational and social forces have done *to* us, but they are not so explicit about what must be done *for* us. They have pointed to the ills and then left us without prescriptions. For example, Alfred North Whitehead saw with rare perception one main area of difficulty.

In the past, the time-span of important change was considerably longer than that of a single human life. Thus mankind was trained to adapt itself to fixed conditions. Today, this time-span is considerably shorter than that of a human life and accordingly our training must prepare individuals to face a novelty of conditions.

But how shall this "training" proceed? How can one go about learning how "to face a novelty of conditions"? By what specific patterns shall we be oriented? Jan Christian Smuts has pointed to another area.

Amid the evils of the world today where the tendency is to follow slogans, to run after catchwords, to worship ideologies or exalt party politics, the sovereign remedy is . . . the spirit of science which exalts fact above sectional loyalties and ideologies.

But where can one go to captutre that "spirit"? Does it come with mere preachment? What precisely must one do before that "sovereign remedy" can be put to work?

In short, we have need of methods—simple, teachable, and usable—by which to break through the conventionalized, stiffly resistant, and confusing habits of evaluation. It is all very well for John Dewey to say that we lack "freed intelligence with understanding and informed conviction to guide it." But in the business of living, in the face of people and situations, we must have not merely the philosophically enriched objective, but also the practical devices, the things to do, the ways of thinking, sharply and crisply understood and at hand. This view takes us to Whitehead's definition of education: "The acquisition of the art of utilization of knowledge." And this objective lies at the heart of Alfred Korzybski's formulation of General Semantics. In that discipline the *ways* to accuracy, discrimination, and proper evaluation are sought at every point, ending in terms and methods which even five-year-olds have been able to learn.

How does it happen that it should be necessary to emphasize the need for discrimination in our language habits today? There are many ways of answering that question. We shall focus on one that has not been given its due.

The sharp separation of the art of gaining assent from the art of making accurate statements is, perhaps, one of the most widely accepted legacies of the Platonic Dialogues. In the *Gorgias*, Socrates described two species of speech-making, "one which conveys belief without knowledge, [whereas] the other conveys knowledge." The one sought to effect belief, the other instruction. The separation, in its most debased form, is well summarized in the line often attributed to Antisthenes, a follower of Socrates: "If a boy is destined to live with Gods, teach him philosophy; if with men, rhetoric [the arts of propaganda and persuasion]."

One result of Plato's attack on the rhetoricians and public speakers of his day, along with his defense of the philosophers, was the splitting of these disciplines into two hostile, antithetical camps. Even though there is danger of oversimplifying what is in fact a long and complex history, it might well be said that most of the great disputes concerning the psychological responses of human beings, the sources of human motivation, the function of the curriculum, the nature of the educative process, the obstacles to human achievement, the role of the scholar, the place of public opinion in a democracy, etc., are built around the oppositely defined attempts, on the one hand, to influence people to believe and act, and on the other, to teach them how to know how to think and act. This schism is manifest in many forms, and whenever one digs to the heart of most of the public controversies concerned with how and why people are oriented as they are, this dichotomous monster peers through. Thus, it is a nice exercise in analysis to discover its manifestations in the following pairs of notions: Education and Propaganda, Science and Poetry, Reason and Emotion, Logic and Rhetoric, Discussion and Debate, Romance and Life, Science and Religion, Nature and Life.

In the wake of the splitting, moreover, came many important by-products. Not the least of these (and by no means insignificant today) is the practice of teaching the arts of influence separate from the arts of accuracy and adequacy. The craft of the ancient Sophists is well represented by those public practitioners who promise in the space of a semester "to teach you, too, how to influence people." The vast battery of procedures for ingratiation, the blandishments, the ways of wheedling, "the tested sentences that sell," the disguised flatteries, the easy glibness, the devices of oversimplification—all these are purchasable, like goods over a counter. Now there can be little quarrel with such instruction in so far as it results in more easy and complete communication. But when men are taught and come to be able to use the techniques of rhetoric divorced from a concern with accuracy, without regard for either the obligation or the necessity of speaking in sentences that are correct-to-fact—then the instruction will have been sold too cheaply to the buyers, and the men and women who listen may have to pay too dearly. For when their lives are guided by statements which do not correspond to what is to be found in life, then low predictability is inevitable, adaptation is complicated, and survival is made difficult.

In *Mein Kampf* Adolf Hitler has shown how he gains acceptance (pistols and brass knuckles helped, too). Guided by his dominant purpose—to get his notions across—he urges these simple rules: (1) Arguments must be directed to the "least intelligent" of the people; (2) avoid "scientific ballast" as much as possible; (3) give the simple points "thousandfold repetition"; (4) seek ever to hold the attention of the great masses; (5) seek not "the many-sidedness of scientific teaching"; (6) restate the main few points as slogans; (7) never try to become versatile, altering the methods, for the masses will not retain the idea; (8) never permit the faintest suggestion that there is "right on the other side"; (9) no halfway urgings will do; things are either "positive or negative, love or hate, right or wrong, truth or lie"; and (10) regardless of all else, keep focused on the fundamental principle, limit the program, and repeat it eternally.

Let such a program be considered part of the ground-work of the Art of Propaganda, the techniques by which to "enchant the souls" of listeners. Should this art and its attendant techniques be condemned because they work, because people are affected and overpowered by them? Our view would maintain that it is not too relevant to focus on Hitler's rhetoric, his methods of influencing his audiences. Of more importance is the question: What is the relationship of what he says to what happens, to the observable life facts which his talk is supposed to represent? How verifiable are his claims? To what extent are his judgments and conclusions manifested as statements of fact? To what degree do his assertions *properly evaluate* with discrimination and closeness the world situations about which he talks? These are the questions which the student of General Semantics wants answered.

The student of the traditional rhetoric might go on to analyze the climaxes, the elements of emphasis, euphony, metaphor, sentence length, ways of beginning, developing, and ending, etc.; and we should then know how the speaker went about his business. But if there is tragedy in Europe, we dare not stop there; we should check on the factual adequacy of the speech as well. How corrosively pedantic to discover that digressions and the personal pronoun predominate in Hitler's assertions of peacefulness, while at the very moment of utterance his armored divisions move directly and impersonally to lay waste another town!

When a Thomas Mann, a John Dewey, or an Albert Einstein speaks, he, too, will abstract but some features of the subject for discussion. He, too, will seek to limit his program, and he will repeat it. There, too, will be emphases, metaphors, and beginnings. The differences between these men and Hitler will emerge when we look at the correctness to fact, the human adequacy of the evaluation in their analyses. The methods of *presentation* may be of a piece (though with varying effectiveness), but the differences will appear when we apply the apparatus of "factual" criticism.

It is precisely at this point that the mischief of the Platonic splitting should be realized. Hitler, the ardent student of rhetoric, shaping quickly and terribly the destinies of men, and the Manns, Deweys, and Einsteins, devoted to philosophy, give us the dichotomy in practice in our time. What we need now understand is this: that that separation cannot be permitted, that we must train ourselves and our students in the two arts together. We must come to see that rhetoric without philosophy is blind, and philosophy without rhetoric empty for the multitudes of men.

If the men of science and philosophy are without the abilities to frame their formulations so laymen can both understand and use them, we shall ever be in danger of the insurrections of the ignorant. And if the men of business and law and politics know how to sell us their wares and their doctrines without the buttress of factuality and proper evaluation, then we shall be ever limping, slowly and ineffectually, through the mazes of indecision, harassed victims of the eternal dueling for our assent.

Now, perhaps as never before, are we ready for the reorientation in purpose which will unify the now dissociated arts of language use. Many teachers of Speech and English have already made the *rapprochement*. If they have been hindered in its application, it is because they do not possess the critical methods by which to get at the numerous and varying expressions of the inaccurate and the inadequate. These teachers should find the materials of General Semantics valuable because they can be applied directly and sharply.

One of Alfred Korzybski's commonplaces is the assertion that the two easiest ways to slide through life are (1) to believe everything and (2) to believe nothing. We have been exposed in the last two decades to innumerable books, speeches, and essays bent on debunking, on revealing the sham and duplicity in hundreds of areas in our public life, from the atrocity stories of World War I to the misbranding of corn-removers. Wherever those public utterances had falsified the facts, the debunkers had rendered invaluable service. One could point to the many gains in legislation and education for consumers, if nowhere else, where that agitation had positive results. But because the restiveness for accuracy was without systematized method, it too often took on the character of sheer negativism, of simple protest, so that vast numbers of the post-war second generation came to distrust whatever was said positively. Unless it was couched in terms of denial and negation, the utterance was marked "Propaganda." To dub something thus, was with one undiscriminating swoop to dismiss it. The result was a kind of critical nihilism which carried status only because it then seemed unnecessary to do the hard work of discovering whether or not, and to what extent, the statements corresponded to life facts.

Those who say that the younger generation (not "all," of course) are without "ideals" are wide of the mark. It has "ideals," but they consist too much of arguing from the premises of *some* of the earlier well-established findings without the vigorous study to see if the same factors are characteristically true today. Thus, students who read and digested Lasswell's *Propaganda Technique in the World War* and Ponsonby's *Falsehoods in Wartime* were eminently justified in their revolt against that early deception. But when they carry over their revulsion, indiscriminately and without the will to check, to the stories which come today from Poland and other Nazi-dominated provinces by arguing "That's just atrocity-story propaganda," then they are unwittingly the dupes of a tragic education and an incompletely methodized system of criticism.

It may be unkind, though unfortunately necessary, to suggest here that the Directors of the Institute for Propaganda Analysis may before long (if they have not already) have to do some soul-searching about the effects of their work. Let it be said that this writer has the utmost respect for the objectives, the integrity, and the good will of the sponsors of that organization. They have done remarkable work in making thousands of students conscious of distortions and misdirections in so much contemporary public speaking and writing. But they, too, have not been guiltless, if after studying their bulletins, students throughout the United States come to distrust in undiscriminating fashion whatever they hear and read. If students have learned to *resist* rather than to *analyze*, then the harm has been done. It is true, of course, that the Institute Secretary and his fellow workers want and try to get Propaganda Analysis, but the net effect of following their advice explicitly and closely has, with this writer's students at any rate, resulted unfortunately in the creation of attitudes of undifferentiated skepticism and resistance. To the charge that he has taught poorly, this instructor has no defense. But if the same effects have been noticed by other teachers, then other factors must be studied. Incidentally, several reviewers of the Institute's recent publication, *War Propaganda in the United States* by Wechsler and Lavine, have pointed to the something less than "objective analysis" to be found there.

Our purpose, again, is not to deride or malign the Institute. It is rather to suggest that the analytical method urged by this organization is defective. That method focused primarily on what was described above as rhetorical considerations, on how audiences are influenced and persuaded, and only secondarily on the many variants of the correct-to-fact considerations. Now there is nothing "wrong" with the study of rhetoric, but students will be hopelessly misled if they assume that a rhetorical analysis gives them the results of a semantic analysis. This confusion is particularly destructive for "intelligence" because of the neglect of the peculiar character of the rhetorical process. Rhetorical criticism, whether we like it or not, can be turned back on the critic of rhetorical practices in others. For example, the first of their devices (used in "bad," undemocratic propaganda), the giving of "bad" labels, is called *Name Calling*. But is not the Institute guilty of using "subversive" tactics when it *name calls* the process of giving names *Name Calling*? Is not that term used with intent to describe the process invidiously? There is something involved here of importance, but it will be got at not by a rhetorical but by a semantic approach (see Chapter XI).

And because of the rhetoric-semantic confusion, one could with much relevance proceed to apply a seven-common-propaganda-devices analysis to the bulletins of the Institute, for they, too, must use the devices (it can't be helped) in the effort to persuade readers to use them on others. There can be no persuasion, no system of inducement without the giving of names, the use of witnesses and testimony, the making of general statements, the methods of transfer, etc. These are, after all, merely characterizations of the elements of discourse in use. And if the Editors sought to be thorough, they could have gone to the rhetoricians of the last three centuries where they should have found in the figures of thought a hundred additional tricks.

If the Propaganda Analysis people come to grief with their devices, it will probably be because, as one critic put it, they did not add an eighth, "Not Distinguishing Fact from Opinion." A systematic exploration of the ramifications of this notion would, perhaps, have brought them to the *malaise* of our time, and in addition, to a set of critical instruments for which there is stout defense.

Starting with "facts and opinions," the analyst will have to see that statements of fact are not life facts. In old-fashioned terms, *noumena* are not *phenomena*. Language acts to represent both words and non-verbal life facts; the relationship is the same as that between a map and the territory. It would then follow, because life and nature are complex, that any discussion of human affairs must leave out some details and that conclusions cannot encompass "all" of any life facts. A thoroughgoing consciousness of abstracting on the part of the reader or listener will serve to disclose and correct his own weaknesses and egotisms. The Propagandist of the Lie can function at his best when the human object of his work ceases "thinking." The task of the teacher is ever that of giving the means by which the student can by himself discipline himself. We must be equally vigilant in seeing that we do not spend our energies warning against the depredations of others. The first line of defense is the fortification of our own "ways of looking" at the world. Only after we have overcome the impulse to dogmatize and project our judgments on to others will we be ready for the larger criticism of what others do.

It will be necessary, then, in the task of self-analysis to realize that, no matter what anyone says, the hard facts of nature, the surrounding phenomena with which we can be acquainted, are never modified by talk. Only human responses can be affected by the value of words. Not until a set of words is accepted, consciously or unconsciously, by someone has the propagandist's work been effectual. But statements which influence people are not all alike, and enormous difficulties result when we fail to distinguish at least two differing varieties.

The one is closely related to what can be found on observation and from direct experience. If in life we discover that objects, situations, people, etc., are definitely diverse, each unique and different in some respects from others, then our talk about them should express that diversity, that uniqueness. And if public discourse would deny or obscure those differences, informed students must act as public defenders. And when a Mortimer J. Adler lumps together "semanticists" for public flaying, he rather readily emphasizes the uncritical character of his utterance. Any careful inspection must reveal *many* (at least five current today) differing semantic systems and modes of training, each moving from different premises, with different methods, to different goals. To talk and write as if they were *identical* is with little subtlety, in this one area at least, to argue the virtues of any kind of educational discipline.

If the findings of our "best" researchers today indicate that "things" exist as wholes, we shall be misled if we act as if they existed in parts. If in our talk we split what is not to be found so split in nature, our talk is better classified as fiction and fancy. And if social legislation and public policy are forever built on such atomistic evaluation, we should not be surprised if somewhere the lives of some are tragically misshapen. There is little harm if we talk fancifully so long as we are conscious of what we do and do not then proceed to act as if we had talked factually. Thus, there is little reason to object to conversation about "heredity" *and* "environment" as if these *elementalistic* terms did not artificially split the unitary, non-separable (except verbally) influences in a man's life. But when doctrines and laws are formulated in favor of one group *on the assumption* that by "heredity" it is "superior," then the full fury of a Nazi persecution seems to have both foundation and justification. Careful study of the discordant relationship between the language and the life facts must reveal the falsity of that claim. When we have learned something of the scope and possibility of incorrect-to-fact talking, we may for the first time glimpse the tragedy of any study which does not take it into account.

To be able to know when talk fits the discoverable aspects of life and nature is, thus, to understand one significant set of language habits. This notion of "fitness" as the ingredient of accurate language use is by no means current in popular discussion, though it should be.

The other kind of talk, by and large, is in terms which do not sharply relate to concrete and specific observations and experiences. This sort cannot be tested by the familiar notions of "trueness" and "falsity." We refer here to talk which represents primarily what goes on *inside-the-skin* of the speaker or writer, his attitudes, "sensations," "feelings," etc., and not *outside*. Only he can judge the adequacy of this verbal representation. Urgings, pleadings, exhortings, harangues belong in this classification, as do all efforts of one person to make another, by a kind of "sympathetic induction," *feel* similarly. Here, too, belong all utterances which deal with personal preferences, choices, desires, and wishes based on no public modes of testing. Inferences, judgments, hypotheses, hunches, and opinions are likewise different from statements of fact, as are highly general, unlimited, and inclusive terms and sentences which represent no particular actions, people, situations, etc.

In too many areas public discussion today fails to discriminate between these two kinds of discourse, which, in effect, describe two modes of orientation, the one by life facts, the other by verbal association. There may be little new in such description, but there is much here that is neglected in daily practice. When men react to one as if it were the other, confusion must inevitably result. Any attempts to provide a basis for propaganda analysis, "good sense," "clear thinking," etc., must first build a fundamental consciousness of and ability to recognize each when it is met.

Starting here, the student of General Semantics proceeds to set up systematically (1) the characteristics of life facts about which speakers must be aware, (2) the host of language habits which represent those life facts inadequately, and (3) specific, usable, and teachable devices by which to make his language habits produce proper evaluation of what he talks about.

In 1939, talking to freshmen, Robert M. Hutchins said, "It is hard to think that education is important when the world is on fire; the temptation is to rush out and join the fire department." We should here translate the issue this way: Firemen have to learn how to be efficient in the handling of ladders and hoses; and should students find themselves amid the conflagrations of prejudice, social confusion, and unreflecting disorder, they, too, had better learn how to deal with them before the flames consume *them*.

I am obligated to some fifty writers and publishers for permission to quote from their works. The references for each appear in the footnotes. Without this body of available material it would have been most difficult to show (1) that there already exists a favorable climate of opinion, that the doctrines of General Semantics represent a systematization of what has long been "known" but not applied, and (2) that examples of "bad" language habits abound in as many areas of human life as one can read about.

Many others had a role in the preparation of this book. I am grateful to the Deans and members of the faculties of the School of Speech and University College of North-western University for the opportunity to offer courses on Language and Thought in which most of the formulations were tested and discussed.

I am happy to record my thanks to Miss Mildred Waltrip of Chicago, commercial artist and fine student, who made the twenty-eight line drawings. These are worth close study. Indeed, one of the sharpest measures of the reader's understanding of the principles is his ability to apply them to the drawings, and, in reverse, to use the drawings to clarify his own utterances.

The careful reading and criticism which Miss M. Kendig, Educational Director of the Institute of General Semantics, gave the manuscript did much to clarify and sharpen the statements on almost every page. Her understanding of the problems involved in teaching this subject matter proved invaluable in the decisions which had to be made about the mode of presentation. It is a pleasure to acknowledge my debt to her.

My obligation to Count Alfred Korzybski is a great one, for it was only after study with him that this book became possible. In one sense I do little more here than provide documentation for points of view already developed in *Science and Sanity*, and summarized in his seminars. My awareness of obligation stems not only from the fact that the basic views were his, but from the experience of working with a man whose "uncommon common sense" was leavened with the will to give freely of his time and energy without concern for personal considerations. The time-binding functions are encouraged and well represented by such unselfishness.

I am eager, also, to acknowledge that the existence of this book is due in large measure to the patience and effort of my wife, Laura Louise Lee, whose assistance in the preparation of the manuscript was immeasurable.

Irving J. Lee

Evanston, Illinois
October, 1941

LANGUAGE HABITS
IN HUMAN AFFAIRS

CHAPTER I

LANGUAGE FOR THE LIVING

This book has to do with words.

They can be studied in many different ways. How does a language develop? How does English differ from Aramaic or Sanskrit? What are the peculiar features of the structure of our language? Why bother with grammar? How can words be put together so that listeners or readers will be influenced by them? What are the methods of enlarging one's vocabulary? What is wrong with slang? How are words taught to the deaf? Can one who stammers over his words be helped? How are sounds produced? What constitutes correct pronunciation? Can a man speak words unless he has ideas? What are the elements of an interesting short story, a lovely lyric, a beautiful sonnet, a piece of sparkling prose? Why do we forget some words and remember others? How does a child learn to talk? How can one acquire the precision and modulation of a radio announcer? Why is it difficult for a foreigner to speak English without an accent?

These questions will receive little attention in this book, for the grammarians, phoneticians, psychologists, pathologists, rhetoricians, and teachers of English have dealt with them elsewhere.

But they have not exhausted the problems of language. There remain almost as many. When does language become reliable? Why do people so often misunderstand each other? How much of anything can anyone talk about? How can our language habits be brought up to date to fit the most advanced findings of science? How can language be made true to fact? What are the methods of definition?

Does silence have any value? What about prophecies, prejudice, and propaganda? What uses of words breed conflict? What characterizes the speaking of men who appear cynical, cocksure, and overly certain? Is it possible to speak without bias and partiality? Under what conditions does language make for survival, and when does it make for maladjustment? How do the little words "is" and "all" often lead us to confusion? Why are we afraid of using certain four-letter words in "good company"? What are the dangers of oversimplification? How must we speak to be discriminating and critical? Is there a place for gossip, party talk, nervous chatter?

These are the questions about which this book is written. Somehow, they come to grips with human living. They have something to do with the problems mankind faces in the twentieth century. "The strategy of terror," "the mobilization of minds," "the white war," "the psychological offensive"—these phrases suggest that wars are fought with words as well as with weapons.

In the home, the office, the conference room, talk is essential and too often marked with disaster. The snarling in strikes, the bitterness of divorce trials, the mute tragedy of suicide notes, the incoherence of nervous breakdowns—here, too, words have a place.

In hoaxes, up-country witchcraft, palmistry, handouts, patent medicine testimonials, confidence games, circus barkers' spiels, shadowy promises—here, too, words are used.

When a teacher advises a student, when mediators help settle disputes, when men quietly deliberate courses of action, when marriage vows are made, when contracts are drawn up—here, too, words are necessary.

In the formulations of an Einstein, in the pages of Webster's Dictionary, in a Freud case history, in the prescription of an Ehrlich, in the technical analysis of a Russell or a Whitehead or a Dewey, in the plans of a Frank Lloyd Wright, in the reports of an Amundsen or a Byrd, in the papers of a Marconi and an Edison—here, happily for us, words also serve.

Of Beasts and Men

To be concerned with language as used by living people is to bring us to the heart of things *human*. Try, if you will, to think of human existence bereft of speech. Imagine this world within the next ten minutes rendered dumb and mute and wordless. For without language, life suddenly takes on a humanless garb. Without language, written and spoken, the silence of the day would be broken only by shadowy forms, primitive cries and grunts, the sounds of the winds and the waves, the rustle and murmur of moving things.

Language is the unique ingredient in man, for where it does not exist, there abides little that is human. A visit to the zoo may be instructive. Observe only the animals— the cockatoos, crocodiles, kangaroos, chimpanzees, sea lions, jaguars, *et al.* How shall they be described? In the simplest terms, two kinds of acts mark their lives. They subsist on plants—the produce of the energies of sun, soil, and air—and the meat of other animals. Secondly, they move about in space, crawling, running, flying, swimming. Chemistry and mobility—these terms define the functioning of the beasts.

This power of movement is not unimportant outside of the zoo. Animals do not produce food; when the natural supply is gone, they die. They must find and fight for what they eat. Survival is only for the quick and the strong.

That picture of life with the animals somehow does not commend itself to the fullness of living. Something is omitted. The sense is one of flatness, incompleteness, of too few dimensions.

Visit now a human city. Observe the elevator operators, workers with electric drills, accountants, cashiers, teachers, salesmen, actors, preachers, policemen. What marks them? What happens in their lives? They, too, eat and move about. And they do something more. They live on and off the labor and achievements of the dead and the contemporary. They can gather and use the experiences of the past as capital for their work in the present. They can accumulate. They can begin where others left off. They can learn from the agony and sweat of those who have gone before. They can produce artificially because others produced the instruments. Here, then, is a unique ingredient—the manipulation of what happens in *time*. Men can draw from the PAST, in and through the PRESENT, and make ready for the FUTURE. The experience of the race can be accumulated, worked over, magnified, and transmitted. This *time-binding capacity* marks the peculiar and characteristic feature of man.

In short,

. . . man improves, animals do not; man progresses, animals do not; man invents more and more complicated tools, animals do not; man is a creator of material and spiritual wealth, animals are not; man is a builder of civilization, animals are not.[1]

But how is this possible? In man new adjustment mechanisms, larger cortical layers, and complex associational tracts inside his skull give rise to language-using abilities. The power of symbolization gave the means by which the skill and wisdom of the race could be recorded and preserved. Our libraries serve as a gigantic memory of ideas and their fruits. And now we can use them as if they were our own.

Lin Yutang has given a sharp statement of the differences.

Man alone has invented a civilization, and this is not something to be lightly dismissed. There are perhaps finer animals with better forms and nobler structures, like the horse; with finer muscles, like the lion; with a finer sense of smell and greater docility and loyalty, like the dog; or better vision, like the eagle; or a better sense of direction, like the homing pigeon; with greater thrift and discipline and capacity for hard work, like the ant; with a sweeter temper like the dove or the deer; more pa-

[1] Alfred Korzybski, *Manhood of Humanity*. New York: E. P. Dutton & Co., 1921, 186.

tience and contentment like the cow; better singers, like the lark; and better-dressed beings, like the parrot and the peacock. . . . Granted that ants are more rational and better-disciplined beings than ourselves . . . still they haven't got a library or a museum, have they? Any time ants or elephants can invent a giant telescope or discover a new variable star or predict a solar eclipse, or seals can discover the science of calculus or beavers can cut the Panama Canal, I will hand them the championship as masters of the world and Lords of Creation.[2]

A bird builds a nest. A man builds an engine. Each used time, effort, and materials. But soon their purposes have been served. A new generation comes. The new bird builds again and the nest is little different. And the next nest not unlike it. With the new man, however, come new possibilities, new searchings, new ways of looking, new experimenting, so that when the engine is built, it is built anew. To the work of the past something is added from the present. For with the symbol-using class of life, "the power to achieve is *reinforced* by past achievement."[3] In the words of Abraham Lincoln,

Fishes, birds, beasts, and creeping things are not miners, but *feeders* and *lodgers* merely. Beavers build houses; but they build them in no wise differently or better now than they did five thousand years ago. Ants and honey bees provide food for winter; but just in the *same way* they did when Solomon referred the sluggard to them as patterns of prudence. Man is not the only animal who labors; but *he is the only one who improves his workmanship*. This improvement he effects by discoveries and inventions.[4]

To see the uniqueness of man's time-binding capacity is to begin to realize the significance of language. If we discover the creative uses of words, we may begin to know what it is to function *humanly*.

[2] Lin Yutang, *The Importance of Living*. New York: Reynal & Hitchcock, 1937, 65-66. Reprinted by permission of The John Day Company.

[3] Cassius J. Keyser, *Mathematical Philosophy*. New York: E. P. Dutton & Co., 1922, 430. Reprinted by permission.

[4] Quoted by W. N. Polakov, *Man and His Affairs*. Baltimore: Williams & Wilkins Co., 1925, 61-62. Reprinted by permission.

Think what speech has done for man. It has given him the earth. Report of a small invention in Chicago is printed in a Tokyo newspaper, in that way it becomes added to a small invention made in Tokyo, to another made in London, to another in Rome, and an airplane in consequence is accelerated fifty miles an hour. On Thursday last a discovery is completed in the Rockefeller Institute, is telephoned to Shanghai, and on the following Tuesday in consequence a life is saved in China.[5]

Similarly, if we learn how sometimes language is used to defeat those purposes, how the perversion of information comes about, how unconsciously confusion obtains, how misunderstanding is born and conflict generated—if, perhaps, these phenomena can be explained, we may in the very process be dealing with some of the deepest aspects of human living.

General Semantics

It was Henry James who said, "All life comes back to the question of our speech, the medium through which we communicate with each other." Because that has somehow been felt, an interest in words is by no means anything new. From the questionings of Socrates to the present, the roster of men who have written about the problems of language and thought is a long and distinguished one. No one who would understand the depth and complexity of what is involved can afford to neglect the questions they raised and the answers they have given. Just an introduction to the literature requires a survey of this minimum list:

1. Aristotle, *Categories; Rhetoric.*
2. Francis Bacon, *The Novum Organum.*
3. Jeremy Bentham, *Theory of Fictions.*
4. Edmund Burke, *Philosophical Inquiry into the Origin of Our Ideas of the Sublime and Beautiful.*
5. Thomas Hobbes, *Leviathan,* Book I.
6. William James, *Principles of Psychology.*
7. John Locke, *Essay on Human Understanding,* Book III.

[5] Gustav Eckstein, "Ancestors," *Harper's Magazine,* Dec., 1940, 66. Reprinted by permission.

8. J. G. Romanes, *Mental Evolution in Man.*
9. G. F. Stout, *Analytic Psychology.*
10. V. Welby, *What Is Meaning?; Significs and Language.*

It would take the pages of a long book to outline the kinds of problems they have defined with the data and arguments in support of their answers. We need not here decide why they chose to deal with the matters they did. Neither need we decide the value of their efforts. On one point alone shall we urge a judgment: that they did not come to grips with the problems we here find most relevant and absorbing. It is a question not of antithetical but of different interests. What we would emphasize finds expression in the writings of Alfred Korzybski, whose book *Science and Sanity,* first published in 1933, deals directly with matters which have not occupied the focus of attention of the other writers.

Korzybski was trained as a mathematician and an engineer in Warsaw. His work in the General Staff Intelligence Department of the Russian Army in World War I and intensive experience in the handling of prisoners had whetted his interest in human affairs, in the problems of human adjustment. That war had put into sharp focus the achievements of the physical scientists as compared with the failures of those who guide and advise us in our everyday living. On the one hand, we see bridges and buildings standing up, guns and airplanes working, steam shovels and dynamos functioning efficiently. When the engineers planned, they ended with structures which were *reliable.* When they make *predictions* in their specialties, things have a way of turning out as per specifications. But how about the men who govern our economic, political, and legal affairs? Too often for them "Prosperity is just around the corner," or "Germany just couldn't finance a war," or "If this bill is passed there'll be an end to drinking." The security we have with the engineers we do not have with the social "scientists"—if we measure their achievements. We cannot be as sure that when they predict, things will so happen.

The question that Korzybski then posed was this: If both the physical structures and the social institutions are products of human nervous systems, what does an engineer do when he builds a bridge that the social scientists do not as invariably do when they go to work? He put the answer in terms of the most easily observed activities of each— their talking. The engineer talks to himself (or calculates) in varied languages (words or figures) which are appropriate or similar in structure to the facts with which he has to deal. That is, he looks at the life facts and then makes what he has to say fit. His major effort is to make his talk, formulas, equations, etc., adequate to represent the facts. And when that is achieved, the bridges don't break down. But what of our everyday language habits in our personal affairs, in matters of community and national importance? Do we follow the efficient patterns of the engineers? Korzybski's investigations led him to a negative answer. In dealing with direct experience in the business of daily living, men were too frequently speaking in ways that did not fit the situations they were speaking about. If reliability was not consistently found, it was because the utterances too often did not fit the facts.

His study then moved to the practical, to an analysis of the ways of language use which were inadequate and mis- leading. With similarity of structure as his criterion of adequate talking, he was able to classify a host of "bad" language habits. And when these were systematized along with techniques and devices for correcting them, Korzybski had succeeded in formulating a theory and method which gave a means of proper evaluation whenever language is used. This body of data and method leading to habits of adequate language-fact relationships he called General Semantics.

One misconception may here be corrected. Korzybski's system, concerned with accuracy and predictability, must be considered as something different in emphasis from the pursuits of other "semanticists." I should distinguish several varieties of semanticists: (1) those popular writers who would debunk abstraction-makers by shouting "define your terms," (2) those students of linguistics who seek to study the history of the changes of meaning of individual words in our language, (3) the anthropologists who study the grammatical and syntactical make-up of languages of different people, (4) the lexicographers who chart the ways individual words have been used, (5) the logicians who emphasize the problems of verbal coherence and the avoidance of inconsistency *within* discourse, (6) the rhetoricians who work to discover the ways of using words for their effect in influencing attitudes and actions, together with the techniques of expression by which to achieve clarity, strength, harmony, melody, elegance, etc.

Another feature of Korzybski's effort is worth noting here. If those not trained in the habits of the engineer-at-work are to "talk sense," then the methods to be evolved must be entirely *general*—usable by a housewife, a sociologist, a lawyer, a teacher, a psychiatrist, a journalist, the engineer-at-home, or by anyone. If predictability is what we want as a function of language use, the methods of testing for its correspondence-to-facts must be applicable wherever speech occurs. That is to say, if he has uncovered methods of "proper evaluation," they should be workable in testing and prescribing for as many different kinds of speech-using situations as there are. That Korzybski's findings do give *general methods* is attested by reports of workers in a large number of special fields. It may be useful here to list some titles of published materials, enough to give a sense of the general applications in which Korzybski's influence has been acknowledged:

Dentistry

Louis G. Barrett, "General Semantics and Dentistry," *Harvard Dental Record,* June, 1938. Also, "Evaluational Disorders and Caries: Semantogenic Symptoms," *Journal of the American Dental Association,* Nov., 1939.

Ecology

Edward F. Haskell, "Mathematical Systematization of 'Environment,' 'Organism' and 'Habitat,' " *Ecology*, Jan., 1940.

English and Speech

S. I. Hayakawa, *Language in Action*, 1941.

Wendell Johnson, *Language and Speech Hygiene: An Application of General Semantics*, 1939.

Irving J. Lee, "General Semantics and Public Speaking," *The Quarterly Journal of Speech*, Dec., 1940.

General Education

Vernon L. Bowyer, "Some Educational Implications of Semantics," *Chicago Schools Journal*, Nov.-Dec., 1940.

D. G. Campbell, "General Semantics in Education, Counseling, and Therapy," *National Education Association Proceedings*, 1939.

M. Kendig, "Language Re-Orientation of High School Curriculum and Scientific Control of Neuro-Linguistic Mechanisms for Better Mental Health and Scholastic Achievement," Presented before Educational Section, A.A.A.S., Dec., 1935.

Sarah Michie, "A New General Language Curriculum for the Eighth Grade," *Modern Language Journal*, Feb., 1938.

Philosophy

Oliver Reiser, *The Promise of Scientific Humanism*, 1940.

Physics

Alvin M. Weinberg, "General Semantics and the Teaching of Physics," *The American Physics Teacher*, April, 1939.

Psychiatry

D. G. Campbell, "General Semantics: Implications of Linguistic Revision for Theoretical and Clinical Neuro-Psychiatry," *American Journal of Psychiatry*, Jan., 1937.

C. B. Congdon and D. G. Campbell, "A Preliminary Report on the Psychotherapeutic Application of General Semantics," in *General Semantics*, comp. by Hansell Baugh, 1938.

A. Korzybski, "General Semantics, Psychiatry, Psychotherapy, and Prevention," *American Journal of Psychiatry*, Sept., 1941.

John G. Lynn, "Preliminary Report of Two Cases of Psycho-

pathic Personality with Chronic Alcoholism Treated by the
Korzybski Method," in *General Semantics*, comp. by Hansell Baugh, 1938.

Sociology

George Devereux, "A Sociological Theory of Schizophrenia,"
Psychoanalytic Review, July, 1939.

What Should You Get from This Book?

Students who read this book carefully should get (1) a
sense of the problems and difficulties involved in making
accurate statements about themselves and the world in
which they live, and (2) a sense of the maladjustments,
both personal and social, that have their roots in improper
evaluation, because of false-to-fact language habits.

Given this awareness, none of the principles set forth
need be taken on "faith." There is nothing mystical or mysterious in their origin, their analysis, or their use. Having
come from the empirical findings of modern science, they
should be checked by the same methods.

Because this book was designed as an introduction, no
effort was made to exhaust the possibilities of adequate
language habits. There remain enough to fill many books.
There are, however, a sufficient number of "new" habits
outlined here to keep one busy for a long time—and the
experience of teachers shows that it is likely to be even
longer than you think.

For Further Study

1. For more reading on Time-binding, see
   1. Cassius J. Keyser, *Mathematical Philosophy*. New York:
      E. P. Dutton & Co., 1922, Lectures XX-XXI.
   2. Alfred Korzybski, *Manhood of Humanity*. New York:
      E. P. Dutton & Co., 1921.
   3. Walter N. Polakov, *Man and His Affairs*. Baltimore:
      Williams & Wilkins Co., 1925.
2. For more reading on the scope of language study, see
   1. Franz Boas, "Introduction," *Handbook of American In-*

dian Languages, Bulletin 40, Part I. The Bureau of American Ethnology, Washington: Government Printing Office, 1910.

2. Kenneth Burke, *Permanence and Change*. New York: The New Republic, 1935.

3. Albert Guérard, "International Language and National Cultures," *The American Scholar*, Spring, 1941.

4. Otto Jespersen, *Language: Its Nature, Development, and Origin*. New York: Henry Holt & Co., 1922.

5. D. V. McGranahan, "The Psychology of Language," *Psychological Bulletin*, XXXIII (1936), 178-216.

6. C. K. Ogden and I. A. Richards, *The Meaning of Meaning*. New York: Harcourt, Brace & Co., 1936.

7. Edward Sapir, "Language," *Encyclopædia of the Social Sciences*, Vol. IX.

8. V. Welby, "Significs," *Encyclopædia Britannica*, 11th edition, Vol. XXV.

9. Leslie A. White, "The Symbol: The Origin and Basis of Human Behavior," *Philosophy of Science*, VII (Oct., 1940), 451-463.

CHAPTER II

THE USEFUL USE OF WORDS

×××

A scheme for entirely abolishing all words whatsoever was urged as a great advantage in point of health as well as brevity. For it is plain that every word we speak is in some degree a diminution of our lungs by corrosion, and consequently contributes to the shortening of our lives. An expedient was therefore offered that, since words are only names for things, it would be more convenient for all men to carry about them such things as were necessary to express the particular business they are to discourse on . . . which hath only this inconvenience attending it, that if a man's business be very great and of various kinds he must be obliged in proportion to carry a great bundle of things upon his back, unless he can afford one or two strong servants to attend him. I have often beheld two of those sages almost sinking under the weight of their packs, like pedlars among us, who, when they meet in the streets, would lay down their loads, open their saddles, and hold conversation for an hour together, then put up their implements, help each other to resume their burdens, and take their leave. —Jonathan Swift[1]

And I remember in frequent discourses with my master concerning the nature of manhood in other parts of the world, having occasion to talk of lying and false representation, it was with much difficulty that he comprehended what I meant, although he had otherwise a most acute judgment, for he argued thus: That the use of speech was to make us understand one another and to receive information of facts; now if anyone said the thing which was not, those ends were defeated, because I cannot properly be said to understand him, and I am so far from receiving information that he leaves me worse than in ignorance, for I am led to believe a thing black when it is white, and short when it is long. And these were all the notions he had concerning that faculty of lying so perfectly well understood among human creatures. —Jonathan Swift[2]

><<<><>>><

What do you think of this suggestion to abolish words? How would you describe the mechanism of a lie?

[1] Jonathan Swift, "A Voyage to Laputa," *Gulliver's Travels.*
[2] Jonathan Swift, "A Voyage to the Houyhnhnms," *ibid.*

THE USEFUL USE OF WORDS

>×××

The Work of Words

Though widely differing in statement, much agreement may be found about what it is that words are supposed to do for us. Some typical definitions:

A sign or expression may concern or designate or describe something, or, rather, he who uses the expression may intend to refer to something by it, e.g., to an object, or a property, or a state of affairs.[1]

Words are vocal sounds or letter combinations which symbolize or signify something. They . . . have no other function except to direct attention. The words now being read by the reader for instance are directing his attention to something; to the fact that words are attention directors. . . . Thus the word gold directs attention to a yellow, incorrodible, dense metal of atomic weight 197, and the word vertebrate to a class of animals having a spinal column.[2]

Words may be thought of as signs which *name* that for which they are signs: "*table* is the name of an object, *red* of a quality, *run* of an activity, *over* of a relation."[3]

Thus, words may be considered as *pointers, indicators, forms of representation,* which are intended to correspond to anything whatsoever that may exist, that may be experienced, or that anyone might want to talk about. Or put another way, words may be used for the almost *endless naming* of the inexhaustible electronic events, objects, per-

---

[1] Rudolf Carnap, *Foundations of Logic and Mathematics.* Chicago: The University of Chicago Press, 1939, 4. Reprinted by permission.

[2] James MacKaye, *The Logic of Language.* Hanover, N. H.: Dartmouth College Publications, 1939, 21. Reprinted by permission of Dartmouth College.

[3] Gustaf Stern, *Meaning and Change of Meaning.* Goteborg: Elanders Boktryckeri Aktiebolag, 1931, 19.

sons, situations, relations, etc., observed in the world out-side-our-skins, along with the sensations, feelings, beliefs, opinions, values, tensions, affective states, etc., experienced inside-our-skins.

Note the Two Media

Such an analysis of the work of words makes one point inevitable: the phenomenon of language is different from the non-verbal phenomena which we represent by it. We live in two worlds which must not be confused, a world of words, and a world of not-words. If a word is not what it represents, then whatever you might say about anything will not be *it*. If in doubt, you might try eating the word *steak* when hungry, or wearing the word *coat* when cold. In short, the universe of discourse *is not* the universe of our direct experience.

If a word *were* what it used to stand for, that is, a "complete reproduction," it would then be no word, but one more non-verbal fact. For words have aspects and functions quite different from the non-verbal facts which they may represent. William James once remarked that words should be taken as "summaries of things to look for," and not, it

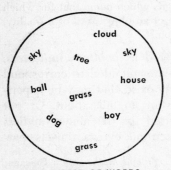

THE WORLD OF WORDS

THE WORLD OF NOT-WORDS

should be added, as the actual existent "things." A book on astronomy is not the heavenly bodies, distances, and movements which make up the stellar universe, and the calculations and hypotheses which result from studying the stars clearly are not the phenomena in space. And the names and addresses on envelopes are not the human beings who receive them.

There exists, then, a world of words which must be sharply distinguished from a world of not-words about which talk occurs, even though frequently we tend to identify them.

Fitting the Two

Language will have maximum usefulness when it properly corresponds to what it is supposed to represent. We need to know what constitutes adequate representation. This may be illustrated in reverse. Suppose that a thermometer registered at freezing point when the liquid in which it was placed boiled furiously; a speedometer recorded only a thousand miles when the auto had been driven from New York to Denver; a road-marker showed the arrow pointing to the left, while the actual road turned to the right. One can say that each of these symbolic recording devices was "wrong," "inaccurate," "erroneous," "misleading," etc. Such evaluations, however, though understandable, do not in themselves account for the wrongness. We get that in the suggestion that the recording did not *fit* the facts.

But what of words? When are they "adequate" and "useful"? Korzybski has said, "If we reflect upon our languages, we find that at best they must be considered *only as maps.*" And further, "A language, to be useful, should be similar in its structure to the structure of the events which it is supposed to represent."[4]

An example may help. Suppose you receive a book entitled *Guide to Beautiful Bali,* which you read carefully. Never having been there, how can you know that such a place exists, and that what is said is correct to fact? A friend who has been there asserts that the book can be read with con-

[4] Alfred Korzybski, *Science and Sanity, an Introduction to Non-Aristotelian Systems and General Semantics.* Lancaster, Pa.: The Science Press Printing Co., 1933, 58, 412. Reprinted by permission.

fidence. He argues further that if passage be taken to Bali, the directions followed, and the places visited, the book will be found to correspond to what is seen. If the trip is taken, and if the book is verified—that is, if the descriptions of Bali parallel the experienced Bali—then we can say that the language of the book was an accurate representation of the non-verbal facts. In the normal run of affairs we cannot personally corroborate what we read. But whenever we do, this notion of correspondence of words with facts will become clear.

Korzybski's famous analogy makes the point even more graphically, so that the notion of "usefulness" becomes readily apparent.

Let us take some actual territory in which cities appear in the following order: San Francisco, Chicago, New York, when taken from the West to the East. If we were to build a *map* of this territory and place San Francisco *between* Chicago and New York thus:

Actual territory   *_____*_____*
                  San Francisco   Chicago   New York
Map   *_____*_____*
                  Chicago   San Francisco   New York

we should say that the map was wrong, or that it was an incorrect map, or that the map has a *different structure* from the territory. If, speaking roughly, we should try, in our travels, to orient ourselves by such a map, we should find it misleading. It would lead us astray, and we might waste a great deal of unnecessary effort. In some cases, even, a map of wrong structure would bring actual suffering and disaster, as, for instance, in a war, or in the case of an urgent call for a physician.[5]

With Words Alone

Even though language can be made to fit life facts, it is essential that another point be clearly understood, that words can be manipulated independently without corresponding to any non-verbal facts.

Just as it is easy to make a map without bothering to survey the terrain, or address letters to imaginary people,

[5] *Ibid.* 58.

so one can indulge in verbalism, using words at random. No inner necessity governs the use of words in their relationship to things, feelings, and circumstances. Stories of people may be manufactured, nonexistent places may be talked about, situations may be verbally distorted beyond recognition, and denials and affirmations may be made regardless of what happens. Nothing *in the nature of language* could have prevented Bismarck from altering the Ems telegram, could have stopped the writing of the letter which helped convict Alfred Dreyfus, or hindered Mencken's hoax about the first American bathtub.

If in 1938 Adolf Hitler could say that he "wants no more land in Europe," even as his armies mobilized for invasion; and if astrologers can assert that those born under Libra should have musical talent, while a researcher finds that the birth dates of 1498 musicians show that almost "fewer are born under Libra than under any sign except Scorpio"[6] —if these things can be said, it should begin to be clear that words *may be used according to the whim of the user*. Without checking and testing with life it is impossible by merely looking at statements to know whether or not they represent some existing territory in the world of happenings. Without an "inner check" one may turn out a false war communiqué, forge the "Protocols of the Elders of Zion," concoct non-verifiable racist dogmas, maintain the prophetic virtues of crystal-gazing, tell a yarn in contest for the "Liars' Championship," and on occasion provide pleasant diversion:

Two of Joe Cook's favorite "gags" in *Why I Will Not Imitate Four Hawaiians* are a note reading "See frontispiece" and another "See page 226," the frontispiece being totally irrelevant to the matter in question, and the book having only 64 pages. Josh Billings had a similar gag. At the bottom of the card advertising his lecture on milk—in which, moreover, the subject of milk was never mentioned—he printed the word *over* in large type, and the other side was blank.[7]

[6] *Time*, Jan. 27, 1941, 38. Reprinted by permission.
[7] Max Eastman, *The Enjoyment of Laughter*. New York: Simon & Schuster, 1936, 55. Reprinted by permission.

John Locke argued that "in inquiries after philosophical knowledge . . . names must be conformable to things."[8] More recently Bridgman agreed that language "owes whatever success it attains to its ability to set up and maintain certain correspondences with experience."[9] However, one who uses words does not have to be governed by such demands. By itself language cannot force a user to seek that correspondence with actual facts. Indeed, there is a certain convenience in avoiding it. As Vilfredo Pareto says,

It is much easier to talk about antipodes than to go out and see if they are really there. To discuss the implication of a "principle of fire" or "damp" is much more expeditious than to prosecute all the field studies that have made up the science of geology. To ruminate on "natural law" is a much more comfortable profession than to dig out the legal codes of the various countries in various periods of history. To prattle about "value" and ask when and under what circumstances it is said that "a thing has value" is much less difficult than to discover and comprehend the laws of economic equilibrium.[10]

Relevant here is a story of the small Austrian village under attack from hostile forces. To preserve the priceless possession of the community, a bell in the tower of the *Rathaus*, three of the elders rowed with it to the center of a nearby lake. To remember the place where it was dropped overboard, a deep mark was cut on the side of the boat.

Just as that boat mark can be moved, unrelated to its object, so, too, can words be handled and bandied about without regard to what they are supposed to represent.

On Adjustment

Mr. George had never given a speech to youngsters. But the Principal assured him that they would listen quietly and

[8] John Locke, *Essay Concerning Human Understanding*. Boston: Cummings and Hilliard and J. T. Buckingham, 1813, II, 51.

[9] P. W. Bridgman, *The Nature of Physical Theory*. Princeton, N. J.: Princeton University Press, 1936, 19. Reprinted by permission.

[10] Vilfredo Pareto, *The Mind and Society*, ed. by Arthur Livingston. New York: Harcourt, Brace & Co., 1935, I, 58. Reprinted by permission.

eagerly and that it was as easy to talk to them as to adults. Mr. George was satisfied and looked forward to the occasion. For the first three minutes the children paid careful attention. Then a few up in front began to wiggle. Then the group burst into laughter at something he thought not at all funny. When a door at the other end of the corridor slammed, they all turned in that direction. And after that they began to whisper. . . . In the next five minutes the confusion increased, and Mr. George, much distraught, mumbled a "Thank you" and sat down.

That the speaker lost control is not too surprising. He was led to expect simplicity and found complexity. His adjustment was affected when the circumstances ran counter to what he expected. The verbal assurances given him had low predictability value.

This suggests a general principle: Our adjustment (and ultimately, survival) is correlated with our expectations, that is, our ability to predict happenings accurately. This is a way of saying that the correctness of our expectations depends upon the similarity of structure of the language used and the happenings represented. If the statements by means of which we are oriented are not adequate representations, it will be difficult to prepare for what is to be met in the world of direct experience.

But a nice problem thus emerges. If it becomes necessary to check everything anyone says with our own personal experience of the life facts, we should have time for little else. In this highly technical and minutely specialized civilization much must be taken on "faith," on the say-so of those who are supposed to know and expected to be responsible. One of the great sources of confusion in our time, however, lies in the fact that many find it profitable and expedient to betray this faith by making "maps" which do not fit the facts. This may be readily documented by reference to the findings of the Better Business Bureaus, the Food and Drug Administration, the Department of Weights and Measures, the Underwriters' Laboratory, the Bureau of Investigation of the American Medical Association, the Federal Trade Commission, Consumers Union, Federal Bureau of Investigation, Senate Investigating Committees, etc. In one form or another these organizations serve as reminders that *complete* faith in what is said, and expectations based on that faith, too often end in disappointment and disaster.

Awareness, then, of the different characteristics of words (map) and what they stand for (territory) should lead to the understanding that all utterance is to be neither blindly rejected nor blindly accepted. To know that language can be false to fact should make for more searching consideration of the nature of language. Those who argue that *all* public statements must be discounted suffer in their cynicism from delusions no less harmful than those who insist that if important men and official statements say so, then it must be so. What is urged here is something quite different: that men and women should be conscious of the *possibility* of structural dissimilarity between words and "things," and further, that a large step is taken toward proper evaluation, predictability, and adjustment, when they begin to ask whether or not the map fits the territory.

In Short

A map is not the territory. To be most useful, statements must fit, must be similar in structure to the life facts being

represented. Words can be manipulated independently of what they represent, and so made false to fact both consciously and unconsciously. In either case their reliability and our predictability are impaired.

The basic question: not, What did he say? but, Did what he said fit the life facts?

For Further Study

1. Such books as
   1. Joseph Jastrow, ed., *The Story of Human Error*. New York: D. Appleton-Century Co., 1936,
   2. C. D. MacDougall, *Hoaxes*. New York: The Macmillan Company, 1940,
   3. C. Mackay, *Memoirs of Extraordinary Popular Delusions*. London: Routledge, 1856,
   4. Vilhjalmur Stefansson, *Adventures in Error*. New York: R. M. McBride & Co., 1936,

will provide innumerable examples of both conscious and unconscious dissimilarity of structure between map and territory. *It is important that students make the distinction between statements that do not fit as a result of ignorance of the structure of life facts and those in which the deception is carefully planned.*

2. From the materials of this chapter you should be able to describe the characteristics not of "Truth," but of truthful statements. Can you?

3. Have you ever had any personal experiences with advice, directions, definitions, etc., by which you were led astray? What should be your attitude henceforth? Remember that the two easiest ways to slide through life are "to believe everything and to deny everything."

4. Do you know the work of any of the many institutions in our country whose job it is to reveal false to fact statements in particular areas?

5. Do you understand this chapter to say that you should go around checking *everything* you read and hear for its fitness with facts?

6. Read the interesting fourth chapter on "Maps" in Van Loon's *Geography*. (New York: Simon & Schuster, 1932.)

7. How would you explain the principles given in this chapter to a six-year-old child?

8. "We have already seen that the chunk of nature which we call a 'pencil' *is not* 'matter' nor 'space' nor 'time,' the terms being only *terms*. Is such *elementalistic language* structurally appropriate for the purpose of speaking about the world

around us? . . . 'Matter,' 'space,' and 'time' can *never* be experimentally divided. . . .

"All that we deal with in the outside world involves indivisibly 'matter,' 'space,' and 'time.' Using the old language, there cannot be something somewhere at 'no time,' or something at some 'time' and 'no where,' or 'nothing' 'somewhere' at 'some time.' Everything which happens must be structurally represented as something, somewhere, at some time. If the structure of the world happened to be such that 'nothing' would happen 'nowhere' at 'no time,' then we should have nothing to talk about, and all we would or could say would deal with our fancies." (*Science and Sanity*, 243.)

What has this to do with map-territory relationships?

9. William M. Thackeray's *Paris Sketch Book* and *Book of Snobs* should provide amusing reading when considered in the light of map-territory relationships.

10. What can we do when people take advantage of our "faith" in what they say? Put your answer in terms of the following example:

"Not long ago, an important center for the match industry in Japan was renamed 'Sweden' so that its matches could be dumped on the world as 'Made in Sweden.' The result of this trick has apparently been so successful that a further development in this direction may be expected. Two other towns have recently been re-christened 'Sheffield' and 'Solingen.' It goes without saying that this is no more than a mere bagatelle to offer oriental razors under the clever camouflage of 'Made in Sheffield' or 'Made in Solingen.' " (Excerpt from a letter in "Letters from the People" in St. Louis *Post-Dispatch*, Jan. 14, 1935.)

11. The question of free speech is not unrelated to the basic task of making our maps fit. Taking the famous words of Justice Holmes as a basis, what relationship do you discover?

"Persecution for the expression of opinions seems to me perfectly logical. If you have no doubt of your premises or your power and want a certain result with all your heart you naturally express your wishes in law and sweep away all opposition. To allow opposition by speech seems to indicate that you think the speech impotent, as when a man says that he has squared the circle, or that you do not care wholeheartedly for the result, or that you doubt either your power or your premises. But when men have realized that time has upset many fighting faiths, they may come to believe, even more than they believe the very foundations of their own conduct, that the ultimate good desired is better reached by free trade in ideas—that the best test of truth is the power of the thought to get itself accepted in the competition of the market, and that truth is the only ground upon which their wishes safely can be carried out. That at any rate is the theory of our Constitution. It is an experiment, as all life is an experiment. Every year if not every day we have to wager our salvation upon some prophecy based upon imperfect knowledge. While that experiment is part of our system I think that we should be eternally vigilant against attempts to check the expression of opinions that we loathe and believe to be fraught with death, unless they so imminently threaten immediate interference with the lawful and pressing purposes of the law that an immediate check is required to save the country.

"Only the emergency that makes it immediately dangerous to leave the correction of evil counsels to time warrants making any exception to the sweeping command, 'Congress shall make no law abridging the freedom of speech.'" (Justice Holmes, Dissenting Opinion in *Abrams* v. *U.S.*, 250 U.S. 616 [1919].)

CHAPTER III

THE MANY USES OF A WORD

Lately an English visitor to the U. S. was confronted by the daughter of his hostess. "Let's put the show on the road, sugarpuss," she commanded. "We're going to a rat race." Although her remarks bore a certain resemblance to his native tongue, the Englishman was only able to deduce that he was being asked to assist in a traveling show whose main feature would be an athletic contest between rodents. This impression was false. In Subdebese, he was being invited to a dance. —Life[1]

First—All general provisions, terms, phrases and expressions shall be liberally construed in order that the true intent and meaning of the Legislature may be fully carried out.

Second—Words in the present tense include the future.

Third—Words importing the singular number may extend and be applied to several persons or things, and words importing the plural number may include the singular.

Fourth—Words importing the masculine gender may be applied to females. —27.13 General Rules, Section 1[2]

Let me claim the honour of one pure neologism. I ventured to introduce the term of FATHER-LAND to describe our natale solum; *I have lived to see it adopted by Lord Byron and by Mr. Southey, and the word is now common. A lady has even composed both the words and the air of a song on "Father-land." This energetic expression may therefore be considered as authenticated; and patriotism may stamp it with its glory and its affection. FATHER-LAND is congenial with the language in which we find that other fine expression MOTHER-TONGUE. The patriotic neologism originated with me in Holland, when, in early life, it was my daily pursuit to turn over the glorious history of its independence under the title of* Vaderlandsche Historie—*the history of FATHER-LAND!*
—Isaac Disraeli[3]

>≪◇≫<

Do you know any law or authority which might prevent people from using words in *new* ways? Are you surprised or outraged when someone uses words in ways to which you are not accustomed? When you read a book or listen to a speech, do you usually assume that the writer or speaker uses words to represent the same things you do?

[1] *Life,* Jan. 27, 1941, 78. Reprinted by permission.
[2] 4 Jones. Ill. Stats. Ann.
[3] Isaac Disraeli, "History of New Words," *Curiosities of Literature,* ed. by B. Disraeli. London: G. Routledge & Co., 1858, III, 31.

THE MANY USES OF A WORD

>>>

The Conventional Character of Word Usage

How does it happen that a word comes to represent what it does? One answer is to be found in *Genesis* II:19-20.

And out of the ground the Lord God formed every beast of the field, and every fowl of the air. And brought them unto Adam to see what he would *call* them: and whatsoever Adam called every living creature, that *was* the name thereof. And Adam gave names to all cattle and to the fowl of the air, and to every beast of the field.

However, this version seems unable to account for the more recent naming of scientific and technical developments, the inventions of the advertising men, slang, specialized jargons, journalese, etc. The origin of these is more simply explained by reference to the individuals who made them up in much the way parents name babies and numbers are assigned to prison inmates. Let it be said that objects, situations, feelings, etc., are called so because someone (who lived after Adam) wanted them to be called so.

This view emphasizes the arbitrary and conventional character of word origin and word usage. It asserts that words are to be understood as the accidental or conscious creations of someone with a purpose. And that it is a matter of indifference what sounds or marks are used to represent anything. Historical accident and development appear sufficient to explain the use of the word *man* in English, *Mensch* in German and *homme* in French. In each of these languages the human being could have been represented by any other word with similar results. Would anything be lost if men agreed to interchange "big" and "small"? There is no discoverable law or necessity which requires that such and such a word must be used to designate such and such a characteristic. The point is nicely made by MacKaye in

the story of the lady who said to a famous astronomer: "I feel *such* an admiration for you astronomers because of your many wonderful discoveries about the universe. But the most wonderful of all it seems to me is your discovery of the names of the planets. How for instance did you ever manage to find out that the red planet named Mars really *is* Mars?" The notion that the red planet, so conspicuous among the heavenly bodies, was first observed, and the name Mars later arbitrarily attached to it for convenience as we attach a street number to a house, did not occur to this lady.[1]

It is perhaps not irrelevant to point out the argument in the *Cratylus* of Plato that "names belong to things by nature," from which it follows that "the artisan of words must be only he who keeps in view the name which belongs by nature in each particular thing." It may be this strange notion that is at the heart of the humor for some when it is discovered that Dr. L. Pullem is a dentist, and Mr. E. Z. Rake is the owner of a hardware store. These observers will argue, too, that "it doesn't seem right to call a big strong man Mr. Little." Mark Twain once wrote that the name Do-do was given the bird by Eve because to her it "looked like a Do-do." This is reminiscent of the youngster who said that "Scrooge was so named because that's the kind of a man he was."

In Boswell's *Life of Johnson*, Wilkes says,

The last city poet was Elkanah Settle. There is *something* in *names* which one cannot help feeling. Now *Elkanah Settle* sounds so queer, who can expect much from *that name*? We should have no hesitation to give it for *John Dryden* in prefer-

[1] James MacKaye, *The Logic of Language*. Hanover, N. H.: Dartmouth College Publications, 1939, 95-96. Reprinted by permission of Dartmouth College.

ence to *Elkanah Settle*, from the *names only*, without knowing their respective merits.[2]

Montaigne once observed,

A gentleman, one of my neighbors, in over-valuing the excellence of old times, never omitted noticing the pride and magnificence of the *names* of the nobility of those days! *Don Grumedan, Quadragan, Argesilan,* when fully sounded, were evidently men of another stamp than *Peter, Giles,* and *Michel.*[3]

The assumption that some words are more apt than others, that some are incongruous for what they designate, and that the quality is inherent in the words themselves (rather than in the reactions of human beings) may be accounted for by the fact that so many know only their own language. So familiar does one become with certain designations that these seem "real and inevitable," all others being "unnatural." This parochial attitude finds affirmation in the oft-told story of that patriot who held that his language was the most useful one, for, as he put it, "Foreigners are funny. Look how they talk. The Germans call cabbage *Kraut;* the French call it a shoe (*chou*). But you have to come to good old English to find cabbage called *cabbage.*"

From the Ideal to the Practicable

Popular (and sometimes academic) talk about the abuses of language often voices the hope that ambiguity and vagueness be done away with by efforts toward *exactness.* "If only," someone invariably remarks, "we could stabilize the meanings of words the way the chemist does, for example! Think how our confusions would vanish. We'd know what others mean." "That's so," another invariably adds, "we've got to know what words mean and use them that way always. One meaning, one word. That's what is needed."

This somewhat free adaptation of attempts at linguistic

[2] Quoted by Isaac Disraeli, "Influence of a Name," *Curiosities of Literature.* London: G. Routledge & Co., 1858, II, 65.
[3] *Ibid.,* II, 69.

reconstruction reveals the often deeply felt desire that in some way the logicians and philologists ought to get together to devise a language which will "exactly fit the particular situation in which the words are used. For otherwise, the same word will be permitted to mean one thing in one context, another in another."[4] This is a way of describing an "ideal" language, which to Jespersen is one that "would always express the same thing by the same means and similar things by similar means,"[5] and which would also satisfy Ramsey, who says that "in a perfect language each thing would have its own name."[6]

Is such an ideal a possibility?

In the preceding chapter we pointed out the dual existence of words and whatever they are intended to represent. Words were described as forms of representation or maps of non-verbal life facts. Consider the number of possible life facts which a language may be called upon to stand for—the objects, people, relations, happenings, feelings, submicroscopic events, etc., in all their kaleidoscopic, myriad, infinite, and inexhaustible details and characteristics. Imagine the size of the library of dictionaries if each existent, unique "thing" had to be named so that each had its own differentiating name! Consider, too, that the number of such names would be steadily increasing so long as investigators in all areas of life continue their findings. Every time a new observation, a new word. One conclusion seems clear: To erect a language with an uncountable number of words for the infinitely complex variety of life facts is to establish the impossibility of communication. A Shakespeare used less than twenty thousand different words in his plays, and estimates of the vocabulary size of the intelligent intellectual fall far short of two hundred thousand including compounding of words, formation of other parts of speech, etc. Indeed, the 1934 unabridged

[4] F. C. S. Schiller, "How Is 'Exactness' Possible?" *Our Human Truths.* New York: Columbia University Press, 1939, 343.

[5] Quoted in F. C. S. Schiller, *Logic for Use.* New York: Harcourt, Brace & Co., 1930, 56-57. Reprinted by permission.

[6] *Ibid.*

Webster's Dictionary has but a total of six hundred thousand. Teachers today faced with the task of building students' vocabularies with much more modest ends would be driven to quick despair.

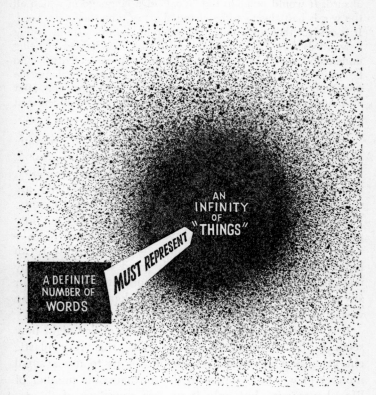

In short, merely to formulate in these terms the demands of an "ideal" language is to doom any hopes of achieving it. Schiller's argument sums up the case:

For if a word has a *perfectly* fixed meaning it could be used only once, and never again; it could be applied only to the situation which originally called for it, and which it uniquely fitted. If, the next time it was used, it retained its original meaning, it could not designate the actual situation but would still hark back to its past use, and this would disqualify it for all future use. Thus, if the meaning of "Nero" had been tied down to a certain historical Roman Emperor, I could not call my dog "Nero." And this would not only be inconvenient but in the end absurd. It would point to the "ideal" of a language in which all the words had always to be changed every time they were used. It is evident that the intellectual strain of continuously inventing new words would be intolerable, and that the chances of being understood would be very small. Thus the price of fixity would be unintelligibility. The impracticability of such a language might not be regarded as its "theoretical" refutation; but after all languages are meant to be used, and human intelligence at any rate could make no use of it.[7]

All of which forces us to a different sort of program. First, to reckon with the infinity of "things," and second, to trust in the use of a language made up of a smaller, more definite number of words which human beings are capable of learning and adapting to represent that infinity. Whether by accident, design, or necessity, that is our language situation now. We have "a language whose signs— which cannot be infinite in number—are extensible to an infinity of things."[8] That is, each word may have many mapping purposes, capable at any moment of standing for any of a number of possible territories, depending upon the wish and attitude of the user.

It is this fact of manifold service which at first sight may seem to be a drawback; nevertheless, this very plastic character is what makes it possible for us to use a small number of words to represent the inexhaustible number of life phenomena—but only if we are conscious of the inherent difficulties.

That this one-word-for-many-uses condition is a working part of our daily (though too often unconscious) experience is not difficult to demonstrate. Let the following assortment of examples bear witness:

[7] *Ibid.*
[8] From Wilbur M. Urban, *Language and Reality,* 1939, 108. By permission of The Macmillan Company, publishers.

X is the Roman notation for ten
X is the mark of illiterate men
X is a ruler removed from the throne
X is a quantity wholly unknown
X may mean Xenon, a furious gas
X is a ray of similar class
Xmas is Christmas, a season of bliss
X in a letter is good for a kiss
X is for Xerxes, a monarch renowned
X marks the spot where the body was found.[9]

P.S. has many significations—here it signifies Post Script—On the corner of a Handkerchief Polly Saunders—Upon a Garter Pretty Secret—Upon a Band Box Pink Satin—At the Theatre Princes Side—on a Pulpit Parson's Snuffle—and at a Country Ale House Pail Sider.[10]

You will recall, for example, his remarks in excited and broken English concerning the absurdities of the word "fast." A horse was fast when he was tied to a hitching post. The same animal was also fast under exactly diametric circumstances— when he was running away. A woman was fast if she smoked cigarettes. A color was fast if it didn't fade. To fast was to go without food. Et cetera.[11]

The Myth of the One-and-only Meaning

In spite of the ease of demonstrating that a relatively few words are used to represent a vastly greater number of life facts, there persists, rather widely spread among those eager to philosophize, the curious notion that it is possible to discover the one "real and proper" meaning of any word.

In discussions on Democracy, Personality, Morality, Liberty, etc., the assumption often prevails that there exists by divine or lexicographical right some one verbal definition

[9] The Chicago Herald-American, Oct. 4, 1939, 24. Reprinted by special permission of King Features Syndicate and Believe-It-or-Not Ripley.

[10] The Complete Poetical Works and Letters of John Keats. Letter No. 54, to Miss M. and S. Jeffrey. The Cambridge Edition. Boston: Houghton Mifflin Company, 1899, 305.

[11] "The Notebook of M. Ravel" (The Contributor's Club), The Atlantic Monthly, April, 1930, 562. Reprinted by permission.

which belongs to it and to it only. "But what is Democracy?" someone will ask on the theory that there can be little point to further talking unless that elusive absolute is found. The hope is often fed by a kind of through-the-looking-glass notion that just because one hunts for something, it must be there. In any event, the verbal playing makes for interesting discussion, particularly if there are several who have *the* definition.

Of course, such talk must end either in agreement on some statement, in postponement of the search until another occasion, or in frustration, for there is no ultimate statement that cannot be modified or changed at will. Such a pursuit is marked at the outset by the failure of its participants to realize that "the meaning" of a word in use is roughly synonymous with what a word is used to represent on any particular occasion. As Welby says, "There is, strictly speaking, no such thing as the sense of a word, but only the sense in which it is used."[12] If the word *strike* does many duties we shall look in vain for "the real, proper, absolute duty" it should perform. At best we can merely decide to use it in one way to stand for one set of experiences rather than another. But even after reaching agreement there is little in the nature of language to prevent others from deciding differently. Linguistic wisdom begins with the consciousness that words can be and are used to represent different aspects of ever-changing experience as, for example:

> The workers voted *to strike* for better pay.
> He promised not *to strike* her again.
> It is not easy *to strike* a match on glass.
> The batter did not wish *to strike* out.

The confusion of purpose may further arise from the tendency to think of words as unique and separate entities apart from the sentences in which they appear. Just as the physiologist isolates for purpose of study the functioning of individual organs in a body, so, too, individual words may be isolated. But the physiologist is not misled into thinking

[12] V. Welby, *What Is Meaning?* London: Macmillan & Co., 1903, 5.

that any organ functions apart from the rest of the body. Similarly, one must not be misled into supposing that a word can function apart from the sentence or totality of discourse in which it may be used.

A word may be related to its context in the way a letter is related to the word in which it appears. In each case word and letter are but parts of a larger unit, and their characteristics are best studied only as they appear in those units. Just as it is not possible to describe the sound- or stress-value of a letter before it exists in a word, so, too, it is pointless to assume a use-value of a word distinct from its use in discourse.

In sum, then, it is more true to say that a word does not have a real, single, unique meaning, but that it means what it does when it is used within the limits to be pointed out. Of course, in any period of cultural history there will be common uses. People will be able rather readily in discussion to discover the uses of a vast number of terms without questioning. Nevertheless, the inherent ambiguity of our language should give us pause and make us less ready to take the meanings for granted. It is better to ask than be misled without asking.

Concern with Words Only

An important problem that arises from the search for the specific "content" of the key words that are so much a part of the speculation of students is the failure to realize that what is important in their lives is not the word and how it is defined, but the non-verbal facts the words are used to represent. We have seen that words are conventional marks or sounds which may be applied in any way we wish to whatever we wish. Important for the student are those first-order experiences he has, the way he feels during examination week, when with other people, and in those moments of frustration, fear, or hope. What is important is what he does, how he evaluates and reacts when at work or play, when he is alone or with other people, when facing problems or retreating from them, when handling and making things, when eating, walking, dancing, swimming, writing, etc. These are what he knows and responds to. These constitute the business of living. And the words used to describe them are as nothing, for while the "things" stand, the words may be taken away and others used without in any way changing what has happened.

To ask the question "What is Propaganda?" is often to ask about and be concerned with the *word*, while deflecting attention away from concern with what people are doing when we label their talk "Propaganda." The only effective answer to such a question is this: *Propaganda* is a word of ten letters, four syllables, two p's, three a's, etc. When one asks what propaganda *is*, he shows by the form of his question that his attention is centered on a word and secondarily on the utterances, evaluations, and life actualities which the word merely keeps track of. Of course, the word *Propaganda* has a place in the analytical schemes of the student. What is so disturbing is the futility of those speculations when they neglect the territory for concern with the map only. Such emphasis might be justified only by the following line of argument:

There is something unknown that acts upon language and gives rise to the word "propaganda." *Since ordinary words are exact copies of the things they represent*, we can understand the thing by studying the word. So by finding out what propaganda is, we shall come to know the thing unknown.[13]

Obviously, the italicized notion, which is the source of the justification, is false to fact. Words merely stand for something else. They act as "labels for keeping track of things." When we are aware of this naming we will say, "Such and such a thing we are going to call *A*," or, "We suggest calling it *A*." We do not say—an entirely different matter—"Such and such a thing is *A*."[14] In short, we can call "things" whatever we choose. Inquiry about the word may proceed indefi-

[13] Vilfredo Pareto, *The Mind and Society*, ed. by Arthur Livingston. New York: Harcourt, Brace & Co., 1935, I, 63. Reprinted by permission.
[14] *Ibid.*

nitely without ever revealing the character of what it is the word was used to represent.

Similarly, discussions about the "hard words" often get under way with the question "What does the word come from?" with the thought, as Jespersen says,

that some light is thrown thereby on the nature of the thing itself. This is a learned form of superstitious belief in the power of the name, related to the primitive superstition that the name has a magical potency. We get no further at all towards understanding what a tragedy is when we are informed that the word must once have meant "goat-song," nor in understanding what a comedy is by learning that it means "festal-song," "banquet-song," whatever the Greek *kōmos* comes from.[15]

The natural procedure of the empirical worker is of a different sort. First he considers, analyzes, and works with objects, situations, relations, etc., *after which* he finds a name by which he generalizes his observation.

First one considers the substance formed by combining oxygen and hydrogen, and then a term is sought to designate it. Since the substance in question is present in great quantities in the vaguely defined thing that the ordinary vernacular designates as water, we call it water. But it might have been called otherwise—"lavoisier," for instance—and all of chemistry would stand exactly as it is. We would simply say that the liquid present in rivers and in the sea contains great quantities of lavoisier.[16]

The Function of a Dictionary

The dictionary's function, if not carefully recognized, can generate the illusion that words have fixed, proper, and absolute designations. It is widely assumed (1) that if a usage is stated in a dictionary, then that is *the* sacrosanct usage of the word, and (2) that the Samuel Johnsons, the Nathaniel Baileys, the Noah Websters are legislators who have handed down immutable decisions about what *shall*

[15] Otto Jespersen, *Mankind, Nation and Individual from a Linguistic Point of View.* Oslo: H. Aschehoug & Co., 1925, 217. Reprinted by permission of the President and Fellows of Harvard College.
[16] Vilfredo Pareto, *The Mind and Society*, I, 63-64. Reprinted by permission.

be the meaning or use of any word. The existence of these beliefs merely adds to the confusion that comes from a failure to realize the pluralistic functioning of words. A study of the making of a dictionary may therefore be useful.

In 1735 there appeared two massive folios entitled "A / Dictionary / of / the / English Language / in which / the Words are deduced from their Originals, / and / illustrated in their different significations / by Examples from the Best Writers. / By Samuel Johnson." Each word was intended to be illustrated in its various uses by a selection of literary quotations. Johnson sought to show the many senses of each word as used by different writers. Thus, by his very method of compilation, he sought to indicate the primacy of usage. In some cases Johnson showed his personal inclinations or a fine sense of humor by giving *his own* uses. *Whig, Tory, excise, pension, pensioner, oats, Grub-street, lexicographer,* are the well-known examples of his attempt to establish significations which were far from being customary.

Eighty-one years later Charles Richardson published "A New Dictionary of the English Language . . . Illustrated by Quotations from the best Authors."

Observing how much light was shed on the meaning of words by Johnson's quotations, he was impressed with the notion that, in a dictionary, definitions are unnecessary, that quotations alone are sufficient; and he proceeded to carry this into effect by making a dictionary without definitions or explanations of meaning, or at least with the merest rudiments of them but illustrating each group of words by a large series of quotations.[17]

The quotations provided a practical device by which to indicate the senses of a word from an inspection of a variety of sentences. He went back to 1300 to authors such as Chaucer and Gower and on up to his contemporaries for quotations. His project was impracticable only to the extent

[17] James A. H. Murray, *The Evolution of English Lexicography.* Oxford: At the Clarendon Press, 1900, 44. The following discussion draws heavily on this paper.

that it was not possible to list in quoted form *all* the ways any word had been used.

The Oxford English Dictionary reveals most completely the recording and historical character of a dictionary. It represents an attempt to list the body of words that have appeared and that have been used for the last eight hundred years. Of unique importance is the biography of each word, which seeks to give the date of its first known appearance and

in the case of an obsolete word or sense, of its last appearance, the source from which it was actually derived, the form and sense with which it entered the language or is first found in it, and the successive changes of form and developments of sense which it has since undergone.[18]

All the materials and data are obtained from historical research. The source material investigated represents the written heritage of our culture. Some two thousand readers going over many thousands of books and documentary records collected more than five million extracts and quotations representing the sum of English literature. From this body of research the history of each word was written.[19]

What now can be said about the function of a dictionary? Analysis of the way one is constructed reveals that the compilers can give us guidance with respect to word "meanings" by listing the way or ways they have been used by other people. The method is mainly one of counting and classifying uses. To find a definition in a dictionary is to find the sense in which someone found a word useful to represent what he wanted it to. That sense may suggest both convenience and practice for some other user. At least it will indicate the limits of its usage in the broad frame of our culture. But the dictionary cannot place for any word the use of that word in any given sentence or paragraph. That is discoverable by a reader or listener only in relation to its setting, both verbal and non-verbal. Thus, no matter what

[18] *Ibid.*, 47.
[19] *Ibid.*

the dictionary listing for the world *flag*, no specific sense can be assigned to the word until its place in some context is found. For one may wave a *flag*, enthusiasm may *flag*, one may *flag* a train, etc.

In practice this historical recording function is neglected by people who look upon dictionary definitions as legislative promptings to which usage must conform. There is an interesting connection between this view and widely held views on the nature of economic and political "laws." The Congress of the United States enacts laws designed to regulate and govern the behavior of people in this country. But in this sense there are no laws in the dictionary. No dictionary-maker intends that "this is the way that words must be used." The dictionary statements are rather the organized presentation and codification of what have been the actual language habits of men. The force of custom is the only law revealed in a dictionary.

The student of the sciences learns another kind of law, Newton's Laws of Motion, Mendel's, Boyle's, etc. The unsophisticated may assume that these *govern* the behavior of moving bodies, the transmission of biological characteristics, and the behavior of gases under pressure. But a scientific law is merely a statement of someone's observations of the matter in question checked by the observations of many other persons. And if other observation reveals different behavior, the law (i.e., a generalization) must be modified to fit the new conditions. The law of economics, first stated by Sir Thomas Gresham—"that bad money drives out good money"—is a case in point from a social science. As Queen Elizabeth's Finance Minister, he saw that it was impossible in his time to keep the two kinds in circulation. The existence of the one tended to affect the existence of the other money. There is nothing of the legislative order in this law. It is merely a statement of observations capable of being revised should the ways people regard money in circulation change. (Incidentally, notice here the many different uses of the word *law*.)

If a speaker uses a word in a way which varies from the customary dictionary definitions, it is often described as a "violation." Such description, however, is not accurate, just as it would not be accurate to say that the action of moneys different from the way Gresham indicated was a violation of his law. It would be more to the point to say that the law must be restated in a broader formulation so that it covers the behavior of the money in this particular case. Similarly, if new usages represent different facts from the "meanings" written in dictionaries, then the latter's definitions must be revised so that they also cover the new usages.

There must be the clear recognition that

language is a living thing, and the great law of life and growth is change. Dictionaries, grammars, books of rhetoric are not eternal statutes handed down from heaven like the tables of Mosaic law. They are history, not dogma; description, not command—descriptions of the changing speech habits of the mass of men. As speech changes, so do dictionaries and grammars change; so must they change if we are to prepare our students to speak the language of their own time, or to secure from the better speech of our own day reenforcement of our teaching.[20]

How to Avoid Confusion

Given a limited number of words which must serve to cover an unlimited number of possible life facts, along with the full freedom, so far as language itself is concerned, of using any words to represent whatever one wishes, we should begin to see why confusion and misunderstanding may readily occur. One kind of explanation is given by Ogden and Richards:

Normally, whenever we hear anything said we spring spontaneously to an immediate conclusion, namely, that the speaker is referring to what we should be referring to were we speaking the words ourselves. In some cases this may be correct; this will prove to be what he has referred to. But in most discussions

[20] Ruth Mary Weeks, "Foreword" in *Current English Usage* by Sterling Andrus Leonard. Chicago: The Inland Press, 1932, xiv. Reprinted by permission.

which attempt greater subtleties than could be handled in a gesture language this will not be so.[21]

As George Cornewall Lewis says, "Where all people talk on the same subject, they should be agreed about the vocabulary with which they discuss it: or, at any rate, they should be aware that they are *not* agreed."

To the extent then, that an individual assumes when reading or listening that words have "fixed" ways of being used, there is increased likelihood that he will assume further that he automatically "knows" in what sense another's terms are being used. And so long as this egocentric attitude prevails there appears no reason to ask "Does he use his terms, as I think he does, to refer to what I do?"

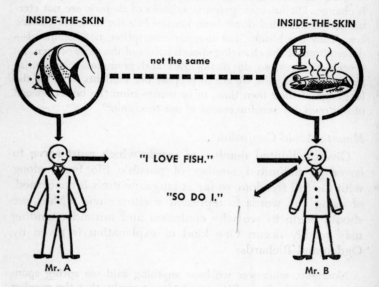

INSIDE-THE-SKIN   INSIDE-THE-SKIN

not the same

"I LOVE FISH."

"SO DO I."

Mr. A   Mr. B

Thorough acceptance and application of the fact of plural duty should do something to force one not to rest content that what *he* thinks a writer or speaker intended is what was actually intended. Mere examination of the utterance

[21] C. K. Ogden and I. A. Richards, *The Meaning of Meaning.* New York: Harcourt, Brace & Co., 1923, 20. Reprinted by permission.

will reveal little about what the words are being used to represent, no matter who does the writing, unless further statements attempt that revelation. It is not possible, regardless of the accuracy of both the reading and the instrument, to discover what highways an auto traveled over from a mere reading of the speedometer. Similarly, study of the amount indicated on a cash register will show little of the kinds of money in the drawer. And to hear someone shout "Hey, Extra!" is not to know without further investigation, either in the life situation or in the rest of the statement, whether it was a newsboy selling papers, an assistant director on a movie set, or the source of excitement on a radio program. In each case, the words must not be taken for granted. Since each can be used variously, we must investigate to see what in any case is being represented.

Failure to comb the statements and question those who make them is often the source of confusion both conscious and unconscious. Notice the neglect in the following random examples:

Private Clyde Ross of Greensburg, Ind., fled into the woods when a motor convoy sped up to his company, and the commander shouted: "Bear to the right."

Found later, he explained: "I'm scared of bears."[22]

When photographers began taking pictures of Anthony Eden during a speech, he raised his hand, said, "Don't shoot, please." Next day the German radio reported that "An attempt was made on the life of Mr. Eden, English War Minister, yesterday."[23]

We all declare for liberty; but in using the same word we do not all mean the same thing. With some the word liberty may mean for each man to do as he pleases with himself, and the product of his labor; while with others the same word may mean for some men to do as they please with other men, and the product of other men's labor.

Here are two, not only different, but incompatible things, called by the same name, liberty. And it follows that each of

[22] St. Louis *Daily Globe-Democrat*, Feb. 6, 1941, 8A.
[23] *Life*, Feb. 10, 1941, 26. Reprinted by permission.

the things is, by the respective parties, called by two different and incompatible names—liberty and tyranny. . . .

The shepherd drives the wolf from the sheep's throat, for which the sheep thanks the shepherd as his liberator, while the wolf denounces him for the same act, as the destroyer of liberty —plainly, the sheep and the wolf are not agreed upon a definition of the word liberty—and precisely the same difference prevails today among us human creatures—and all professing to love liberty. Hence we behold the process by which thousands are daily passing from under the yoke of bondage hailed by some as the advance of liberty, and bewailed by others as the destruction of all liberty![24]

I learned something of the intricacies of plain English at an early stage in my career. A woman of thirty-five came in one day to tell me that she wanted a baby but that she had been told that she had a certain type of heart-disease which might not interfere with a normal life but would be dangerous if she ever had a baby. From her description I thought at once of mitral stenosis. This condition is characterized by a rather distinctive rumbling murmur near the apex of the heart, and especially by a peculiar vibration felt by the examining finger on the patient's chest. The vibration is known as the "thrill" of mitral stenosis.

When this woman had been undressed and was lying on my table in her white kimono, my stethoscope quickly found the heart-sounds I had expected. Dictating to my nurse, I described them carefully. I put my stethoscope aside and felt intently for the typical vibration which may be found in a small but variable area of the left chest.

I closed my eyes for better concentration, and felt long and carefully for the tremor. I did not find it and with my hand still on the woman's bare breast, lifting it upward and out of the way, I finally turned to the nurse and said: "No thrill."

The patient's black eyes snapped open, and with venom in her voice she said: "Well, isn't that just too bad? Perhaps it's just as well you don't get one. That isn't what I came for."

My nurse almost choked, and my explanation still seems a nightmare of futile words.[25]

[24] From a speech by Abraham Lincoln quoted by Franklin D. Roosevelt at Wilmington, Delaware, on Oct. 22, 1940. The Chicago *Daily News*, Oct. 23, 1940, 8.

[25] Frederic Loomis, M.D., *Consultation Room*. New York: Alfred A. Knopf, 1939, 47. Reprinted by permission.

Positive advice to readers and listeners would consist, then, of two warnings. First, learn to be conscious of the fact that any word may have a whole list of uses and not only one. Second, develop a habitual awareness that what is being said may not represent what you assume it does. Do not try to project your impressions on to the discourse. The uncritical assumption of the similarity in word use and the often resulting misinterpretation may sometimes be avoided in conversation by the regular use of some lubricating phrase such as, "Because terms may be used in many ways, will you give me an example which will explain what you are using it to represent?" For after all, this is but to take heed of ancient wisdom.

Humpty-Dumpty said: "There's glory for you." "I don't know what you mean by 'glory,' " Alice said. Humpty-Dumpty smiled contemptuously. "Of course you don't—till I tell you. I meant, 'There's a nice knock-down argument for you.' " "But 'glory' doesn't mean 'a nice knock-down argument,' " Alice objected. "When I use a word," Humpty-Dumpty said in a rather scornful tone, "It means just what I choose it to mean, neither more nor less."[26]

In Short

Relatively few words are available to represent an infinity of objects, situations, happenings, feelings, etc. Any one word may have many uses. We waste time looking for but one-and-one-only-"meaning." Misunderstanding and confusion arise when readers and listeners assume that their word uses are also the word uses of writers and speakers. Only study of the utterance and direct questioning can reveal the use.

The basic question: not, What do I represent by the terms, but What does he?

For Further Study

1. The next time you are near a good-sized library, have a look at the Oxford English Dictionary. Study its make-up.

[26] Lewis Carroll, *Through the Looking-Glass,* Ch. VI.

2. Take a paragraph or two from a newspaper or magazine editorial or speech. Read it carefully line by line with a friend. Then, together, see if the two of you can agree on (a) what the author *said*, (b) what non-verbal life facts his words represented, and (c) whether at any point his words may possibly represent life facts different from your usual uses.

3. Try this during the next discussion in which you participate. Pick out the word or words around which the talk goes. See if you can discover whether the participants are using these words similarly, or whether the argument is prolonged and made confusing by varied uses.

4. Books to read on the fact of many uses.

    1. Isaac Goldberg, *The Wonder of Words*. New York: D. Appleton-Century Co., 1938.

    2. H. L. Mencken, *The American Language*. New York: Alfred A. Knopf, 1936.

    3. Progressive Education Association, *Language in General Education*. New York: D. Appleton-Century Co., 1940.

    4. I. A. Richards, *The Philosophy of Rhetoric*. New York: Oxford University Press, 1935.

    5. Allen Upward, *The New Word*. New York: Mitchell Kennerly, 1910.

5. Study carefully the paragraphs which follow. Attempt to state the points made in terms of advice which you can follow. Has the point been treated in this chapter?

"Smith₁, who is *not* conscious of abstracting, makes the statement, 'A circle is not square.' Let us suppose that Brown₁ contradicts him. Smith₁ is angered; for [him], his statement 'is' the 'plain truth,' and Brown₁ must be a fool. He objectifies it, ascribes to it undue value. For him, it 'is' 'experience,' a 'fact,' etc., and he bursts into speech, denouncing Brown₁ and showing how wrong he 'is.' From this . . . attitude, many difficulties and tragedies arise.

"But if Smith₂ (conscious of abstracting) makes the statement, 'A circle is not square,' and Brown₂ contradicts him, what would Smith₂ do? He would smile, would not burst into speech to defend *his* statement, but would ask Brown₂, 'What do you mean? I do not quite understand you.' After receiving some answer, Smith₂ would explain to Brown₂ that his statement is not anything to quarrel about, as it is verbal and is true only by *definition*. He would also grant the right of Brown₂ *not* to accept *his definition*, but to use another one to satisfy himself. The problem would then, naturally, arise as to what definition both could accept, or which would be generally acceptable. And the problem would then be solved by purely pragmatic considerations. Words appear as creatures of definitions, and optional; but this attitude involves important and new [attitudes and modes of evaluation]." (*Science and Sanity*, 419.)

6. In terms of the way our language works to represent the infinity of aspects of our world, account for the mechanism of the pun. Try your explanation on this example in "A Visit to the Asylum for Aged and Decayed Punsters" written by Oliver Wendell Holmes:

"The Superintendent, who went round with us, had been a noted punster in his time, and well known in the business world, but lost his customers by making too free with their names.

" 'Do you know'—he broke out all at once—'why they don't take steppes in Tartary for establishing insane hospitals?'

"We both confessed ignorance.

" 'Because there are nomad people found there,' he said with a dignified smile."

7. In his *Pragmatism*, William James tells the story of a dispute which grows out of the fact of many uses. Suppose, while walking in the forest, you see a squirrel clinging to the side of a tree. As you walk around the tree, imagine that the squirrel moves at the same speed in the other direction so that you do not get to see him. The question is this: Do you go round the squirrel or not? The question is quickly solved free of wrangling when you see that "going round" may represent (a) passing from the north, east, south, and west, to the north again of the squirrel and (b) passing from front to right to behind to left of the animal's body. You would do (a) but not (b). Begin making a collection of disputes which become solved as soon as the "other" uses of the terms are revealed.

8. "We all of us, whether we have given a distinct account of the matter to ourselves or no, believe that the words which we use, some at least of them, stand in a more or less real relation to the things which they designate—that they are not arbitrary signs, affixed at random, for which any other

might have been substituted as well. And this sense of the significance of names, that they are, or ought to be—that in a world of absolute truth they ever would be—the utterance of the innermost character and qualities of the things or persons that bear them, speaking out in various other ways, speaks out in none more clearly than in this—namely, in the amusement and interest which children find in any striking agreement between a name and the person who owns that name— or, which naturally lays hold on their attention far more, in any striking contradiction between the name and the name-bearer; as, for instance, if Mr. Strongitharm is a weakling, or Mr. Black an albino; the first striking from a sense of fitness, the other from one of incongruity.

"Nor is this a mere childish entertainment. It continues with us through life; and that its roots lie deep is attested by the earnest use which is often made, and that at most earnest moments of men's lives, of such agreements or disagreements as these. Thus Shakespeare shows his own profound knowledge of the human heart, when he makes old John of Gaunt, worn with long sickness, and now ready to depart, play with his name, and dwell upon the consent between it and his condition; so that when his royal nephew asks, 'How is it with aged Gaunt?' he answers,

"'Oh, how that name befits my composition,
Old *Gaunt* indeed, and *gaunt* in being old—
Gaunt am I for the grave, *gaunt* as the grave.'
with much more in the same fashion; while it is into the mouth of the slight and frivolous king that Shakespeare puts the exclamation of wonder,

"'Can sick men play so nicely with their names?'"
(Richard Chenevix Trench, *On the Study of Words*. New York: W. J. Widdleton, twenty-fifth American from the ninth English edition enlarged and revised, n.d., 29-30.)
Do you believe that?

9. "There is nothing more common," said Voltaire, "than to read and to converse to no purpose. In history, in morals, in law, in physics, and in divinity, be careful of equivocal terms."

For a novel and most useful method of dealing with equivocal terms read Chapter V in James MacKaye's *The Logic of Language*. (Hanover, N. H.: Darmouth College Publications, 1939.)

10. Franz Boas once said, "The same words may be used

with different significance, and by assuming the word to have the same significance always, erroneous conclusions may be reached." Students ought to make a collection of such examples of the onset of misunderstanding.

11. "A father said once, 'My son, in water exists a principle which is destructive of life, and in brandy a principle preservative of life.' The father meant, that immersion in water would produce death, and that a small quantity of brandy was occasionally salutary. The proposition was correct while confined to the particulars to which the father alluded; but the son, supposing its application universal, refrained from the use of water, and substituted brandy. We all err in a similar manner, though not always in a like degree, when we consider any proposition significant of more than certain particulars; and if those who promulge general propositions, will not announce the particulars to which they refer, we have still every thing to learn." (A. B. Johnson, *Treatise on Language: or the Relation Which Words Bear to Things.* New York: Harper & Brothers, 1836, 113.)

Have you read such doctrine before? Note the date of this book.

12. "We cast into a tub of water a small piece of indigo, and the water becomes tinged with blue; we cast into another tub of water a lump of sugar, and the water becomes sweet; we open our shutters, and light becomes perceptible throughout our room; we ignite a few sticks of wood, and the mercury will rise in a distant thermometer:—these results possess a certain congruity, hence we say, the indigo and sugar are *diffused* through the water;—the light and heat are *diffused* through the room. If, however, we wish to discover the sensible meaning of the word diffused, in these several uses, we must resort to our senses, and not to our dictionaries. The sensible meaning is so diverse in the above different applications of the word diffused, that a blind man will possess no conception of the diffusion that refers to the light and indigo; while a man who never possessed tasting, will possess no conception of the diffusion which refers to the sugar." *Ibid.,* 100.)

Study carefully this statement about the limitations of a dictionary. What practical effects might result from its awareness?

CHAPTER IV

ACQUAINTANCE, ABSTRACTING, NON-ALLNESS

I was told some time ago of a lawsuit which was being tried before a justice of the peace. When the attorney for the plaintiff had just about concluded his argument, the justice said, "Counsel, it will not be necessary for you to proceed further." He said, "You have convinced me. I have made up my mind. I have my decision ready."

Of course, the attorney for the defense was immediately on his feet protesting, and said, "Your Honor, certainly you are going to hear what the defendant has to say."

The justice said, "No, I have made up my mind."

"But," the attorney said, "I insist that you hear the viewpoint of the defendant."

The justice said, "Well, I have my mind all made up; and if I listen to you, it might confuse me. So I guess I won't do it."

—REXFORD S. MITCHELL[1]

"Fust-rate," "prime," "a prime article," "a superior piece of goods," "a handsome garment," "a gent in a flowered vest,"—all such expressions are final. They blast the lineage of him or her who utters them, for generations up and down. There is one other phrase which will soon come to be decisive of a man's social status, if it is not already: "That tells the whole story." It is an expression which vulgar and conceited people particularly affect, and which well-meaning ones, who know better, catch from them. It is intended to stop all debate, like the previous question in the General Court. Only it doesn't; simply because "that" does not usually tell the whole, nor one-half of the whole story.   —OLIVER WENDELL HOLMES[2]

There will be omissions, and how can they be avoided? In all great battles there are thousands of men on the field of operations, formed into companies, regiments, brigades, divisions, and corps, with private soldiers, captains, colonels, brigadier generals, major generals, and marshals. In describing these conflicts the newspaper correspondent and the historian mention the chief officers, the corps, the divisions, the brigades, sometimes a regiment, but rarely a company or a private soldier. Space, on the pages of history, has never permitted a detailed description of Waterloo or Gettysburg. Waterloo, where all Europe were engaged, was described in one-third of a column of the London Morning Chronicle in 1815!   —FREDERIC HUDSON[3]

〰〰〰✕〰〰〰

What conclusions about "good" and "bad" language habits do you draw from these paragraphs? Can you formulate some specific rules from your conclusions which should guide your own speaking and thinking?

[1] *University Debater's Annual.* New York: The H. W. Wilson Co., 1931, 145. Reprinted by permission of the publishers.
[2] Oliver Wendell Holmes, *Autocrat of the Breakfast Table.* Boston: Houghton Mifflin Company, 1891, 28.
[3] Frederic Hudson, *Journalism in the United States.* New York: Harper & Brothers, 1873, xxiii.

ACQUAINTANCE, ABSTRACTING, NON-ALLNESS

×××××○××××○××××○××××○××××○××××○××××○××××○××××○××××○××××○××××

Getting Acquainted with the Territory

What an individual experiences depends upon which specialized structures in his nervous system are stimulated. Note the paper on which this is written. In what ways can an observer have relationships with it? He can see it, touch it, smell it, taste it, lift it, tear it, etc. Each sort of response provides one avenue of acquaintance, because the receptors (the eyes, nostrils, skin, etc.) are so differentiated that each is sensitive only to particular stimuli. The wave lengths of radiations which affect the rods and cones in the retina of the eye do not also affect the nerve endings, membranes, and canals in the ear. Each nervous receptor will thus be excited by but some stimuli from the paper. And since none is "all-engaging," it follows that our acquaintance with the paper through any one nervous means will be *specific and partial*.

Second, variations in sensitivity in the specialized nervous receptors in different observers will make for differences in the reports of their experiences. Deafness, color blindness, near- and far-sightedness, fatigue, adaptation, reaction time, etc., influence both the kind and the quantity of impressions, thus making acquaintance with anything *personal and individual*.

Third, the character of an individual's habits and interests affects the working of the nervous mechanisms so that his responses to stimuli are individualized. Objects viewed by several persons may thus give rise to widely varying evaluations. How different the reactions of a hungry baby, a dairyman, a bacteriologist to a bottle of milk. " 'Milk,' Barrymore looked horrified. 'I tried the stuff once,' he said

55

shuddering, 'but the stuff turned to chamois in my stomach!' "[1] "The fool sees not the same tree that a wise man sees," said William Blake.

Fourth, what is experienced varies with the position of the observer. "Where you are determines what you see." It makes a difference whether your seat at the opera is in the orchestra or in the top gallery on the side; whether you study New York City from the tower of the Empire State Building or the lush surroundings of an exclusive night club; whether you are in a bomb shelter or near a radio getting the news summary of an air raid. In the foreground of a famous Holbein painting one can see an oblong yellow patch, but from one particular position the patch looks like the top of a skull. The notion of perspective thus further emphasizes the *partial* character of experience. "There is no possible point of view from which the world can appear as an absolutely single fact."[2] And when different observers are located in different places, it should not be surprising if they get different impressions and so make different maps.

Fifth, the fact that human reactions occur in "time" makes impossible our acquaintance with any object from all sides at once. At best, human study can proceed only serially, i.e., viewing the various aspects in turn. Details must be missed as observation goes on. A blade of grass as well as a three-ring circus defies coverage at any instant. But even if there were time to use the full resources of the nervous system, our acquaintance would still be partial, for microscopes and atom-smashing chambers would reveal new details. And special investigators, chemists, physicists, technicians, etc., could extend the areas of observation indefinitely, so that the process of becoming acquainted with anything must ever remain incomplete. In the words of George Santayana,

[1] Excerpt from *PM*, Feb. 28, 1941, 22, copyrighted by The Newspaper PM, Inc., N. Y. Reprinted by special permission of the copyright owners.

[2] William James, *The Will to Believe*. New York: Longmans, Green & Co., 1912, ix. Reprinted by permission.

The most exhaustive account which human science can ever give of anything does not cover all that is true about it. All the external relations and affinities of anything are truths relevant to it; but they radiate in space and time to infinity, or at least to the unknown limits of the world . . . before we could know all about [the flower in the crannied wall] we should have to explore for ourselves the whole universe in which it grows. Evidently complete knowledge of anything, if we include all its natural and ideal relations, is incompatible with mortality and with the biological basis of thought.[3]

Language and Abstracting

Here the Red Queen began again. "Can you answer useful questions?" she said. "How is bread made?"

"I know that!" Alice cried eagerly. "You take some flour ———."

"Where do you pick the flower?" the White Queen asked. "In a garden or in the hedges?"

"Well, it isn't picked at all," Alice explained, "it's ground ———."

"How many acres of ground?" said the White Queen. "You mustn't leave out so many things."[4]

Our analysis of the ways of acquaintance as a means of asserting the inexhaustible characteristics of nature, its manyness, its legion of details, and the segmented, isolating, and limiting character of human awareness should make clear the difficulties involved in the White Queen's admonition, for Alice could not do otherwise. Whenever we respond we *abstract* some details from a total situation, so that some others must be left out. Every way of looking brings with it some areas of blindness. "A way of seeing is also a way of not seeing—a focus upon object A involves a neglect of object B."[5] As Korzybski says, "We see what we see because we *miss* all the finer details."[6]

[3] George Santayana, *Obiter Scripta*, ed. by Justus Buchler and Benjamin Schwartz. New York: Charles Scribner's Sons, 1936, 132. Reprinted by permission.

[4] Lewis Carroll, *Through the Looking-Glass*, Ch. IX.

[5] Kenneth Burke, *Permanence and Change*. New York: The New Republic, 1935, 70.

[6] Alfred Korzybski, *Science and Sanity, an Introduction to Non-Aristotelian Systems and General Semantics*. Lancaster, Pa.: The Science Press Printing Co., 1933, 376.

What applies to the workings of the nervous system applies also to the coverage "capacities" of language as a form of representation. A map of any piece of territory will of necessity be diagrammatic, that is, indicate only a few of the many relationships which exist in the territory. The map can never cover all the minute aspects of the land, growths, markings, buildings, streets, conditions due to weather, etc. The map-maker, according to his purposes, selects and indicates some of the aspects while ignoring others.

Bloomfield approaches the matter this way. Any object or situation includes a wide range of stimuli, and any observer possesses a wide range of predispositions and ways of becoming acquainted with the object or situation. The stimulation and response "are to all practical purposes continuous," whereas the forms of language are discrete and specific. This being so, it follows that when we use language we must abstract, must fail to include in any report "all the features of a situation." Thus, for example:

If we do not consider the extension of an object, we may call it a "line"; if of two only, we call it a "surface"; terms like "straight line," "plane," "triangle," etc., add further characteristics, but still leave unmentioned certain simple features which are present in every object.[7]

What is said here has been said before.

[7] Leonard Bloomfield, *Linguistic Aspects of Science*. Chicago: The University of Chicago Press, 1939, 37. Reprinted by permission.

There is indeed nothing that admits of *complete* description, for things are so interrelated that however much we may say of a given thing, there ever remains more to say of it; and complete description of one object would involve—in fact it would *be*—complete description of every other.[8]

No language can give a complete account of any situation or experience in the sense that given only the language we can produce the situation. . . .An essential distinction between language and experience is that language separates out from the living matrix little bundles and freezes them.[9]

No philosophy an ever be anything but a summary sketch, a picture of the world in abridgment, a foreshortened bird's-eye view of the perspective of events.[10]

Symbols can only represent certain selected phases of nature and society, never the totality of "reality" in all its complexity. . . . No single language, frame of reference, or system of symbols can capture all the aspects of nature.[11]

We need to realize . . . that nature transcends our . . . abstractions, in the sense that nature contains more than the scientific law or equation expresses.[12]

We must conclude that just as no map can have in it "all" the features of the territory it represents, so, too, no verbal utterances can give "*all*" the characteristics or details of whatever it is used to represent.

What Happens When Abstracting Is Forgotten?

How easy it is to stop when a principle has been explained. How obvious this business of abstracting, and how oblivious to it we can be when it comes to application. And what dire consequences when in what we do and say we

[8] C. J. Keyser, *Mole Philosophy and Other Essays.* New York: E. P. Dutton & Co., 1927, 132. Reprinted by permission.

[9] P. W. Bridgman, *The Nature of Physical Theory.* Princeton, N. J.: Princeton University Press, 1936, 20, 24. Reprinted by permission.

[10] William James, *A Pluralistic Universe.* New York: Longmans, Green & Co., 1909, 8. Reprinted by permission.

[11] Sidney Ratner, "Presupposition and Objectivity in History," *Philosophy of Science,* VII (Oct., 1940), 504. Reprinted by permission.

[12] Oliver L. Reiser, *The Promise of Scientific Humanism.* New York: Oskar Piest, 1940, 51.

are not conscious of the workings of the nervous system and the inherent difficulties in the functioning of language.

But men have forgotten and continue to forget. The list of those who have taken the adequacy of language coverage for granted is a long one. It includes the social scientists who wait for decisions "until the evidence is all in"; the demagogues and panacea-makers who assert the single principles which promise to solve the whole of life's complexities; the guardians of doctrines who require that "Ye shall not add unto the words, neither shall ye diminish aught from it"; those who would burn the papers of an Abélard because he would argue the usefulness of "doubt"; the Hitlers who exalt the finality of one-sidedness ("Once I have decided on my course I am filled with boundless fanaticism"); the historians who insist that their cullings and sortings somehow piece together into the "definitive history as it actually was"; the debaters who erect their approximate descriptions into compelling totalities; the Renans for whom "the world today has no more mysteries"; the Ciceros who know that "mental stains can neither be blotted out by the passage of time nor washed away by any waters"; the cosmologists who find axioms in postulates and who argue for *the* geometry and universe-picture of a Euclid and a Newton, forgetful that each is but *a* geometry and *a* universe-picture; the gullible taken in by the lures and soft words of the confidence men; the psalmic quoter, "I said in my haste all men are liars"; the practical men, "who believe only what they see"; the judges who, quoting but a few passages from the shelf of his books, pronounce the "immorality" of a Bertrand Russell; the researchers whose reduction of *a* situation gives *the* facts; the academicians who could see only "romantic dreams" in the diathermy treatments of Arsene d'Arsonval; the students who so readily assume they "understand" whatever they read for the first time; those who "keep up with affairs" by reading but one newspaper; the men who so confidently predict the outcome of games on the basis of small shreds of information; the pundits and columnists so ready with prophecies based so often on local gossip; people whose fears and worries are intensified because they focus full attention on the possibilities of failure, danger, and defeat; the paranoiacs who see only the persecution aspects of the behavior of other people; those who feel "inferior" because they see only their relationships with those who are "superior"; those who feel "superior" because they see only their relationships with those who are "inferior." . . .

What to Do?

That the impossible assumption of "allness" has had destructive effects in generating conflicts, in preserving obscurantism and ignorance, while preventing our plumbing the vast areas of human existence, has not been unrealized. In the words of a columnist:

> No addition to the total of human knowledge was ever made by one who was convinced that the end of knowledge had been reached. No one ever learned anything who thought he had nothing to learn. . . . The civilized man may have convictions, but he tries to keep them from crystallizing.[13]

Attacks on the "closed mind," arguments for the necessity of tolerance, and pleadings for the fertilization of curiosity are also nothing new. Here is an editorial putting the matter in most practical terms.

> Do your mental muscles feel stiff? Are your convictions, hates, resentments, tooling a deep crease between your eyebrows? Do you feel sometimes as if you could scream at this world and all the rot that's in it?
> Here's a suggestion. It may do you good to pick out your pet hate or your deepest conviction, and force yourself to think just the other way for, say, four or five minutes.
> Suppose you detest John L. Lewis, just for instance, above anybody else now treading this mortal earth. Well, for just five minutes, tell yourself with all the earnestness and resolution you can call up that you admire Mr. Lewis, think he's great, believe he's got something or other nobody else has. . . .

[13] Howard Vincent O'Brien, "All Things Considered." Chicago *Daily News*, Dec. 11, 1939, 14. Reprinted by permission.

You can always go back at the end of such a period to hating John L. Lewis . . . or whatever you hate most.

But during that period you've been relaxing your mental and spiritual muscles, so to speak—same principle as flexing and relaxing muscles for exercise.

Give it a try. Our estimate is that six out of every eight persons who do so will feel mentally refreshed and rejuvenated after each session of this kind of mind-limbering, and that anybody who makes a practice of it will gradually deepen and broaden his or her whole outlook on life.[14]

If this advice does work with "six out of every eight persons," then it is here recommended with the hope that more will try to make it work. But it is necessary to demur because much experience has shown differently. How difficult to "see another side." The man or woman who approves vigorously of the continuance of the "private enterprise system" is not likely to have either the data or the arguments or the methods and techniques with which to "think" otherwise. To have the will without the wisdom is usually to end in frustration. Further, such advice is offered as a means of dealing with a particular case whereas the problems of "allness" crop up continuously. We need a method so deep-seated and general that it makes the recurrence of those rigidity habits less frequent.

In this quest a twofold program is offered involving the consciousness of a process and the use of a device.

First, one must be convinced of the *fact of non-allness*, which Korzybski has summarized in these words:

Let us take any actual object; for instance, what we call a pencil. Now, we may describe or "define" a "pencil" in as great detail as we please, yet it is impossible to include *all* the characteristics which we may discover in this actual objective pencil. If the reader will try to give a "complete" description or a "perfect" definition of any actual physical object, so as to include "all" particulars, he will be convinced that this task is humanly impossible. These would have to describe, not only the numerous

[14] "Look At the Other Side," *Collier's,* March 23, 1940, 86. Reprinted by permission.

rough, macroscopic characteristics, but also the microscopic details, the chemical composition and changes, submicroscopic characteristics and the endlessly changing relationship of this objective something which we have called pencil to the rest of the universe, etc., an inexhaustible array of characteristics which could never be terminated. In general, physical abstractions, including daily-life abstractions, are such that *particulars are left out*—we proceed by a process of forgetting. In other words, no description or "definition" will ever include all particulars.[15]

If, then, the achievement of "allness" is prevented by the characteristics of the nervous system, it should be clear that in speaking and acting one can only abstract *some* details while omitting *others*. *Consciousness of abstracting* as a habitual reaction will lead directly to attitudes of non-allness. This consciousness is the coveted first step in *proper evaluation*, for when men act as if what they say says "all," delusions and improper evaluation are inevitable.

Second, the new attitudes may be coached into practice by the memory of a simple device which summarizes the fact that details are invariably left out in speaking. A hint of it is found in a statement by William James, that "the word 'and' trails along after every sentence. Something always escapes. 'Ever not quite' has to be said of the best attempts made anywhere in the universe at attaining all-inclusiveness."[16] We here adopt a variant in the contraction, ETC., used to indicate that "more could be said." Habitual use of the ETC. silently or orally should dissolve the "all-ness-growths" by producing consciousness of factors left out. Which suggests a "new" slogan: Remember the ETC.

Maximum Probability and the Business of Prophecy

For the astrologers, the investment counselors, the readers of tea leaves and palms, the political seers, the columnists, etc., the assertion of things to come is an important and

[15] Alfred Korzybski, *Science and Sanity*, 68.
[16] William James, *A Pluralistic Universe*, 321. Reprinted by permission.

profitable stock in trade. But how shall we take their insistent utterances? Under what conditions do we get useful predictions?

The work of a man like Pasteur may suggest an answer. In one of his many achievements he was able to devise methods by which disturbing microbes could be kept from getting into liquids. He was able, too, to bring about the growth of one variety of microbe without having it contaminated by other kinds. Having tested his procedures in a variety of circumstances, aware of what those circumstances were and of his role in the process, he could say something like this: If you will do this and that under these conditions with this kind of material, these things are *very likely* to occur. Because he controlled the *important,* but not *all* the circumstances, he was never able to say what would happen with *absolute certainty.*

Now back to prophecy. The "perfect" prophet would know "all" there was to know about the subject, "all" that had occurred before, "all" that was now occurring, and "all" the possible factors which might occur to affect the outcome. If but one solitary new factor were to be introduced, the first conclusion might be invalid in some respects. The "perfect" prophet must see *all* and not merely *some* of the possibilities.

The trouble with most prophecies, however, should now be evident. The nervous systems of human beings function by *abstracting* from the totality, not by exhausting it. And if some factors or aspects of the situation are neglected but nevertheless do influence the course of circumstances, then what happens in life is very often quite different. The pattern of prophecies which do not turn out appears something like this: The seer argues that with facts B, C, and D operating, then action A must inevitably occur. But other factors X, Y, and Z intervene, giving rise to action M. In short, the prophecy went askew because some factors were not (or perhaps could not be) taken into account.[17]

[17] See Robert Lord, "About a Book," *Rob Wagner's Script,* Oct. 21, 1939, 8.

At least two attitudes can be taken toward the business of prophecy. One is to disregard everyone, on the ground that no prophet can be "completely certain," that in discussions of our complex social, economic, and political life the control that gave Pasteur authority cannot be achieved. The shifting of a single factor far off might at any moment introduce a chain of influences far-reaching and upsetting. A second attitude implies discounting on our part and a recognition that the fallibility of prophets is not something unusual, given the enormous possibilities of new factors. A full consciousness on our part that prophets, like the rest of us, abstract from the totality will prevent despair and cynicism on the one hand and disappointment on the other. Prophecies must be looked upon not as infallible truths but as *possible* guides and hints of what probably will happen. If Pasteur could not claim omniscience in the little area in which he operated, humility in the big matters should not be too much to ask for.

In Short

We see what we see, but human nervous systems cannot get to "all" the details of anything. Our speech abstracts

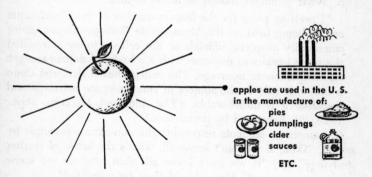

apples are used in the U. S.
in the manufacture of:
pies
dumplings
cider
sauces
ETC.

some details and neglects others. Partial descriptions must not be defined as "complete." The assumption of "allness" leads to tension and conflict, the preservation of ignorance, and the blockage of further learning.

Habits to be acquired: (1) a consciousness of abstracting, and (2) memory of the ETC.

FOR FURTHER STUDY

1. The first time you come upon a "dogmatic" person, try to engage him in the game of trying to say "all" about anything. Use the first object at hand. Be sure to explain that "what he sees he sees," but that since the nervous system abstracts, not "all" can be said.

2. A group project is most useful in demonstrating non-allness. Let a group visit a museum, movie, ball game, public institution, well-known locality, etc., after which let each individual report orally or in writing what he "saw." To what extent did they see the "same things"?

3. Read three or four different biographies of any well-known historical figure—Lincoln, Napoleon, Marie Antoinette, Henry VIII, etc. Did the same picture emerge?

4. What silent assumptions are made in the following?
    1. La Martine: "History teaches everything, even the future."
    2. Francis Bacon: "I have taken all knowledge as my province."

5. What comment should be made to this?

"Upsetting plans for the feature number of the Chautauqua course being held on the Morningside College campus under community auspices, officials of the college today compelled the show leaders to dispense with a scheduled debate tonight on companionate marriage. The college heads declared there is only one side to the subject of companionate marriage and therefore it is undebatable. (*The American Mercury,* Sept., 1928, 29. Reprinted by permission.)

6. Sometimes students respond to the non-allness principle by saying, "Well, if we can't know all, what's the sense of further studying?" and "If we can't know all, then how do we know we know anything?" How should they be answered?

7. At any place in the chapter is it said that we *do not* see what we see? What is said?

8. You should begin the collection of "allness" statements which you find in newspapers, magazines, speeches, conversa-

tions, etc. Even more important than what is said, take notice of the "allness" attitudes of speakers, their tension and rigidity.

9. What happens in discussion groups when participants assume they say "all"?

10. What are some of the popular recipes for overcoming "allness"? Are they workable? Compare their efficacy with "consciousness of abstracting."

CHAPTER V

A WORLD IN PROCESS

Amyclae *in ancient Greece had been harassed so often by false reports of an invasion by the Spartans that a stringent law was passed forbidding anyone to mention the enemy again. Shortly afterward, the Spartans did arrive and, as no one dared to give the alarm, Amyclae was captured and went down in history as "the city that perished through silence."* —Freling Foster[1]

> No single thing abides; but all things flow.
> Fragment to fragment clings—the things thus grow
> Until we know and name them. By degrees
> They melt, and are no more the things we know.
>
> Globed from the atoms falling slow or swift
> I see the suns, I see the systems lift
> Their forms: and even the systems and the suns
> Shall go back slowly to the eternal drift . . .
>
> Nothing abides. Thy seas in delicate haze
> Go off; those mooned sands forsake their place;
> And where they are, shall other seas in turn
> Mow with their scythes of whiteness other bays.
> —Lucretius[2]

The scientific spirit requires a man to be at all times ready to dump his whole cartload of beliefs, the moment experience is against them. The desire to learn forbids him to be perfectly cocksure that he knows already. C. S. Peirce

※※※◇※※※

What has the notion of change to do with language habits? Are you usually aware that nothing "stands still" when you talk and act?

[1] Freling Foster, "Keep Up With the World," *Collier's*, May 10, 1941, 8. Reprinted by permission.
[2] Lucretius, from *On the Nature of Things*, trans. by W. H. Mallock. Used by permission of Dodd, Mead and Company, Inc.

A WORLD IN PROCESS

No "Rest"

Max Born has given our text: "It is odd to think that there is a word for something which, strictly speaking, does not exist, namely 'rest.'"

The winds, the rains, and the snows; the ebb and flow of the waves and currents of the sea; the shifting clouds; the rhythm of the seasons ceaselessly changing; the growth and aging of animals and men; the nervous dartings of the vehicles on the streets; the hum and drive of the dynamos and power houses; the turning colors and dimensions of the things that grow in the fields—these are but a hint of the gross changes we perceive about us, an ever so brief list of the endless and sometimes haphazard flux of our "restless universe."

To one who will read the books on the history of "ideas," the panorama of our cultural development is marked with no "rest" either. The "march of mind in time" is too apparent. Compare for a moment the differences within the last century in our views in the U. S. A. on the role of women, the rights of labor, the place of charity, the virtues of democracy, the authority of scientific methods, the necessity of education, the spread of technology, and the significance of the Bible. The fashions in criticism, the new attitudes on morals and art, the changing folkways, the codification of custom in laws—these are but chapter headings attesting to the change and evolution in our attitudes and evaluations.

More immediately, reflect on your own patterns of re-

[1] Max Born, *The Restless Universe*. New York: Harper & Brothers, 1936, 1. Reprinted by permission.

sponse from moment to moment and hour to hour. From boredom to excitement, from fatigue to alertness, from hate to love, from interest to satiety, from despair to hope, or from faith to cynicism one moves with and without purpose, sounding the changes on the gamut of response with ever-varying vividness and intensity. As Keyser says so eloquently:

> For the most obvious, the most embracing, the most poignant and the most tragic fact in the pageant we call the world is the fact of *Change*; in the world of sights and sounds, in the world of *sense*, nothing abides. "The life of man," said the Spirit of the Ocean, "passes by like a galloping horse, changing at every turn, at every hour."[2]

At Deeper Levels

Long before our time Leucippus and Democritus had postulated the existence of atoms—minute, indivisible, unchanging bits—as the basic stuff of all material things. It remained for J. Dalton, father of so-called modern atomism, followed by Gay-Lussac, Berzelius, *et al.*, to codify the theory that the earth, planets, human beings, animals, houses, radios and pencils—in short, everything with which we can be acquainted—is made up of similar kinds of elementary stuff.

More recent scientific interpretations of chemical changes, of heat and cold, the phenomena of electrolysis, the electromagnetic theory of light, studies of isotopes, Brownian movements, spectra analyses of X-rays, researches in the radioactive disintegration of radium and uranium, etc., have, however, modified the early notions that the atom is "the basic indivisible particle of matter." By cunning manipulation of heat, explosions, magnetic fields, high voltages, caught by gravity or detected by fluorescent light or smashed in massive cyclotrons, the atom has been revealed as a universe in itself, as complex as anything that exists. So that now in 1941 the atoms of whatever one might mention

[2] Cassius J. Keyser, *Mathematical Philosophy*. New York: E. P. Dutton & Co., 1922, 181. Reprinted by permission.

can be broken down to electrons, positrons, protons, mesons, neutrinos, neutrons . . . and the full picture of the sub-atomic organization is not yet drawn.

Attempts to picture the atom have been many, from Bragg's description, "like someone's head, a nucleus with a cloud of mosquitoes [electrons] buzzing around it," to Swann's, a region of "wiggling knottiness" free to behave at random.[3] Garbedian has summarized some other efforts:

The solar system atom of Rutherford, in which electrons re-volved around a central nucleus in the manner of planets about the sun, has lost its popularity and has been abandoned. Bohr gave us a new picture of the atom as a shell which housed jump-ing electrons—electrons which jumped from orbit to orbit and radiated energy as they did so. Then came DeBroglie with his picture of the atom as a tiny particle accompanied by waves, somewhat in the manner of a boat which is followed by a train of ripples. DeBroglie's scheme has now been replaced by the Schroedinger theory, which pictures the atom as a pulsating sphere of electricity, a diffuse cloud of electricity, a kind of halo vibrating around an undefined center. Heisenberg has recently modified the Schroedinger atom with the concept that the cen-tral nebula of the atom consists of concentrated particles of electricity, the electrons, dancing around the nucleus. Heisen-berg has made this perplexing problem of the nature of the atom even more difficult with his principle of indeterminacy—gen-erally termed "the uncertainty principle"—according to which a particle may have position or it may have a velocity, but it cannot in any exact sense have both.[4]

At the heart of the analysis of the atom in modern physics is the sense of a perpetual, energetic "mad dance"; a hurry-ing, oscillating, vibrating existence at submicroscopic levels. Thus, our primitive atomistic view of a dead, indestructible,

[3] *Time,* Nov. 11, 1940, 41. Reprinted by permission.

[4] H. Gordon Garbedian, *The March of Science.* New York: Halcyon House, 1936, 73-74. Reprinted by permission of Covici Friede, Inc.

"Scientists do not try to visualize the atom; its mechanics are too complex, too alien to the familiar things of life. Laymen can visu-alize it after a fashion by imagining a heavy nucleus composed of protons and neutrons clumped together surrounded by a sort of throbbing mist of electrons." (*Time,* May 12, 1941, 72.)

solid "matter" must be replaced by a view which emphasizes the *process character* of the world. If, below the ordinary macroscopic and microscopic levels of sense perception, there exists a level of motion and high velocity, we believe in a delusion when we view the world about as static and enduring "matter." We must "see" it, also, as at its deeper levels, a very lively world in *process*.

On occasion students are disturbed by such pictures of the nature of the world at deeper levels. Belief is at first not easy, for the hard chair or table does seem at "rest." But a host of everyday experiences should have made them conscious of phenomena that are not seen, such as voltage in wires, radio waves, chemicals in solution, the rusting of iron, the tarnishing of silver, the fading of colors, etc. Even the process of aging suggests that something is happening which our senses and rough instruments of acquaintance do not register. The chair, if left untouched and unused long enough, will crumble and disappear.

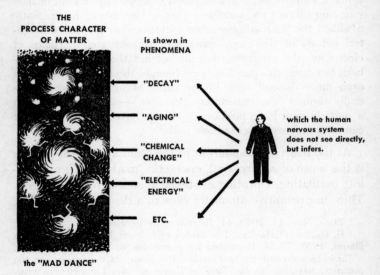

THE
PROCESS CHARACTER
OF MATTER   is shown in
PHENOMENA

"DECAY"

"AGING"

"CHEMICAL
CHANGE"

"ELECTRICAL
ENERGY"

ETC.

which the human
nervous system
does not see directly,
but infers.

the "MAD DANCE"

A student once told this story of the way he came to an understanding of the process character of "things." From the veranda of a cabin in Glacier Park he could see a row of mountains, and directly in front between two peaks a thin patch of white stretched vertically as if to provide a boundary line. The patch appeared "still and unmoving." But once he set out to see it and found a swirling waterfall. What was "immobile" six miles away turned out to be something very much in motion up close.

And so it is with the chair. What is seen at the levels of sense perception is quite different from the picture we get from the theories the physicist makes to account for what goes on slowly at gross levels. As Born says:

> We distinguish between living and dead matter; between moving bodies and bodies at rest. This is a primitive point of view. What seems dead, a stone, or the proverbial "doornail," say, is actually for ever in motion. We have merely become accustomed to judge by outward appearances; by the deceptive impressions we get through our senses.[5]

Giving Process Character to the Language

What is the significance of this process view of the world for our attitudes toward language and its use?

A starting point is found in this statement by Levy:

> It is possible that in his effort to build up an environment on which he could rely and which he could control, man has striven always for permanence, to find and to use unchanging elements in a changing world. On these he has attempted to build up a solid basis for his life. And so it is not surprising that his language is honeycombed with words that suggest fixed, static, unalterable things—*tables, mountains, I.*[6]

Reflect on the word "table." Does it suggest the dynamic, changing character of the submicroscopic events? Does it even hint at the slower, gross, macroscopic, moment-to-moment changes in the object? Does the word as a word imply anything about the process? Or as you look at the word,

[5] Max Born, *The Restless Universe*, 1.

[6] H. Levy, *A Philosophy for a Modern Man*. New York: Alfred A. Knopf, 1938, 15. Reprinted by permission.

are not the implications static? Are you not led to a sense of the changeless character of the object?

And so it is with the bulk of the nouns in our language. Elaborated in the centuries when the macroscopic world was the only one known, it is not strange that our everyday language should only reflect that seemingly static existence. If, however, for maximum efficiency and proper evaluation our maps should fit the territory they are designed to represent, and if the territory is revealed by our best knowledge as something in process, then a way must be found to make our utterances correspondingly process-like. In short, if change goes on about us, that change must be suggested in our verbal representations, in what we say about ourselves and the world.

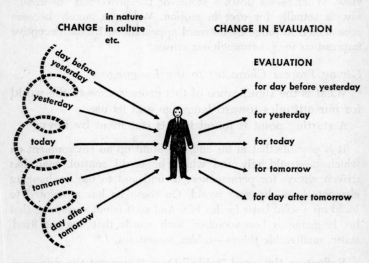

What is needed, then, is a technique of location. If an object exists in process, then statements must place it at some point *in time*. A description of a table should *say when*, at what date in the object's history it is made, so that the description does not mistakenly lead one to assume that it fits for "all time"—which may or may not be the case. Adding a date would tend to prevent settling by language what is not settled in life facts. Furthermore, when the time factor has been differentiated, we get a new sense of discrimination in observing what goes on.

For instance, a man is shot. Where? At the corner of 7th Avenue and 42nd Street, New York. This fixes the place by two coordinates crossing at right angles in a plane. But was it above or below this, on the twentieth floor of the Times Building or in the Subway? Knowing this fixes the third dimension, but we still have to fix its position in a fourth dimension, time. Was it today or last week and what hour? If, then, we find out all four we can distinguish this shooting from any that may have occurred in other places at the same time or at other times in the same place.[7]

In short, what is being urged here is this: the development of the habit of dating, or even better, a consciousness of it in everyday speech. It involves little more than the addition of the date as a subscript to whatever we are thinking or speaking about. Thus, the President $_{1938}$, my automobile $_{May, 1940}$, etc.

Date Your Statements

The systematic and habitual use of the simple device of dating statements would have far-reaching effects.

The immediate result would be to make clear the specific area in which one speaks. The France $_{of\ 1941}$ is not the France $_{of\ 1937}$. The Chamberlain of Munich was not the Chamberlain who read the declaration of war on Germany. The apple on the tree is not the cut apple on the table a month later. The boy sent to reform school is not the same boy on his release a year later. The coddled coed of nineteen is not (and should not try to be) the coddled youngster of five.

Public and private discussions marked by the persistent use of dates (or a consciousness of them in talking) might well become more cautious and less given to great sweeping statements about men and events. Men might be moved

[7] Edwin E. Slosson, *Easy Lessons in Einstein*. New York: Harcourt, Brace and Howe, 1920, 31. Reprinted by permission.

to delay condemnations of the "decadence and materialism of democracies," for there may be times when the actions of the latter appear otherwise. They might even hesitate before extolling the virtues of "fascist efficiency" to reckon with the moments when other judgments are possible. Orators who open the stops on "The American Way" might reflect on conditions before and after the Civil War, the year 1929, and the WPA. Before arguments become heated on "ultimate standards" and "eternal verities," it may be useful to question whether they were always thus. Before asserting the mercenary habits of a "Jew" or a "Scotchman," the habit of dating might lead to the discovery that he appears so only sometimes. In preparation for the delivery of discourses on Freudianism, Marxism, Modern Art, etc., notice should probably be taken of the possibility that their emphases may have shifted from time to time. Debates about the Classics, Great Speeches, or Great Anything might be tempered by the admonition to "say when," for between 1863 and 1941 the *Gettysburg Address* has been considered differently, and even *Hamlet* has had its critical ups and downs between the then and now. Perhaps the memory of Somerset Maugham's plaint will be helpful.

In my twenties the critics said I was brutal, in my thirties they said I was flippant, in my forties they said I was cynical, in my fifties they said I was competent (used with sarcastic implications) and now in my sixties they say I am superficial.[8]

Consider how the failure to date may be involved in human relationships. Miss Jay was insulted by Mrs. Burns on the afternoon of June 12, 1936. It is now 1941. The two have grown older, assumed new responsibilities, and moved far from each other. The feud, however, persists. "An insult is an insult, and I'll not forget it," is Miss Jay's argument in spite of the fact that the insult situation in 1936 does not exist in 1941. Conditions have changed and so have the

[8] From *The Summing Up*, by W. Somerset Maugham, copyright, 1938, p. 223; reprinted by permission of Doubleday, Doran and Company, Inc.

participants. Only the word "insult" remains timeless, unchanging, and undated. Not dissimilar in pattern and effect are the nationalistic rivalries nurtured and fed by aging generations to the young, quite unmindful that rivalries generated long ago are not the rivalries artificially whipped up now.

Unwed mothers, men with prison records, the youngster who "pulls a boner," the man who once was called "yellow" —these know well how it feels to be haunted by people who react as if lives are not in process. Note how the words "thief," "dumb-bell," "quitter" give little sign that the men behind the labels have nervous systems that in life keep going, changing from date to date. Only the labels stick.

For those who insist that "once a criminal always a criminal," the story of John Thomas Cain might be instructive.

Well known to the police of London's East End is 15-year-old Costerboy John Thomas Cain. Often enough they have had him up for piddling misdemeanors, blocking traffic with his barrow, chucking unsold vegetables about at the day's end. Last week, however, the Metropolitan Police would have looked the other way if he had overturned his barrow in Piccadilly Circus. For John Thomas Cain was sporting one of the highest awards for gallantry that his country can give a civilian, the George Medal. He is, so far, the youngest Briton to wear it.

John Thomas Cain has three hobbies: snooker pool, beer drinking, and rescuing bombees (score to date: twelve single-handed rescues, 44 assists). Playing pool one night, John heard the crash of a bomb, looking out of the billiard parlor window saw a paint factory down the street go up in a stinking inferno of flames and fumes. With four policemen John dug into the basement, slithered through a four-foot flood of paint, dodged arcing electric wires. On doors they hauled ten workmen into the street, six alive. As they were carrying the last one away the building shuddered and fell. Then John Thomas Cain went to a pub and had a beer.[9]

Neglect of the date sometimes accompanies profound

[9] *Time,* March 3, 1941, 10. Reprinted by permission.

personal disturbances. When an individual disregards the changing circumstances in his life, describing them in terms that manifest stability so that his adjustments are not consonant with the circumstances, some disorganization is to be expected. Two examples may make the point.

Mr. Eks was thoroughly frightened at the age of five by the roar of an onrushing locomotive. The noise was so loud and so sudden that the fright was justified (aged 5). But for the next sixty years the influence of the situation remained, so that at sixty-five the fear persisted and prevented him from moving into open places more than a mile from his house. Mr. Eks readily admits his "fear of distance" and is willing to discuss it. It is important to realize that the timeless, unchanging, undated character of the phrase "fear of distance" may act to conceal and even to prevent the sense of process in his evaluations, and further, to affect his ability to observe first, that he at sixty-five should understand and not fear what at age five he did not understand and so feared, and second, that the roar of the train in 1880 is not existent now to inclose his movements. "Fear of distance" for the man of sixty-five ought not be the same as for a boy of five. The phrase remains to preserve the pattern of the response, even though the life facts have been in process for sixty years.

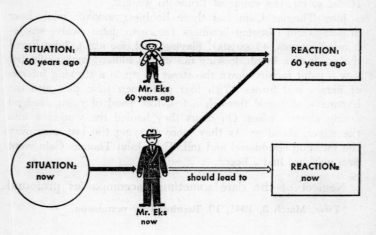

Bill came into the Instructor's office on the tenth of October, worried and depressed. After a short silence he said, "I should like your signature on this drop-slip. I want to leave school."

"Why?" he was asked.

"I'm quitting. I can't make it. I'm a failure," was the blurted answer.

"But what happened?"

"I came here from Fort Wayne with three other boys. We were good friends. Now they've been pledged to fraternities and I haven't. And I can't have them pitying me."

The Instructor sparred for time, then asked, "What did you do last summer?"

"Had a good job," Bill said.

"How good?"

"Made enough to pay this year's tuition and buy my books besides."

"Were you a 'failure' *then*?" the older man asked cautiously.

"Not at all," was the most cheerful note of the talk thus far.

"How about the last year in high school? Were you a 'failure' then?"

"No, I don't think so. I was in the top twenty per cent of the class in grades and played on the tennis team."

"But look," and the Instructor spoke very quietly, "you didn't call yourself a failure in the summer of 1940, nor in the winter of 1939-1940. Yet today, October 10, you do. Do you mean that from now on you'll be called nothing else? Aren't you making assumptions about what is to come?"

"I guess so," Bill replied. "But what should I do?"

"Remember the Date. Bill in 1939-1940 was not Bill in the summer, who is not Bill on October 10. Sure, things are somewhat unpleasant now. But that's no sign that you can't go on to do other things. What is true of today does not have to be true of next month. . . . " It took a half-hour to convince Bill that his description of his plight must take the fact of process into account. Perhaps readers will remember that Jesse Livermore, who had won and lost four fortunes, put a bullet through his head on November 28, 1940, leaving a suicide note which read, "I am tired of fighting. . . . I can't go on. . . . I'm a failure."[10]

Readers may be able to point the moral (and perhaps outline the necessary advice for "making sense") in the following two stories by André Maurois:

The slightest childhood memory may create absurd associations of ideas—that last as long as life itself. When I was five years old one of my uncles took me into his office and showed me the first telephone I had ever seen.

"I am going to call your father," he said, "and you will speak to him."

When he put me in front of this unknown, black object and said: "Speak!" I was terrified and could not say a word.

"This is very serious," said my uncle severely, who liked to tease children. "The law says that, if you ask for a connection and then say nothing, you must have your ears cut off!" And he thrust an enormous pair of scissors at me.

The strange consequence is that to this day I have an unconquerable mistrust of the telephone and a secret fear, every time I take off the receiver, that I will not be able to talk.

When such a memory is associated not with an object, but with a person, it will build up a resentment that can never be forgotten. I know a woman of forty who cannot meet her sixty-year-old mother without experiencing a mixture of fear and anger. Thinking the daughter unfair I said to her:

"Why do you answer your mother so rudely? What she said to you was unimportant and didn't justify your fury."

"Ah!" she replied, "you would not say that if you had known her twenty-five years ago! When I think that, in order to seem younger, she compelled me to wear my hair loose on my shoulders and dresses above my knees, at an age when all my friends had a chignon hair-do and long skirts; when I can hear the contemptuous tone in which she used to say: 'My daughter? Unfortunately she resembles her father—she will never be pretty,' then I cannot judge her by her present actions and words, but only by my old grievances."[11]

[10] The Chicago *Daily News*, Nov. 29, 1940, 10. Reprinted by permission.

[11] André Maurois, "Forget It," *This Week Magazine*, April 5, 1941, 2. Copyright 1941 by the United Newspapers Magazine Corporation. Reprinted by permission of the author.

In Short

In this world "things" and "thinking" are ever in process. There is no "rest." Our language use too often emphasizes the static. We speak as if life facts were not changing, as if our statements fit for "all-time." The time factor must become a part of human orientation.

Habits to be acquired: (1) Consciousness of the process character of nature, and (2) *Date* your statements.

FOR FURTHER STUDY

1. For a full day (or more) look about and observe the *process* that goes on around you. Remember the deeper, submicroscopic level. Try to imagine it when you look at objects and people.

2. For further data on the findings in physics and chemistry, read

   1. Bruce Bliven, "New Miracles of Atomic Research," *The New Republic,* June 16, 1941, 818-821.
   2. Max Born, *The Restless Universe.* New York: Harper & Brothers, 1936.
   3. John Pfeiffer, *Science in Your Life.* New York: The Macmillan Company, 1939.

3. Where have you heard about the notion of process before? In what school studies has it been called to your attention? What people do you know who seem most aware of it?

4. Do you know of consequences other than those suggested in this chapter which come from failure to date?

5. Make a catalogue of the ways you know of giving the notion of process to your speech—without using dates.

6. "On his ninetieth birthday, Mr. Chauncey M. Depew was called upon by a representative of the press who brought him congratulations and good wishes and invited a statement from Mr. Depew as to how it felt to be 90 years of age. 'But,' said Mr. Depew in a tone of startled surprise, 'I am not 90 years of age!' The young journalist, quite taken aback, said, 'But, Mr. Depew, my newspaper is very careful in these matters. Surely, they cannot have made a mistake. Were you not born, Sir, on April 23, 1834?' 'Certainly,' answered Mr. Depew. 'Then,' said the journalist triumphantly, 'surely that makes you 90 years old today.' 'Oh,' replied Mr. Depew with a characteristic smile, 'I see, young man, I see. You are one of those

who measure age by years. There is nothing in it, young man. Nothing in it.'" (From an address of Dr. Nicholas Murray Butler delivered at the 183rd Commencement of Columbia University.)

How would you analyze Mr. Depew's answer in terms of the principle of dating? You may want to come back to this after you have read Chapter IX.

7. "Shortly before dawn March 2, a young Negro named Robert Brady tried for the second time to break into Flynn's candy, hamburger and juke shop in Winchester, Ky. He had worked there once and he knew that on Sunday mornings the cash register was generally stuffed with change. A year ago he had tried to enter through a window but police had caught him and sent him to the reformatory. This time he decided to try the chimney. He didn't know as he eased himself down the rough, sooty shaft that the flue had undergone alterations —that, to improve the draught, it had been narrowed to 10 in. at the throat.

"Brady stuck when he reached the narrow part. He squirmed and kicked, but the black stones gripped his clothes and soon he could move neither up nor down. From the damped-down coals in the grate below rose exhalations. He may have cried for help. He certainly coughed before he suffocated and died. But there was no one to hear him. An employe who opened the store next morning discovered his lifeless feet dangling in the fireplace. Stonemasons had to take down part of the chimney in order to extract Brady's body from its sooted tomb. Then it was noted that, to keep himself warm, rash Robert Brady had on two overcoats, three pairs of pants. (*Life,* March 17, 1941, 42. Reprinted by permission.)

What "moral" do you draw from this story?

8. What relationships can you find between the responses designated by the word *dogmatism* and the principle of *dating*?

9. What does the principle of dating do to discussion of "the absolute"?

10. Do you know any individuals who would resist the application of process thinking in their lives and work? How do you account for that?

CHAPTER VI

INDEXING MAKES THE DIFFERENCES

John Lee, 33, a Negro, is on trial in General Sessions charged with stealing a watch and a dime from one Jeremiah Haggerty. "Would you believe the word of a Negro against that of a white man?" Lee's counsel asked Leo J. Goodwin, a prospective juror. "No, I would not," said Goodwin, manager of a sight-seeing bus concern, who comes from Florida. Judge Jonah J. Goldstein ordered Goodwin's name stricken from the jury panel.

—PM[1]

After he [General Goering] had returned to Berlin (1918), a socialist mob saw him in uniform and forcibly tore his officer's insignia from his coat lapels. Foaming with rage, he swore vengeance. His hatred of socialists, which is psychopathic in intensity, dates from that day. This incident is important to Nazi history. It is not entirely fanciful to assume that much of the Brown Terror was directly motivated by this incident.

—JOHN GUNTHER[2]

The tragedy of the innocent onlooker of a quarrel is only too well known. The anger that should have been felt for the antagonist is not felt for him at all but for the innocent bystander. Sometimes it even transfers itself to the whole class to which the antagonist or even the witness belongs. The woman-hater, or man-hater, the police-hater, or the teacher-hater, are all well-known types. Teachers are often hated and feared by a child on account of an experience with some other teacher. Often any person of authority is hated by some one whose anger has been deeply stirred. The more unwilling the person has been to admit the original cause, the more likely the discharge of emotion is to move on some innocent person. This is too often the basis of criminal behavior. The teacher, the police, and finally society as a whole become the victims of retribution for some act, often minor or even imagined, of the beloved parent. There is a record of this in many folk-sayings and acts. The bearers of bad tidings are usually disliked and were even killed by the Roman Tyrants.

—SMILEY BLANTON AND MARGARET BLANTON[3]

※※※◇※※※

How would you explain these reactions? Would you call them examples of "good sense"? Do you see any relationship between them and language habits? What specific measures do you now know to reorient the responses of the people?

[1] Excerpt from *PM*, May 23, 1941, 10, copyrighted by The Newspaper PM, Inc., N. Y. Reprinted by special permission of the copyright owners.

[2] John Gunther, *Inside Europe.* New York: Harper & Brothers, 1936, 64. Reprinted by permission.

[3] Smiley Blanton and Margaret Blanton, *For Stutterers.* New York: D. Appleton-Century Co., 1936, 54. Reprinted by permission.

INDEXING MAKES THE DIFFERENCES

⋙⋘⋙⋘⋙⋘⋙⋘⋙⋘⋙⋘⋙⋘⋙⋘⋙⋘⋙⋘⋙⋘

Uniqueness in Our World

If it were possible for us to take the time, with and without extra-neural instruments, to examine quietly and closely a host of objects from fingerprints, snowflakes, human skulls, and blades of grass to airplane parts, newly minted dimes, razor blades, and cans of soup, to people, animals, plants, buildings, autos, clouds, colors, sounds—admission of the fact that "things" exist in a vast and varied profusion should come rather quickly. The words *multiplicity, heterogeneity, dissimilarity* would begin to describe the basic structure of whatever we should come upon.

We should learn, perhaps for the first time, of the uniqueness of each thing that exists.

What could seem more nearly alike than the pebbles strewn along the seashore, but do we ever find two really the same? On the maple the leaves all look sufficiently alike to be recognized at once as maple leaves, yet how easy it is to pick any two and notice a difference between them. In some families the common type of feature is so marked that we can recognize even strangers as members. Yet seen together we easily distinguish even the very closely resembling twins. From cases of this near similarity of feature we turn our attention to that of faces in a great crowd. All are distinctly human, but there seem to be never two alike. So we could go on recalling the wonderful variety throughout every type or sort of object in the whole realm of nature. It is true, we should have to stop when we came to objects too small for us to see, or in some way directly to perceive. Thus it is true that you and I may not be able to find any difference between one set of atoms of hydrogen and the atoms of the same element elsewhere. But still there comes to one the belief that could we only see them as we see the leaves of the maple tree, the same wonderful variety would reveal itself here also. Is there any end to it as far as we can judge or as far as the facts of nature lead us to believe? We have to answer No, and thus regard the world as composed of objects admitting of an indefinite variety. Not only do these objects themselves differ, but their motions seem likewise to differ wherever we are able to observe them carefully. Who ever threw a stone through absolutely the same path in the air, landing upon the identical spot of ground as did the stone that he threw before? In short, who of us ever repeated an act with absolute accuracy? A careful measurement or observation would be sure to show parts of the act a little different in the one case from like parts in the other. We may try to play a piece of music twice over, but every time we do so, and are keenly observant, we are sensitive of differences. And what is true in such complicated activities as our own seems equally true, for the best of reasons, of the simple activities in the material world about us. What day is the exact repetition of some previous day in atmosphere and temperature? What river flows two successive days in exactly the same channel? . . . We hear over and over again of human nature being ever the same and of history repeating itself; but we do not mean this except in a rough way. No two instances of human conduct, no two stages in the world's history or in a nation's, are mere repetitions. A new element, and a very large new element, is sure to be found, if our observation and information be but fairly accurate and complete. Thus we find, no matter where we look, and we believe we could find even where our senses fail at present to reveal it, an indefinite variety of objects and an indefinite variety of actions or changes taking place in or through these objects.[1]

The argument may be briefly put this way: In this world "complete sameness" between any two of anything has not yet been demonstrated, for in some respects objects and happenings differ from each other. And the closer to nature we are able to get, the more apparent does this structural fact become.

When the fact of difference has been understood, we should be ready for another—that each item of our acquaint-

[1] Walter T. Marvin, *An Introduction to Systematic Philosophy.* New York: The Macmillan Company, 1903, 22-24.

ance, each object and happening will appear unique, differing in some details from every other one. As Korzybski says,

If we analyse the silent objective level by objective means available in [1941], say a microscope, we shall find that whatever we can see, handle, etc., represents an *absolute* individual, and *different from anything else in this world*. We discover, thus, an important structural fact of the external world; namely, that in it, everything we can see, touch, etc., that is to say, all lower-order abstractions, represent absolute individuals, different from everything else.[2]

And with that fact assimilated there is one more—that the "things" of our experience do not exist the same now as they were, for no "identity" or "external sameness" in their make-up is to be found from one instant to another.

. . . "identity," defined as "absolute sameness," necessitates "absolute sameness" in *"all"* aspects, never to be found in this world, nor in our heads. Anything with which we deal on the objective levels represents a process, different all the "time," no matter how slow or fast the process might be; therefore, a principle or a premise that "everything is identical with itself" is *invariably false to facts*. . . . If we take even a symbolic expression $1 = 1$, "absolute sameness" in *"all"* aspects is equally impossible, although we may use in this connection terms such as "equal," "equivalent," etc. "Absolute sameness in all aspects" would necessitate an *identity* of different nervous systems which produce and use these symbols, an *identity* of the different states of the nervous system of the person who wrote the above two symbols, an identity of the surfaces, etc., of different parts of the paper, in the distribution of ink, and what not. To demand such impossible conditions is, of course, absurd.[3]

From readers to whom the notions of difference, uniqueness, and non-identity are commonplace, we beg patience. But to those who are not persuaded by this description of the discoverable, structural facts of difference, we should urge first, a rereading, or second, that a search be made

[2] Alfred Korzybski, *Science and Sanity, an Introduction to Non-Aristotelian Systems and General Semantics.* Lancaster, Pa.: The Science Press Printing Co., 1933, 262.
[3] *Ibid.*, 194-195.

for two of anything absolutely the same in "all" aspects, or both steps.

Similarities

Despite the discovery of uniqueness and individuality in nature on the levels of direct experience, we also observe similarities. If differences only could be seen in this world, men would be unable to recognize what they had already seen. Each item of existence would have to be studied anew. The invariant relations of "things" to other "things" could not be discovered. Without recognition, continual adaptation to different conditions would be most difficult, and what we know as "intelligence" would be impossible.[4] For daily living and human evaluation, there must come the consciousness of *both* similarities and differences. Nevertheless,

In this work, we start structurally *closer to nature* with unspeakable levels, and make *differences* fundamental, similarities appearing only at a later stage (order) *as a result of higher abstractions*. In simple words, we obtain similarities by disregarding differences, by a process of abstracting.[5]

As this is written there are three pencils on the desk. Each is made by a different company, with different kinds of erasers, grades of lead, shades of paint, lengths, weights, etc. To enumerate the readily observable points of dissimilarity might easily fill a book. It is a relatively simple matter, however, to shift the focus to the points of similarity, the respects in which the three objects resemble each other. And interestingly enough it is on this seeing of similarities in the abstracting process that so much of our training centers. This is, perhaps, what Lynd is concerned with.

"As like each other as two peas," we have said: but *are* two peas like each other? Who knows whether the peas have not the same differences of feature among themselves that Englishmen have? Half the similarities we notice are only the results

[4] See *ibid.*, 165.
[5] *Ibid.*

of our ignorance and idleness. The townsman passing a field of sheep finds it difficult to believe that the shepherd can distinguish between one and another of them with as much certainty as if they were his children. And do not most of us think of foreigners as beings who are all turned out as if on a pattern like sheep? The further removed the foreigners are from us in race, the more they seem to us to be like each other. When we speak of Negroes, we think of millions of people most of whom look exactly alike. We feel much the same about Chinamen and even Turks. Probably to a Chinaman all English children look exactly alike, and it may be that all Europeans seem to him to be as indistinguishable as sticks of barley-sugar. How many people think of Jews in this way! I have heard an Englishman expressing his wonder that Jewish parents should be able to pick out their own children in a crowd of Jewish boys and girls.[6]

Making Our Language Fit

If the language we use is to be similar in structure to a world of differences and unique individuals along with the similarities which may be abstracted, then we must find a method for using our language to represent both characteristics.

Some investigations of structure in the language patterns of primitive peoples indicate an unbalanced emphasis on differences only, so that often common elements are neglected. Werner has summarized some of these findings.

The more primitive the society the less interest there is in the generic name. Names are above all individual names. The Bakaïrí of Brazil have a whole group of expressions for different species of parrots, but the generic name "parrot" is lacking in their language. Among the Australian aborigines there are no such class names as bird, tree, or fish; but on the other hand there are special terms for particular species of birds, trees, and fishes. The same is true in primitive African tongues, and in the languages of the South Sea Islanders. Certain American Indian languages have many names for cloud formations; the Lapps

[6] Robert Lynd, "The Pleasures of Ignorance," *The Pleasures of Ignorance.* New York: Charles Scribner's Sons, 1921, 87-88. Reprinted by permission.

have twenty names for different kinds of ice and forty-one names for the various kinds of snow. Yet in both cases the language has no corresponding generic terms. The Tamo of British New Guinea has no word for "to go," but he has words for "going north, south, east, or west." Even among the more advanced primitive peoples, such as the Bantu or the Polynesians, there is still an extraordinary specialization in names. . . . The old Maoris of New Zealand gave names to each separate thing—their houses, their boats, their weapons, and even their clothing.[7]

The structure of our own everyday speech tends to unbalance in the other direction in an emphasis on similarities. How readily we talk of college professors, labor agitators, juvenile delinquents, damyankees, strikes, movies, seasons, races, fires, etc., so that there is no ready defense against the implication that they are "identical." An argumentative reader may be quick to retort, "Of course I may speak of people and happenings as if they are alike, but everyone knows each is different. You're making overfine, pedantic distinctions." Nevertheless, though the explanation of the fact of unique individuals may be verbally understood, analysis of discussions and living behavior shows that in practice this fact is often neglected by the widespread going-by-similarities of speakers who act *as if* they never knew the principle in the first place.

If it is necessary to make our language habits avoid the excesses of both the primitive and the civilized distortions, how can those habits be reoriented so as to keep us aware of both the differences and the similarities?

One method is to qualify the generalized character of our statements by a reminder that they fail to mention the existing diversity, thus, "I think that college professors are teaching students to be skeptics, though, of course, some are different and they may teach otherwise." This is but a weak and grudging kind of concession to the hard and demonstrable life facts—that each college professor is a

[7] Heinz Werner, *Comparative Psychology of Mental Development.* New York: Harper & Brothers, 1940, 267-268. Reprinted by permission.

unique individual with a set of experiences, interests, abilities, points of view, ways of teaching, etc., which individuality is not suggested by the qualification.

A more thorough consciousness of the diversity is to be obtained by the habitual use of the device of the numbered index as a subscript to the generic (similarity-making) term. Then, merely to speak or think in terms of college professor$_1$, college professor$_2$, etc., is to give an immediate sense of the life facts.

The office secretary who receives a batch of letters does not lump them together pell-mell in a filing cabinet if she will some day have to refer to any one. She is better advised to sort out the letters, noting the uniqueness so that each can be filed separately in some alphabetical or numbered arrangement. The chaos of "sameness" is thus reduced to a more ordered awareness of "similarities in differences and differences in similarities." Moving beyond the lesson of such organizing procedures, Korzybski has widened the scope and application of the method.

Now, returning to the analysis of the object which we called "pencil," we observe that, in spite of all "similarities," this object is unique, is different from anything else, and has a *unique* relationship to the rest of the world. Hence, we should give the object a *unique name*. Fortunately, we have already become acquainted with the way mathematicians manufacture an endless array of individual names without unduly expanding the vocabulary. If we call the given object "pencil$_1$," we could call another similar object "pencil$_2$," etc. In this way, we produce individual names, and so cover the *differences*. By keeping the main root word "pencil," we keep the implications of daily life, and also of *similarities*.[8]

The use of the index would provide in our speech what is to be found on investigation in the world, a sense of the individuals and the uniformities abstracted therefrom. The habit of giving "special names" to the specific facts of existence makes for similarity of structure between language and what it is used to represent. If the language of everyday

[8] Alfred Korzybski, *Science and Sanity*, 381.

use obscures the differences, we are in danger of being oriented by false-to-fact maps which make errors in judgment inevitable.

Identification: the Mechanism of Neglecting Differences

A direct result of the failure to index and to be conscious of differences is a harmful lack of discrimination in our evaluation of daily life situations. Such failure is revealed in the mechanism of identification, a process by which our responses to one situation are carried over indiscriminately to other situations which, being unique, should be evaluated differently. This transfer is understandable when once we discover how easy it is to assume that "things" are "identical," an assumption produced by the habit of going by similarities in our talk. The mechanism may be outlined as shown in the accompanying figure.

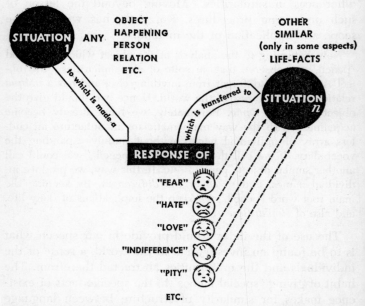

A simple form of transfer appears in grown-up Mary's distaste for orange juice. As a youngster she was given doses of castor oil supposedly made palatable by the orange flavor. Her response, then entirely negative, has carried over, even though orange juice$_1$ *with* the castor oil is not orange juice$_2$ *without* castor oil. Seeing the respects in which the liquids are "alike" brings about "like" reactions. A full consciousness of the difference induced by the index should make for revised evaluation.

A bit more serious was the case of the man, aged forty-two, who suffered from what he described as "fear of people," which was destroying his usefulness in his business and disturbing his relationships with his family and friends. After some questioning (by the author) he explained that he was a sales manager for a well-known company and that an important part of his work consisted of periodic talks to salesmen in various cities over the country. He further admitted that he thought his troubles began the year before when, at a convention of marketing and sales experts, he had "messed up his speech right there in front of fourteen hundred people." And ever since, he has been unable to face any audience, including the men in his own office, without living through "that awful experience."

It must be clearly understood that this man was in great discomfort, that he had "tried to forget it," and that his memories were "making life more miserable every day."

Notice, to begin with, that the "fear" experienced in one situation seemed transferred to other situations, each unique and different. For purposes of therapy, his focus on similarities was taken to be a causative factor. And on that assumption efforts were directed to make him see that Situation$_1$ where the speech failed, was not Situation$_2$ with quite different people in a different place, which was not Situation$_3$ with his family and friends, etc. That he should have been disturbed in the original "failure situation" was to be expected, considering the importance (to him) of the occasion and the prestige he hoped to get. From our point of view he erred only in carrying out that disturbance to situations which should have been evaluated differently.

After four two-hour sessions of steady explanation and

drilling designed to force him to a consciousness of differences and realization that his response to each situation should proceed in terms of each and not as a transfer from any other, he admitted that he "saw his error." At six-month intervals since the first conversation he has reported the elimination of his "fears" and renewed ability to talk "as well as ever."

In the course of a study concerned with the development of critical reading habits, the importance of seeing differences along with similarities for appropriate adjustment was sharply underlined.

A group of fifteen men and women had been meeting and working with reading materials when questions arose about the adequacy of the news presentation of local labor problems in the news columns of the Chicago *Daily Tribune.* They were then instructed to pay special attention to (1) inaccuracies (statements not similar in structure to what was represented as verified by first-hand observers), (2) biases (abstracting on the assumption that there was none), (3) the introduction of the reporter's private judgments, and (4) the suppression of relevant information (as revealed by a reading of other papers, magazines, etc.).

The study proceeded regularly until one evening there emerged a rough oral consensus of opinion that "the *Tribune* could not be trusted for its news coverage of local labor happenings." Each member was asked to turn in one week later a written statement which would embody his views as they had developed during the analysis. Thirteen of them concluded (most significantly for present purposes) that "the news columns (sic!) gave a false-to-fact picture of what goes on," and nine indicated that they "would never believe anything (sic!) if they saw it in the *Tribune.*" A transfer of attitude had already taken place from the labor to the other columns. At that point the group was handed a clipping (previously checked by outsiders and found accurate) from that newspaper reporting the doings of a committee raising funds for welfare work, which they were to read for inaccuracies, biases, etc. Most noticeable at this time was their unwillingness to use the verification techniques set out earlier, and a ready willingness to take for granted that if "the *Tribune* printed a story it would not be a fair one." That is, news column$_1$ with "bad" labor reporting was to them just like news column$_2$ with an accurate account of fund raising, which was just like news column$_n$. Failure to realize the differing character of news columns, when indexed, led sharply to identification, to a transfer of attitude from one to all, with a resulting failure to look at, study, and check the differing individual items of their reading experience. The result in this case was the development not of careful reading habits but of a kind of critical nihilism whose effects were just as destructive as a complete acceptance of everything read.

In another experiment performed as a stunt the transfer mechanism and the usefulness of indexing were taught by example to students in a university class in public speaking. Mr. John had on several occasions given speeches to which most of the class listened approvingly. At one meeting during a discussion of a bill before the state legislature, he suggested they sign a petition to be sent to their representatives. All agreed. A month later he again passed around a sheet which, he explained, carried a statement arguing against an amendment to the original bill which, if passed, would defeat the primary purposes. Again all signed. Two weeks later his appearance was the occasion for a vigorous plea that the class once more urge final passage of the bill, now in danger of defeat. This time the explanatory paragraph at the head of the petition read as follows:

The undersigned do strongly urge the passage of House Bill 722 establishing a fund and agencies for more widespread public education on the dangers and spread of syphilis, and in addition we just as strongly advise public prosecution for all signers of this and similar petitions on the ground that public safety and the general welfare will be thereby aided.

All but two signed. Most interesting was the ease and

rapidity with which the students moved to the assumption of "identity," that since petitions$_1$ $_{and}$ $_2$ were presented in good faith, so was petition$_3$. This is no argument against having faith in those who have established their responsibility to speak. It is an argument for more careful reading and attention to what is said, of going by both similarities and differences.

An arresting and often tragic example of the transfer mechanism is to be found in the onset and development of many forms of social prejudice, those negative reactions to objects, people and situations. *Hate, fear,* and *distrust* are the terms that commonly define the manifestations of prejudice which so frequently grow up as generalized responses from specific experiences.

In 1926 Duffus reported some of the findings of *The Inquiry,* which sought to study the sources of public opinion. Two cases are immediately relevant for us.

Then there was the story of Henry B. "My early childhood," this confession began, "was spent in a suburban district of the city of Chicago, and in this place there lived but one family of Jews. This family consisted of Mr. and Mrs. B., and their son Henry. As we were neighbors Henry and I used to play together until one fatal day. While playing house I happened to break one of Mrs. B.'s white milk pitchers, for which Henry admonished me and frightened me terribly. . . . From that day I never played with Henry again, for I both hated him and at the same time was afraid of him. . . . Since my childhood days I have had many pleasant dealings with Jews and Jewesses. Yet when one mentions the name 'Jew' I am liable to grow very angry or condemn the Jewish race in a terrible manner, for then . . . the recollection of my childhood experience comes to mind."

A trivial incident, no doubt, but a million such trivialities make a mountain of prejudice. Put this beside it: "When I was quite young my mother read me the story of Oliver Twist. I remember quite plainly how angry I became when I learned the full extent of Fagin's operations as affecting Oliver. There was also a picture of the old Jew, showing him in all the horror imaginable—stooped, filthy, ragged, sly, sneaking, all the worst possible traits. Then I saw a few years ago Lon Chaney play the part on the screen. This performance capped the climax. Since then I have looked upon most Jews with somewhat of aversion."[9]

No attempt will be made to diagnose either the manifold forces or the climate of opinion which might have contributed to the solidification of these attitudes. It is enough if but two aspects of these cases be emphasized. First, there occurred a negative response to a specific situation. Second, in each case the persons involved carried over their hate and fear to others not originally present and implicated only because of abstracted similarities. Such identification in terms of our analysis seems aided by the word "Jews" which as written suggests that all are "identical." Any investigation, however, of the life facts should make abundantly clear the existence of individuals, each separate and unique, differing in characteristics each from the other, and each different at different dates. No possible search by known techniques in 1941 could produce "identical Jews." As Lewis Browne writes,

Some Jews are dark, some as fair as Swedes, some are full-blooded Negroes and some real Hindus. Edward G. Robinson is short, swarthy, typically Mongol in appearance; Melvin Douglas is tall, blond, and as typically North European. Both are called Jews, yet racially they are no more akin than the shah of Iran and the Duke of Windsor.[10]

This is no place to describe the vast and terrible destruction visited in our time on unique individuals lumped together by bitter cries of hate built on transferred responses. What must not go unsaid, however, is the misevaluation which occurs when all "Jews" become the objects of aversion growing out of particular cases.

But what would constitute proper evaluation? For the child (a girl?) who was frightened by Henry B. this: the full complement of prejudice should be directed at him (at

[9] Robert L. Duffus, "Where Do We Get Our Prejudices?" *Harper's Magazine*, Sept., 1926, 505-506. Reprinted by permission.

[10] Lewis Browne, "What Can the Jews Do?" *The Virginia Quarterly Review*, Spring, 1939, 219. Reprinted by permission.

a date), the source of her discomfort (at a date). He hurt her. He should be the object of whatever aversion she musters. And as for "the Jewish race," each member of which is unique, different from Henry B., she should respond in terms of the particular relations she has with each. A full consciousness that this world is peopled with indexed individuals might prevent her "terrible" indictment. And to the youngster (a boy?), deeply affected by the story-book character of a Fagin, similar advice. Hate and fear Fagin (at a date) with all the fury that can be commanded (at a date), but remember that each other individual must be indexed and responded to as you find *him* and not as you found Fagin.

There may be little need for pleas of unity, charity, and harmony when men index and study the world as they meet it, a world of heterogeneous elements from which homogeneity is only abstracted. The habitual use of the index, trifling and obvious as it may seem, may yet do something to lubricate the machinery of social feeling while helping somehow to obliterate the savagery that sometimes comes when it is forgotten.

Orientation by Two Values

Another species of the non-indexing habit is to be found in our temptation to talk in terms of but two values, even though many may be found. Involved in this process is a neglect of the differing facts of experience and an assigning to them of few rather than many distinctions. This is a favorite device of the dogmatist, of an Adolf Hitler, in whose program everything must be "positive or negative, love or hate, right or wrong, truth or lie, never half this or half that." To restrict an analysis by reducing the number of evaluations is to introduce a spurious simplicity. The habit of seeing only two sides blurs in the utterance the often myriad variety and ever-changing diversity of what might be discovered if we were released from that too sharp, two-valued verbal orientation.

The following assortment of selections should give a hint of the prevalence of this language habit:[11]

Aristotle: That which other men do under compulsion, I do freely.

Rousseau: Do the opposite of what is being done, and you will be right.

Edmund Burke: My merits, whatever they are, are original and personal; his are derivative.

Jonathan Swift: For all human actions seem to be divided like Themistocles and his company's. One man can fiddle and another can make a small town a great city; and he that cannot do either one or the other, deserves to be kicked out of creation.

Charles Lamb: There are two races of men: the borrowers and the lenders.

Lord Chesterfield: There are but two objects in marriage, love or money. If you marry for love, you will certainly have some very happy days, and probably many very uneasy ones; if for money, you will have no happy days and probably no uneasy ones.

Thackeray: Someone told Thackeray that all his characters were either fools or knaves—to which he replied, "I know no other."

Gilbert and Sullivan in *Iolanthe*:

> Every little boy and every gal
> That's born into this world alive
> Is either a little liberal
> Or else a little conservative.

Dwight Morrow: The world is divided into people who do things and people who get the credit.

William Lyon Phelps: I divide all readers into two classes—those who read to remember and those who read to forget.

Helen Keller: Life is either a daring adventure or nothing.

Adolf Hitler: This war is a fight between two worlds, a world

---

[11] One religious sect makes the orientation by two values a basic doctrine: "The Two-Seed-in-the-Spirit Predestinarian Baptists (16 churches, 201 members), who believe that Adam & Eve were infused with a 'good seed' from God, and that Eve received a 'bad seed' from Satan. Since everything is born of either a good seed or a bad seed, and nothing can be done about it, this church does no gospel preaching, no missionary work." *Time*, August 26, 1940, 40.

of special privilege in which is included the United States, and a world of real freedom and equality as represented by Germany.

What should be said about such strict divisions, rigid classifications, and too sharp distinctions? Simply this: they do violence to the complexity of experience and the diversity of existence; in the world of men and happenings they do not adequately represent what is to be found.

It is possible verbally to call a man "honest" or "dishonest," but living men capable of such total designation are not easily found. When the behavior of specific individuals is studied, each appears somewhat, more or less honest, honest under certain circumstances, honest here, and dishonest there. "Villains" and "heroes" are not always thoroughly villainous or heroic in everything they do or think. Rather each shows these qualities in greater or less degree. Sometimes each is somewhat as described.

Things, situations, human beings appear in endlessly changing roles. Men may be classified verbally as "big" or "small," but when measured individually they are infinitely different in their "bigness" and "smallness." We too quickly rate those about us as "smart" or "dumb," "skillful" or "clumsy," without regard for the fact that they may be only more or less so in certain kinds of circumstances at certain times. In the rating process, however, there is a too-ready tendency to disregard the varied elements, the differences, the degrees, the *nuances* that abound.

We know the word "red." Is there but one color so called? A survey of a pigment catalogue reveals carmine, cerise, crimson, maroon, magenta, scarlet, etc., indicating many varieties of "redness." And similarly with other colors. There is not one specific blue, green, yellow, etc., but a whole series of blues, greens, yellows, etc., visible to the naked eye with as many gradations as there are wave lengths from red (760 millimicrons) to violet (385 millimicrons) and as there are human eyes. Analysis of a spectrum will show that the differing colors go off into each other gradually, yielding a succession of blends rather than one clearly distinguishable "color." Areas in the spectrum may be defined, but the point to be emphasized here is that there are many and not merely a few of them—in terms of millimicrons in the spectrum, at least 375.

It is the failure to apply a spectrum analysis to the many different aspects of natural existence that is our theme. Though the shading off and the uniqueness may be readily seen and not mistaken when the topic is color, the discrimination often does not come when the discussion turns to objects, happenings, feelings, persons. We speak of "sanity and insanity," "beauty and ugliness," "strength and weakness," as if these terms were capable of application without their more or less qualification, without regard for the uniqueness and differences in the non-verbal world. Just as the color spectrum is made up of many wave lengths, so, too, are there degrees and many variants from the more or less "sane" to the more or less "insane." There is no one "redness" and there is no one kind of what we call "beauty," "ugliness," "goodness," or "badness." These terms must be placed on their "spectrum" and indexed so that the diversity of their designations may be realized.

No doubt there are emergencies when we cannot take time to distinguish: we must leave a ship not wholly rotten and take to a dinghy not wholly sound, but creating false emergencies of this kind within a going culture is nothing short of criminal sabotage which leads straight to the evils we would avoid. The all-or-none policy *is* the retreat from reason. It is the dueler's false heroism which risks two lives on a Yes or No. And the habit of giving and taking the challenge, which masquerades as Choice, prepares our minds for tyranny—tyranny being nothing but the forcing and accepting of a single final answer to an infinite diversity of problems. It is a blind, deaf, and dumb machine that repeats the same operation in all circumstances and regardless of what material is thrown to it.

The human mind at its best works in precisely the opposite way: in art, in science, in a truly progressive education or democratic society, it seeks to distinguish differences and to deal with each appropriately.[12]

[12] Jacques Barzun, *Of Human Freedom.* Boston: Little, Brown & Co., 1939, 7-8. Reprinted by permission.

Conflict and the Two-valued Orientation

The pattern of two values projected on a world of infinitely varied men and happenings sets up the conditions of conflict. How readily, given differences$_1$ of opinion between groups, are the differences$_2$ of their subjects magnified by the establishment of one set of values for one side and an opposing set for the other. With that comes the obscuring of the differences that appear in the actions and the individuals involved, with a corresponding highlighting of their similarities. And once a we-group has made manifest the existence of *all* justice and honor with it, of necessity there seems nothing left but *all* injustice and dishonor for the they-group.

Mr. Pickwick and his three companions once encountered such a situation.

It appears . . . that the Eatanswill people, like the people of many other small towns, considered themselves of the utmost and most mighty importance, and that every man in Eatanswill, conscious of the weight that attached to his example, felt himself bound to unite, heart and soul, with one of the two great parties that divided the town—the Blues and the Buffs. Now the Blues lost no opportunity of opposing the Buffs, and the Buffs lost no opportunity of opposing the Blues; and the consequence was, that whenever the Buffs and Blues met together at public meeting, Town Hall, fair, or market, disputes and high words arose between them. With these dissensions it is almost superfluous to say that everything in Eatanswill was made a party question. If the Buffs proposed to new skylight the market-place, the Blues got up public meetings, and denounced the proceeding; if the Blues proposed the erection of an additional pump in the High Street, the Buffs rose as one man and stood aghast at the enormity. There were Blue shops and Buff shops, Blue Inns and Buff Inns;—there was a Blue aisle and a Buff aisle in the very church itself.

Of course it was essentially and indispensably necessary that each of these powerful parties should have its chosen organ and representative: and, accordingly, there were two newspapers in the town—the Eatanswill Gazette and the Eatanswill Independent: the former advocating Blue principles, and the latter conducted on grounds decidedly Buff. Fine newspapers they were. Such leading articles, and such spirited attacks!—"Our worthless contemporary, the Gazette"—"That disgraceful and dastardly journal, the Independent"—"That false and scurrilous print, the Independent"—"That vile and slanderous calumniator, the Gazette"; these and other spirit-stirring denunciations were strewn plentifully over the columns of each, in every number, and excited feelings of the most intense delight and indignation in the bosoms of the townspeople.[13]

When people (unindexed) have not been trained to face the complexity and variety in the facts of experience, they can be expected to respond to the oversimplified, few-valued appeals of those who seek adherents. Besides, see how easy it is to enlist allies if all right is with our side and all evil with the other. Explanations, modifications, and qualifications to care for diverse factors take time and may even diminish the intensity with which our cause is defended. The more data are slurred over, the greater can be the focus of our interests, and the more energy stirred for the attack.

In the heat and fury of such emphases, life distinctions are obliterated and the possibilities of human observation are artificially narrowed down. And when men's eyes are lifted from the variety of things to the phantasms made by few-valued utterances, then books are burned, heretics lashed, concentration camps filled, pogroms organized, and terrors unleashed, for somehow it has ever seemed easier to fight with more fury when life facts give way to exhortations.

Sometimes students take from this discussion the notion that the use of "polar" words should be stopped. But this must be impossible if the sense of similarities would be preserved. The point to be made is this: that two-valued statements tend to conceal the variety and differences of "things," each one of which is capable of many-valued description.

[13] Charles Dickens, *The Posthumous Papers of the Pickwick Club*, Ch. XIII.

For purposes of economy in discussion, it is frequently convenient to speak in terms of few values. Danger arises only when speakers act as if these values exhaust the possibilities or as if these only are to be found.

Further, in the course of investigations it is often useful to mark the boundaries of a problem within which study will occur. Thus, a check on health conditions in a city may begin by assuming the existence of those who are well and those who are sick. This, however, gives no picture of the degrees or differences in the condition of each person. The two values merely serve as an introduction to further discrimination, as directives for study rather than conclusions.

From Few to Many

Our concern with the existence of limited and restricted modes of analysis is shared by many of the seminal writers of our time. To list only a few:

. . . authority is never so absolute in society that there is no liberty in anything; nor is liberty ever so absolute that authority in society is utterly extirpated. The opposites are interlaced in practice and there are usually gradations from one extreme to the other.[14]

Mankind likes to think in terms of extreme opposites. It is given to formulating its beliefs in terms of *Either-Ors*, between which it recognizes no intermediate possibilities.[15]

. . . the loss in importance [in modern physics] of logical dichotomies and conceptual antithesis. Their places are taken by more and more fluid transitions, by gradations which deprive the dichotomies of their antithetical character and represent in logical form a transition stage between the class concept and the series concept.[16]

[The] emphasis upon classes and paired opposites hides the

---

[14] From Charles A. Beard, *The Discussion of Human Affairs*, 1936, 66. By permission of The Macmillan Company, publishers.

[15] From John Dewey, *Experience and Education*, 1938, 1. By permission of The Macmillan Company, publishers.

[16] Kurt Lewin, *A Dynamic Theory of Personality*. New York: McGraw-Hill Book Co., 1935, 10. Reprinted by permission.

fact that one is dealing not with two contrasted poles but with a distribution of frequencies ranging from one extreme to another.[17]

Such [sharp-cut] classification hides the truth that the different modes of natural existence shade off into each other.[18]

Alfred Korzybski has put the problem of "insufficient coverage" in more descriptive terms, from which is derived a solution in terms of a language habit that can be widely and readily applied.[19]

He starts with the verifiable observation that the "facts of experience" are indefinitely many-valued and single and individual. That is, each object, each event, each act, each person, each interpretation, each feeling, etc., is an individual matter, and nowhere in the universe can there be found cases of objects, events, feelings, persons, etc., which are completely identical or absolutely the same in all respects. Now, these many aspects of the world can be responded to or evaluated in our language in different ways.

To the single, different facts of experience we can be oriented so that we ascribe but one set of values instead of many, so that the resulting improper evaluation is projected on the facts. Within the framework of this language pattern come statements of the form, "Negroes are intellectually inferior to whites." This primitive, undiscriminating, unobserving orientation stresses similar characteristics to the neglect of the indefinitely many-valued, different "Negroes" and "whites" that can be found. The shift from this one-valued to the desirable orientation by life facts is to be coached by the systematic use of indexes and dates.

To the single, different facts of experience we can be oriented so that we evaluate by twos, wherein we cover up many of the different facts, and in our talk "boil down"

[17] Robert S. Lynd, *Knowledge for What?* Princeton, N. J.: Princeton University Press, 1939, 28. Reprinted by permission.

[18] Alfred North Whitehead, *Nature and Life.* Chicago: The University of Chicago Press, 1934, 33. Reprinted by permission.

[19] Alfred Korzybski, *Science and Sanity,* 461-466.

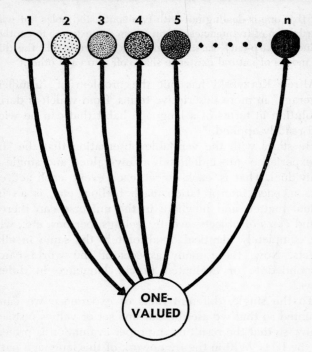

ONE-VALUED ORIENTATION

the many aspects of life to but two. Instead of recognizing that there are indefinitely many varieties of "sanity" and "insanity," we respond to this "manyness" as if there were only the two. This two-valued orientation is obviously not similar structurally to the world of objects, happenings, people, feelings, etc. Our talk, when we see only two values instead of many, thus gives a false, inadequate, misleading evaluation of the world. It is possible to extend the orientations from two to the recognition that perhaps there are three, four, five, and so on, but the number of possibilities remains dissimilar to the actual facts of experience. We may say that there are three modes of describing people verbally: the sane, the insane, and those who are sane twelve hours of the day and insane the other twelve. But the introduction of another value still does not adequately tell us of the indefinitely many varieties of people.

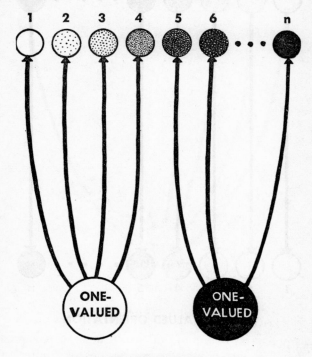

TWO-VALUED ORIENTATION

To the single, different facts of experience we can be oriented so that we evaluate each, that is, so that instead of calling a man "insane," we seek to describe the unique, individual characteristics of his behavior. In this many-valued orientation we seek to respond in our talk to the individual facts in the world, so that when we talk, our talk is directed to each of the indefinitely many-valued facts of experience. Such a language orientation will inevitably be structurally similar to what is talked about, thus making for proper evaluation, predictability, and so adequate adjustment.

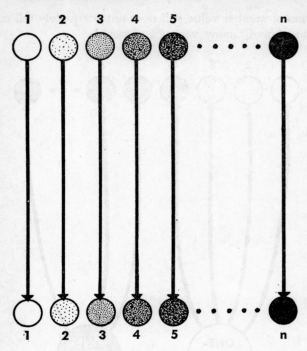

INFINITE-VALUED ORIENTATION

In Short

No two of anything in this world have been found "identical," absolutely the same in all respects. Similarities are abstracted by neglecting the differences. Too often we discriminate *against* rather than *between* individuals. Differences must not be obscured by habits of identification. Language use must represent both similarities *and* differences. An infinite-valued orientation does not project few values on to facts, but starting with the facts of direct experience makes language similar in structure to them. We need devices to give the sense of difference in our evaluations.

Habits to be acquired: (1) Consciousness of "similarities

in differences and differences in similarities," and (2) *Index* your statements.

GEORGE₁   GEORGE₂   GEORGE₃   GEORGE₄   • • • • • •   GEORGEₙ

FOR FURTHER STUDY

1. For further analysis of the two-valued orientation the following should be helpful:

    1. S. I. Hayakawa, "The Meaning of Semantics," *The New Republic*, August 2, 1939.

    2. Wendell Johnson, "War Propaganda and the United States," *Iowa Law Review*, Jan., 1941.

2. You should be able to go through the columns of your favorite newspaper on any day and clip out at least a dozen examples in which people respond to similarities only, neglecting differences. Do this sometime.

3. Whenever you hear someone preaching the values of tolerance, understanding, good will, etc., try asking him *how* they are to be achieved. Do not take vague general statements for an answer. Make him tell you specifically what you should do. Does the advice add anything to the principle of indexing?

4. Go through the pages on "Propaganda" in Adolf Hitler's *Mein Kampf* (New York: Reynal & Hitchcock, 1939) and pick out the statements in which he urges the adoption of the two-valued orientation as a basic strategy in winning assent. Do you know "good" people who use similar methods of evaluation?

5. For a full day (or more) try not to think in terms of similarities. Look at the unique, individual "things" about you. Index everything you say. What would happen if you did that all the time? What would be the effect of excluding similarities from your thinking? Does the advice in this chapter lead to emphasis on the one or the other?

6. Have you ever examined any reports or summaries of the Scopes trial at Dayton, Tennessee, concerning the teaching of

the theory of evolution? Read one sometime with the two- and infinite-valued orientations in mind.

7. "The Nominalists and the Realists, who once filled the world with their brawls, and who from irregular words came to regular blows, could never comprehend their alternate nonsense; 'whether in employing general terms we use *words* or *names* only, or whether there is *in nature anything* corresponding to what we mean by a general idea.' The Nominalists only denied what no one in his senses would affirm; and the Realists only contended for what no one in his senses would deny; a hair's breadth might have joined what the spirit of party had sundered!" (Isaac Disraeli, "Confusion of Words," *Curiosities of Literature*, ed. by B. Disraeli. London: G. Routledge & Co., 1858, III, 66.)

This is no place to open up that old controversy, but an interesting test of your comprehension of the chapter would be your attempt to state a solution of the problem in terms of similarities, differences, indexing, and abstracting.

8. Analyze the two sets of responses in the following:

"Not long ago I had an appointment with a certain man. I had never seen him and knew nothing about him, yet I found myself beginning to dislike him even before he came in. I couldn't imagine why.

"Suddenly it came to me. His first name was Roger! And when I was a boy the neighborhood bully was named Roger. I had loathed him, and that hatred, clinging to me unnoticed through the years, had almost turned me against a complete stranger named Roger.

"Unfortunately, I don't have a monopoly on such foolish prejudices. How many times have I heard people exclaim, 'Of course he's no good. I never knew anybody by that name who was!' Buried deep within all of us are similar emotional judgments, based on ridiculous trivialities. . . .

"Still another man has an illogical dislike for all 'foreigners.' Why? Because in grammar school he sat next to an immigrant's son who always reeked of garlic. 'I hate the smell of garlic,' he says, 'and somehow that smell is tangled up in my mind with the word "foreigner" and I can't get rid of it.' " (William McChesney Martin, "Prejudice," *American Magazine*, Feb., 1941, 150. Reprinted by permission.)

9. How would you explain the reasons why this letter was written?

"Sirs:

"I read with interest your article concerning the preparedness program at Russell Sage College in the Dec. 16 issue of *Life*. You say, 'If needed, they will be able to jump into overalls, take their tools in hand and keep the family car running.' I was unfortunate enough to have a flat tire while on a date with a Sage girl last weekend. I regret to inform you that after having had this course, she still does not know a lug wrench from a jack." (*Life*, Jan. 6, 1941, 4. Reprinted by permission.)

10. Did you understand that the analysis of the habit of going by two values related *only* to the problem of choice? Can you find situations where one has two and only two choices?

11. Lamarck once said, "The classifications are artificial, for nature has created neither classes nor orders nor families nor kinds of permanent species, but only individuals." Can you find any evidence with which to deny this?

12. Read carefully the following analysis of a one-valued orientation:

"I am speaking, I am standing, several persons are present. Each of these assertions is a truth; but if we seek among these truths for truth itself, believing it to be a unit, we are seeking in nature for what is merely a contrivance of language. 'What is truth?' said Pilate. He supposed it a unit, and hence the difficulty of the question. All things that we call truths, possess certain general characteristicks; just as snow, salt, silver, and glass, possess certain characteristicks, which entitle them all to the designation of white: but if we wish to ascertain the meaning of the word white in any given case, we must examine the object to which it is applied; and if we wish to know the meaning of the word truth in any given case, we must examine the circumstances to which the word is applied. The oneness of a thousand whites is verbal; and the oneness of a thousand truths is verbal. The unit is a creation of language; hence the fallacy, ambiguity, and difficulty, when we seek in nature for a corresponding unit. . . .

"Temperature is hot, cold, tepid, freezing, melting, burning, &c. Temperature seems a unit, but these examples exhibit it multiform. Shall we interpret the oneness of temperature by the multiformity of nature, or shall we estimate hot, cold, tepid, freezing, &c., by the oneness of the word temperature? We choose the latter course, and fallaciously perplex ourselves to discover in hot, cold, tepid, &c., the unit which exists in language only. Hot, cold, tepid, &c., may be deemed a unit; but we must estimate their oneness by what we discover in nature, and not by the implication of language. The oneness of the name is a contrivance of language. The oneness of the phenomena is the similarity which induces us to class them under one name." (A. B. Johnson, *Treatise on Language: or the Relation Which Words Bear to Things.* New York: Harper & Brothers, 1836, 59-60.)

CHAPTER VII

FACTS FIRST—THEN WORDS

The farmer studied the horse eagerly.

Good morning, sons of my friend, he said. What is the name of your horse?

My Heart, my cousin Mourad said in Armenian.

A lovely name, John Byro said, for a lovely horse. I could swear it is the horse that was stolen from me many weeks ago. May I look into its mouth?

Of course, Mourad said.

The farmer looked into the mouth of the horse.

Tooth for tooth, he said. I would swear it is my horse if I didn't know your parents. The fame of your family for honesty is well known to me. Yet the horse is the twin of my horse. A suspicious man would believe his eyes instead of his Heart. Good day, my young friends.

—William Saroyan[1]

[1] William Saroyan, "The Beautiful White Horse," *My Name Is Aram.* New York: Harcourt, Brace & Co., 1940, 14-15. Reprinted by permission.

*The disorder of our world was reflected, in a sad, funny way, in the
disordered brain of an old fellow, an alcoholic with delusions of persecution, who was recently brought into the psychiatric clinic of a local
hospital. His persecutors, he told the staff, were a band of little men,
only two feet tall, who followed him day and night, spying on him
and plotting his downfall. And that wasn't all. None of the little men
were citizens of the United States.*

—THE NEW YORKER[2]

*President Kalinin was making an impassioned speech in Moscow about
the great economic progress of the Soviets. With particular emphasis
he described the new 20-story skyscrapers on Karl Marx Street in
Kharkov.*

*"Comrade Kalinin," a worker in the audience rose naïvely to correct
the speaker. "I live in Kharkov. Every day I walk on Karl Marx Street
but I have never seen such skyscrapers ———"*

*"That's the trouble with workers like you," Kalinin shouted angrily.
"You waste your time in promenading the streets instead of reading
the newspapers and learning what is going on in your country."*

—EUGENE LYONS[3]

*The Emperor, to 72,000,000 Japanese people, is simply the present
head of the Sun Family. He is, furthermore, by way of the ancestor
cult, practically identical with the Sun. If you are Japanese, it actually hurts your eyes to look at the Emperor, just as it hurts your eyes
to look into the blazing sun.*

—LIFE[4]

><<<><>><<

Two "ways of life" are embodied in the evaluations in these examples, one explicitly, one implicitly. Try to describe them. Can you
always tell when the "little men" are *inside* your head and when
outside?

[2] "The Talk of the Town," *The New Yorker*, April 26, 1941, 12.
Reprinted by permission.
[3] Eugene Lyons, "Stifled Laughter," *Harper's Magazine*, April, 1935,
559. Reprinted by permission.
[4] *Life*, June 10, 1940, 70. Reprinted by permission.

FACTS FIRST—THEN WORDS

>※<※><※><※><※><※><※><※><※><※><※><※><※><※><※><※><※><

Two Patterns

Up to this point we have catalogued some ways and means of bringing our language use into correspondence with life facts. It should now be apparent that the imposition of language patterns of "completeness," "permanence," and "sameness" on a world of infinite complexity, process, and differences must result in impairing our ability to evaluate properly and adjust ourselves to that world. If a language structure does not fit the facts of experience, then we should expect to find its users talking about what is actually non-existent, and suffering from delusional states of their own making.

A direct attack on our disordered modes of response involves, then, a reordering of our usual habits of observing and talking. This reorientation would make us go to life facts first, before we spoke about them. Our existing patterns usually reverse this order, with speech first, neglecting the facts sometimes until later, and very often entirely.

In the life history of a child the facts are experienced long before he begins to verbalize about them. He wiggles his toes before he learns how to name them. But once he has command over the flow of words there is nothing in the nature of facts to force him to take them into account. Indeed, it may be more immediately satisfying to dodge the labor of going to the facts.

Aristotle was no child when he wrote about the emptiness in the back of a man's head and the single circular suture in a woman's skull. The learned Pliny could announce, "I find that a cold is checked by anyone who will kiss the nostrils of a mule." And Francis Bacon argued persuasively that, because of the similarity of the material, a wooden arrow would penetrate the side of a ship to a greater depth than one tipped with iron. Some observations made in similar circumstances today would force the modification of these assertions.

Two patterns thus become clear: (1) when speakers look to facts first, and (2) when they reverse the order and talk first. This is not to say that any individuals can be found who do one or the other exclusively, but that their behavior may be studied most revealingly from these points of view. We can then ask about them, do they go by facts before talking, or do they burst into speech first? These differences in approach may be clarified by some examples. This story by Edwin R. Embree is worth careful study.

In a little school just outside Baton Rouge, Louisiana, the teacher had been hearing a class read a lesson on birds in one of the standard textbooks. To drive home a point from the lesson, she asked a boy, "When do the robins come?"

The pupil promptly answered, "In the fall."

"Now, Jimmie," urged the teacher, "read the lesson carefully again."

After he had droned out the text a second time, she said cheerily, "Now, Jimmie, when do the robins come?"

More hesitantly and sullenly he answered again, "The robins come in the fall."

"James, James," shouted the teacher, "read that lesson again. Now tell me when do the robins come?"

Almost in tears the boy finally answered, "The robins come in the spring."

And so they do—in Boston where the text was written. But in Louisiana, just in order to avoid the northern winter, they come in the fall, as the boy well knew.[1]

Then there is the Don Marquis story which shows the two habits of looking and speaking at work. Members of a certain tribe were being continually dragged below the surface of the sea, never to return. The remaining tribesmen on the

[1] Edwin R. Embree, "Can College Graduates Read?" *The Saturday Review of Literature,* July 16, 1938, 4. Reprinted by permission.

shore could only watch these strange and terrible disappearances with fear and anxiety. Some concluded that devils, awful and terrifying, were at work. Others argued the presence of gods. Then one day an unsatisfied and curious man decided to look. He found not gods or devils but Giant Oysters. Following his report, the men went to work, and now the Giant Oysters are no more.

The two patterns are likewise revealed in the tale of the experiment performed by Sir Thomas Browne. Ship captains had been trained for a long time in the tradition that their diet must not include onions and garlic. It was believed that their pervasive odors would influence the mariner's compass, deflecting its balance. Skeptical Sir Thomas, bent on testing this belief, placed his instrument in a bowl of onion juice, after which he was able to announce triumphantly that the action of the needle was unaffected by the immersion.

Here is a more up-to-date situation. Frank Lloyd Wright's plans in 1938 for the Johnson Wax plant at Racine, Wisconsin, included columns designed for support which "were neither pillars nor posts, but tall stem forms, tapering from a concrete disc 20 ft. in diameter at the top to a shaft 8 in. thick at the floor. By ordinary reckoning, these slenderizing pencils would take about two tons weight each where they were called on to support twelve." In terms of mere talking the supports thus appeared inadequate, and inevitably members of the State Industrial Commission raised questions about the plans. However, "in an official test the column held up 60 tons."[2]

Henshaw Ward's example epitomizes the differences in response.

Imagine that three philosophers are sitting at an ebony table studying the motions of a Mexican Jumping-bean. The bean is on a sheet of white paper that is lighted by a strong electric lamp hung from the ceiling. Near the table is a case filled with small jars of several hundred species of beans. On a shelf is a delicate pair of scales and a set of drawing instruments. Shelves

[2] *Time*, Dec. 2, 1940, 40. Reprinted by permission.

of books are at hand—learned volumes on gravitation, levitation, kinetics, vital forces, spiritual values, food values, etc. The philosophers are prepared to attack the problem with all the powers of their reason.

For five days they sit in session, pondering, comparing notes, thinking out possible solutions, arguing, developing techniques, laying out a program of methodology for the study of the bean— which continues all the while to give spasmodic hops.

At the end of their deliberations each philosopher writes an essay to set forth his theory of what makes the bean move. The first one argues for an Electrical Hypothesis: that some process of magnetization in growth has made the bean sensitive to the magnetic currents in the earth. The second philosopher has a psychological solution: that some vital principle in the nucleus responds to the ebb and flow of thought which goes on about the table. The third philosopher decides that the bean is demoniac, is possessed by an uneasy spirit which is trying to escape from the hard shell. . . .

If a man is interested in the way beans move, he ought to buy a bag of them, pour them into a dish, select the liveliest one, and cut it open. Inside he will find a small larva that is wriggling vigorously. In every other active bean he will find a similar larva. He can prove by a few observations that the motion is always caused by the activity of one of these little caterpillars. If he cares to study the animals, he can learn details of how the mother moth deposits her egg, what the life of the larva is, and how it develops into another moth that lays its eggs on other bean-plants.[3]

These examples not only show the two habits of evaluation, but they ought to suggest that investigating before talking sometimes uncovers data about the world which can affect our adjustment to that world.

The Doctrine of Facts First

The method of going by facts first may seem a matter of common sense, but the history of civilization contains many pages which tell how it was resisted. A long and bitter bat-

[3] From *Builders of Delusion*, by Henshaw Ward, Copyright 1931, pp. 11, 15. Used by special permission of the Publishers, The Bobbs-Merrill Company.

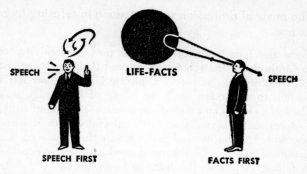

tle had to be fought by those early fact-finders, the men of science, before the power of this pattern came to be accepted. But that story has been told too often to be repeated here.[4] The problem may be glimpsed, however, in the life of the physician Paracelsus, who died in 1541.

All his life Paracelsus was hurling abuse at contemporary medicos and vomiting contempt at the mere mention of their practices. And organized medicine retaliated by hounding him, making his life miserable and trying to paralyze him professionally.

Those were the days when authority counted for more than experiment or the direct observation of nature. Galen had said this and Galen had said that, and Galen was always right. To Paracelsus Galen was often as wrong as he was right. Not what Galen said but what experience taught was important. To be sure, men like Bacon had been preaching the gospel of experience long before Paracelsus appeared. But it was something new for an educated ruffian to clash with the entire medical profession and to tell it that it was on the wrong track. It must have irritated the professors excessively to be told that "all the universities have less experience than my beard" and that "the down of my neck is more learned than my auditors," but it was true.[5]

---

[4] See J. W. Draper, *History of the Conflict Between Religion and Science*. New York: D. Appleton & Co., 1903. See also A. D. White, *History of the Warfare of Science with Theology in Christendom*. New York: D. Appleton & Co., 1897.

[5] Waldemar Kaempffert, "Science in the News," the New York *Times*, Feb. 9, 1941, Sec. 2, p. 5. Reprinted by permission.

The medical profession was not alone in refusing to go by facts first.

Upon the foundation of Scripture passages and quotations from "authorities" the scholastics erected their towering systems of philosophy and "science." Dialectical speculation led from deduction to deduction until the whole of knowledge was enmeshed in a closely knit web of arguments. The test of truth was not experimental verification but conformity with the opinion of accredited authority and inclusion in the approved scheme of deductions. When Galileo conducted his famous experiments with falling bodies at the leaning tower of Pisa, "the Aristotelians, who with their own eyes saw the unequal weights strike the ground at the same instant, ascribed the effect to some unknown cause and preferred the decision of their master to that of nature herself." And when Galileo asked the professors in Florence to look through his telescope and to observe for themselves the satellites of Jupiter, "they would neither see them nor the telescope."[6]

Regardless of the obstacles to acceptance of this "new" kind of human orientation, it was insistently uttered.

Roger Bacon: Without experience nothing can be known sufficiently.[7]

Leonardo da Vinci: All sciences are vain and full of errors which do not terminate in observation.[8]

Descartes: It is possible to attain knowledge which is very useful in life, and instead of that speculative philosophy which is taught in the Schools, we may find a practical philosophy by means of which, knowing the force and the action of fire, water, air, the stars, heavens, and all other bodies that environ us, as distinctly as we know the different crafts of our artisans, we can in the same way employ them in all those uses to which they are adapted, and thus render ourselves the masters and possessors of nature.[9]

[6] W. H. Werkmeister, *A Philosophy of Science.* New York: Harper & Brothers, 1940, 11-12. Reprinted by permission.

[7] Quoted in *ibid.,* 11.

[8] *Ibid.,* 15.

[9] *Discourse on Method,* Part 6. Quoted by J. H. Randall, *The Making of the Modern Mind.* Boston: Houghton Mifflin Company, 1940, 224.

Extension and Intension

Intensional orientations are based on verbal definitions, associations, etc., largely disregarding observations as if they would involve a "principle" of "talk first and never mind life facts." *Extensional orientations* are based on ordering observations, investigations, etc., *first*, and the verbalization next in importance.[10]

In these words Korzybski crisply epitomizes the attitudes we have sought to describe. For him the methods of extension give both clue and guidance in the search for adequate language habits.

To be oriented extensionally is to put great store in the methods of discovery and verification. If something has been found in our universe, then others using similar ways of observing should be able to confirm or acknowledge it. And if the reports have been inaccurate, checking gives the means of correcting them. The virtue of this relationship with life facts is that we permit ourselves further scrutiny. We need not rest with mere statements. We can look for ourselves. Since the process is a public one, anyone may enter freely and show wherein his observations fit or differ. Going by extension thus promotes the fulfillment of man's time-binding capacities.

When people become extensionalized, they are able to get out of the ruts and grooves in which their word habits have kept them. They have less tendency to take what is said for granted. The questions *who* and *how* and *what* become tools of new usefulness; and with them come the birth of inquiry, of curiosity, an attitude of moving on beyond the limits of the verbal patterns. If someone were to say to you, "This is how it has been, how the men of old said it should be done," your reply might well be, "Well, I wonder. Let's see." And in discussion of matters not immediately clear, there is little defeat and much wisdom in your adoption of the slogan of the extensional attitude, "I don't know. Let's see." We should then at least be spared the folly and

[10] Alfred Korzybski, "Outline of General Semantics," *General Semantics*, collected and arranged by Hansell Baugh. New York: Arrow Editions, 1938, 1.

stupidity that so often attend the unwillingness to go and look. For example, consider the protests and declarations against new inventions.

The first successful cast-iron plow invented in the United States in 1797 was rejected by New Jersey farmers under the theory that cast-iron poisoned the land and stimulated the growth of weeds. . . . An eloquent divine in the United States declared that the introduction of the railroad would require the building of many insane asylums, as people would be driven mad with terror at the sight of locomotives rushing across the country. . . . In Germany it was proved by experts that if trains went at the frightful speed of 15 miles an hour blood would spurt from the travelers' noses, and that the passengers would suffocate going through tunnels. . . . It was argued in 1833 that Philadelphia should continue to be lit with oil, because discharges from the gas works into the surrounding waters might drive away the shad and herring. . . . In 1881 when the New York Y.W.C.A. announced typing lessons for women, vigorous protests were made on the grounds that the female constitution would break down under the strain. . . .[11]

The business of looking, of becoming directly acquainted with changing conditions will make evident the unending quantities of details and the necessity for becoming conscious of the ETC., the process character of the world which forces us to "say when," and the existence of unique individuals which are to be differentiated by indexing.

When we have become extensionalized in our reactions, we go *to* life facts (or to the descriptive data of others) prior to making statements, and we go *by* them in making evaluations. The extent to which these habits of response are learned and applied gives us a measure for distinguishing the farthest reaches of human linguistic achievement from infantile babbling and noise-making. To speak without such checking is to indulge in neuromuscular grunts and cries which may interest a voice specialist, but they help us little in dealing with a recalcitrant world.

[11] "Progress Under Protest," *Reader's Digest*, Oct., 1937, 61 Reprinted by permission.

Nevertheless, to take stock of what goes on, to attend to direct experience, to order our reactions in terms of what

THE EXTENSIONAL METHOD

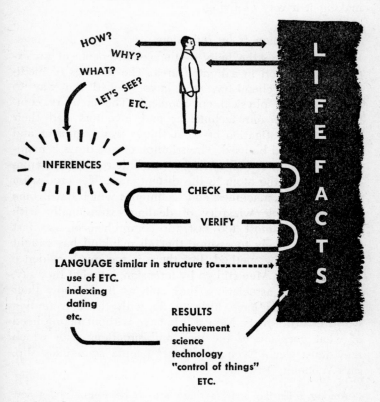

is found in life—this extensional orientation marks the beginning of man's control over his own destiny.[12] This

[12] In some quarters today orientation by facts constitutes basic strategy. Anton J. Carlson (Professor Emeritus of Physiology, University of Chicago) prodded his students back to life facts with his famous caustic question: "Vot iss de effidence?" The resulting search for the data to support assertions "has launched a thousand experiments." (*Time*, Feb. 10, 1941, 44-48.) Theorists in physics, studying the meaning of their important terms, end by urging that those terms be defined by seeing what actual physical operations they represent.

offers no simple design for living. But it is a simple prescription which can be learned. There are men thus oriented in some areas of daily living in their jobs and hobbies. But all too few are they who abide by the pattern habitually, making it a way of living.

When Orientation Is by Intension

Today we are the heirs of the achievements of an extensional method in a limited area. The findings of medicine, physics, chemistry, etc., have opened the way to control of the physical environment. The creature comforts given by our technicians and inventors had their origins in investigation of what things were made of and how they could be used. The triumph of our times is manifest in our mastery of certain areas, hitherto hidden, from the depths of the atom to the distant suns. The procession of instruments, machines, and techniques which have come from the simple wizardry of dealing extensionally with nature goes almost too fast for comprehension—so fast that we are likely to assume that all mankind has caught and lives by the method. But there is too much evidence to the contrary. Men still go by intension, by what they say, by the verbal associations they spin as if somehow their definitions need have little to do with the surrounding world of brute facts. Men still behave without taking heed of what goes on, of the men and situations with which they must deal. Even our "best" people sometimes slip, says Wilhelm Ostwald:

Among scientific articles there are to be found not a few wherein the logic and mathematics are faultless but which are

---

If disagreement arises about the meaning of "pressure of a gas," then you must move to a laboratory and see what someone does, how he measures, etc., to which operations the phrase can be applied. Or whenever you talk about pressure, you should try to visualize the apparatus involved, glass, tubing, a mercury column, and the accompanying actions, until a pointer reading is obtained—all of which is summarized in the term "pressure of a gas." R. B. Lindsay, "A Critique of Operationalism in Physics," *Philosophy of Science*, IV (October, 1937), 456.

for all that worthless, because the assumptions and hypotheses upon which the faultless logic and mathematics rest do not correspond to actuality.

To talk without first observing life facts, and to act without abiding by them—in these primitive modes of response are too many of us held fast. The adequate documentation of this disordering evaluation would take us away from the triumphs of our productive genius to the heart of the crisis of our time as it is seen in the wars, in the degradation of human time-binding capacities committed to waste and destruction, in the tragically mounting numbers in our jails and asylums, in the need for more and more police control, in the persistence of superstition, bigotry, and obscurantism, in the continuing refusal to use what we already "know" for the preservation and release of human creativeness and happiness.

It is impossible in these pages to chart the gamut of intensional manifestations. We must be content with samples of some of the recurring types of situations in which people do go by words and not by facts.

1. *When people pay more attention to what is said about "things," to what they are called, than to the facts themselves.*

Note how reactions may be totally changed by a word:

When Basil Rathbone was handed a scenario titled "The Monster," he gave it back to Paramount without reading it. A wise man in the studio retitled it "Destiny" and sent the same script back to Rathbone. He read it, liked it, and assures me on the set that it is not a horror picture. "I'm through with horror and villainy," says Basil, "a man has only so many villains in him, and I've played all mine."[13]

A friend of mine, the owner of a department store, sought to test the intensionality of customers by a practical experiment. One morning he set out at different ends of a counter

[13] From a column by Sheilah Graham, the Chicago *Daily News*, March 6, 1940, 20. Reprinted by permission of the North American Newspaper Alliance.

piles of men's handkerchiefs. On the one he placed a sign reading "Soft-Textured, Genuine Irish Linen Handkerchiefs, Special 3 for 50¢." On the other the sign read "Nose Rags, three for a quarter." During an eight-hour period, twenty-six different persons examined and eleven bought from the "Irish Linen" stock, while but six examined and only two bought the "Nose Rags." The point of this experiment should by now have been guessed: both piles contained the same kind of handkerchiefs. The salesgirl's comment is more than a little in point, "The people just didn't look at the merchandise."

Poffenberger tested this phenomenon by giving to fifty-seven men copies of the following advertisement of a well-known razor company:

A new triumph of American inventive genius of startling interest to every man with a beard to shave . . . for the first time in any razor micrometric control of the blade position made possible by the fulcrum shoulder, overhanging cap, and channeled guard. [A diagram showed] how the blade is biflexed between overhanging cap and fulcrum shoulder. It is flexed once into the inside curve of the cap. This is the minor flexure—the curve for easy gliding action and play of the wrist in shaving. It is flexed a second time—more sharply and in a shorter radius—by the grip of the overhanging cap the whole length of the fulcrum shoulder.[14]

After they had read and studied the copy, he asked a list of seven questions to learn to what extent they believed and understood what they read. This is what he reported:

The answers to these questions showed that all the students agreed that the new razor was better than the old one, and that they would rather pay $5 for the new one than $1 or $2 for the old one. In supporting their belief they were allowed to consult the advertisement as much as they wished. They quoted the "fulcrum shoulder," which made possible "micrometric control of the blade position," but not one of them could explain how

[14] A. T. Poffenberger, "Conditions of Belief in Advertising," *Journal of Applied Psychology,* VII (March, 1923), 2. Reprinted by permission.

the micrometric control was obtained or what advantage there would be in having such a micrometric control. They believed that the "channeled guard" was an improvement although they could not tell why it was an improvement. As to the importance of major and minor flexures they were entirely ignorant.[15]

In 1935 Sherif investigated the existence of aesthetic stereotypes. He first found the preferences of his subjects for certain English and American writers, including Barrie, Conrad, Cooper, Dickens, Poe, etc. Several weeks after receiving their rank-order votes on these sixteen authors, he gave sixteen prose passages, *all written by Stevenson*, but after each passage was written the name of one of the authors in the original list. The subjects were asked to rank the writings in terms of their literary merit. As far as was known, no one of the subjects realized the deception.

Some of the subjects said they had ignored the names appended. As a result, their correlation between the preference for the writers and the preference for the merit of the writing was zero. However, for the remaining nearly two hundred subjects, the average correlation was +.46. Passages attributed to highly rated writers were considered "good," while passages attributed to lowly rated writers were thought to be "bad."

One conclusion is inevitable. Since the passages were all from Stevenson, the rating of the passages in terms of favored and unfavored authors' *names* indicated that the responses were to the names and not to the passages.[16]

In another study along this line, Boldyreff and Sorokin found marked responses to the aesthetic opinions of musical "experts." Two phonograph records of the same recording were played for a number of students. The suggestion was then made that music critics preferred one of the records, as if they were different recordings. A large majority of the students then "heard" two different recordings and indicated that the "one" was to be preferred. They were surely

[15] *Ibid.*
[16] M. Sherif, "An Experimental Study of Stereotypes," *Journal of Abnormal and Social Psychology*, XXIX (Jan.-March, 1935), 371-375.

responding to the names and assertions of the critics rather than to the music.[17]

Bernays tells of responses to words even in moments of crisis.

> In Great Britain, during the war, the evacuation hospitals came in for a considerable amount of criticism because of the summary way in which they handled their wounded. It was assumed by the public that a hospital gives prolonged and conscientious attention to its patients. When the name was changed to evacuation posts, the critical reaction vanished. No one expected more than an adequate emergency treatment from an institution so named. The cliché hospital was indelibly associated in the public mind with a certain picture.[18]

On one occasion at least the influence of a word has been fatal. A certain man in Germany was preparing to meet and welcome his son, who had been gone for many years. The house was being readied, food was stored, arrangements were made for a large party with many invited guests, the boy's room was fixed up, and the old man's expectations ran high. On the day fixed for his return, a telegram came saying that the boy was *ungekommt* (dead), whereupon the father himself fell over dead. That afternoon the boy arrived. The telegram should have read, he has *angekommt* (arrived).

The consequences of such automatic reaction to words cannot be underestimated if we see how the failure to observe the order of facts first produces misevaluation. Readers might ponder the effects of such orientation on the quality of our larger political and social decisions. When individuals are so oriented that their acts of judgment in connection with simple and unimportant matters are rendered impractical and useless as guides to proper evaluation, we should be little surprised (though greatly

[17] J. W. Boldyreff and P. A. Sorokin, "An Experimental Study of the Influence of Suggestion on the Discrimination and the Valuation of People," *American Journal of Sociology*, XXXVII (1932), 720-737.

[18] Edward L. Bernays, *Propaganda*. New York: Horace Liveright, 1928, 51. Reprinted by permission.

worried) if their judgments are equally distorted and unfounded in more significant matters.

2. *When the response is to words as if they were something more, as if they need not be considered as forms of representation.*

We refer here to a kind of naïve, though by no means less disordered, type of reaction which somehow sees in the words themselves the very "things" which the words are intended to represent. The mechanism appears in the disturbance of the girl who "just can't stand stories about blood and death," and in the terror of the man who "breaks out in a cold sweat whenever they mention airplane crashes" because, as he says, "I see again the earth coming up to meet me just as that time." Martin Wolfson's mother provides an excellent illustration.

A play called *Gabrielle* . . . was based on a Thomas Mann short story which takes place in one of Mr. Mann's perennial TB sanatoria on a Swiss mountain peak. In it was an actor named Martin Wolfson.

When Wolfson landed the job in the show he went home to tell his mother. She asked him what the play was about.

"Oh," Martin replied, "it takes place in a sanatorium and there are a lot of sick people in it."

"What's the matter with them?" asked ma.

"Well, they've got tuberculosis, and some of them have social diseases, syphilis and so on."

"Please, Martin," said the old lady, "please. Be careful."[19]

In this category also should be placed the experience G. K. Chesterton had with a woman selling fish. Strolling by, he stopped quickly, and pointing to her, said, "You are a noun, a verb, and a preposition." The woman was taken aback. Wherewith Chesterton began again, "You are an adjective, an adverb, and a preposition. You are a pronoun. . . ." But by that time the woman had lost patience

[19] Robert Rice, "Broadway Report." Excerpt from *PM*, April 1, 1941, 22, copyrighted by The Newspaper PM, Inc., N. Y. Reprinted by special permission of the copyright owners.

and, as she called the police, struck Chesterton squarely with a flounder.

The crew in Lewis Carroll's "The Bellman's Speech" seemed satisfied with words only.

> He had bought a large map
>   representing the sea,
> Without the least vestige of land;
> And the crew were much pleased
>   when they found it to be
> A map they could all understand.

The literature dealing with the inducement of "emotion" in subjects in experimental situations shows in clear-cut fashion how reactions of all sorts can be set off by mere utterances without efforts on the part of the subjects to find out what the words represent in a particular situation. We are saying that the very responses of the subjects which made them useful in the situation should be recognized as disordered to start with. For individuals to react simply because another individual talks, without waiting to understand the life facts he is talking about, is to demonstrate sharply the neglect of extensional procedures and to reveal how unwittingly "scientists" themselves help to establish, or at least do little to prevent, disorienting modes of response. From this point of view, read carefully this typical example.

In a dark, quiet room the investigators put the patient on his back. They passed a slender tube through one nostril into his stomach, so that a sample of the stomach fluid could be tapped at any time. They talked soothingly to him, urged him to relax and think peaceful thoughts. When he was in a good frame of mind they took a stomach sample. Then they began to talk with him about other things (with the tube through his nostril he could talk well enough)—unpleasant things, things that made him resentful, anxious, angry, frustrated. They continued their calculated tactlessness till his voice and manner showed that he was in a good dither. Then they took another stomach sample. The experience was painful but it served the cause of science.

This experiment . . . was intended to measure something

that psychologists and doctors have long believed and all sufferers knew anyway—that distressing emotions cause increased amounts of hydrochloric acid to be poured out in the stomach, are thus linked to such stomach disorders as "heartburn," dyspepsia, gastric ulcer. The experimenters were Drs. Bela Mittelman of New York Post-Graduate Hospital and Harold Wolff of Cornell Medical College. Not only did they find that emotion induced increase of stomach acid, but they also measured the increase.[20]

Again, the pattern of response by which words are taken for granted is revealed in the prevalence of accounts of happenings which are passed from person to person on the unstudied assumption that they originated from observed life facts. An excellent illustration of intensional rumor-mongering ferreted out by an extensionally oriented listener appears in a newspaper column by Ben Hecht:

I heard [a legend] first from a writer named Charles Boswell who lives at 260 W. 11 St., N. Y. Mr. Boswell believed the story and related it as follows:

A Brooklyn woman put her cat in a cat and dog hospital. It died and she called for its remains. She wished to bury the pet herself. The dead cat was put in a neat box and the lady started for home. On the way she stopped in Stern's department store on 42nd St. to make some purchases. While shopping she noticed suddenly that the box she had placed on the counter near her was gone. Store detectives began a search for the missing dead cat. Ten minutes later a woman was found slumped on the floor of a telephone booth. Beside her was the box, just opened, and the feline corpse staring out of it. The woman was dead. She was immediately identified as a notorious shoplifter for whom this and other emporiums had been gunning these last six months. She had obviously stolen the box, taken it to a telephone booth to open, sighted the dead cat and fallen lifeless to the floor with a heart attack—the victim of a macabre justice.

Mr. Boswell said the story had been told him by two actors in the apartment above him, Oscar Stirling and his wife Edna Peckham, recently on view in *Kind Lady*. Mr. Boswell said these two knew the full truth of the story.

[20] *Time*, Sept. 16, 1940, 50. Reprinted by permission.

Interview with the Stirlings revealed that they had got the story from their Christian Science practitioner, a Mr. Charles Simmonds of 450 W. 24th St. Mr. Simmonds, a man not to be doubted, had told them the story as gospel.

Mr. Simmonds repeated this gospel. He had heard it, he said, from a woman who was a friend of the dead cat's owner. This woman was Mrs. Katherine Luebbers of 28 Mile Square Rd. in Yonkers. Mrs. Luebbers would give me the names of all the people involved.

And Mrs. Luebbers turned out to be full of the dead-cat wonder. She did not know the name of the animal's owner, but the story had been told her by her son-in-law, Ronald Schaeffer, who knew all about it. And Mr. Schaeffer turned out to know everything about it. He had heard the story firsthand from a passenger on a commuter's train whose aunt knew the lady who owned the dead cat.

At Stern's the tale was firmly, and a little indignantly, denied, by W. F. McCue, chief store detective. And at the W. 54th St. Police Station there was no record of any feline or shoplifter corpses being reported.

By this time you may have heard the tale of wonder elsewhere. There are probably scores and hundreds of wonder-lovers broadcasting it from table to table and office to office. And if you have nothing to do, like myself, take a few days off and play ring around a rosy with this Dead-Cat-Come-to-Judgment rumor.

You will come upon no dead cat or stricken shoplifter, but you will get an instructive look into that well of rumor which is deeper and more crowded with fact apparently than that other well out of which no wars, massacres or religions are ever born.[21]

In so far as pictures (moving and still) can be considered forms of representation, we should expect to see responses to them follow the patterns of intension and extension, and we do. People forget that the picture is not what it represents and so they react to it as if it *were* the facts represented. Rosett's behavior not only describes the mechanisms, but it should make evident how deep organismal responses can be stimulated by other than life facts.

[21] By permission of PM and The Viking Press, Inc., publishers of "1001 Afternoons in New York," by Ben Hecht, *PM,* April 4, 1941, 13.

A vivid picture on the cinema screen represented a boy and girl pulling down hay from a stack for bedding. I sneezed— from the dust of the hay shown on the screen.

On another occasion a colored picture of lilacs—a favorite flower—moved by a gentle breeze, was shown on the screen. I smelled the odor of lilacs distinctly.[22]

Then there was the girl who insisted that she was "allergic" to cats, so much so that she would sneeze and suffer the pangs of "hay fever" until she could get far from the "beasts." A friend gave her the *Autobiography* of William Lyon Phelps. Upon reading the first two pages of the chapter dealing with his fondness for cats, she began to sneeze and suffer. No cats for her, only words.

3. *When men, though exposed to life facts, do not abide by them.*

It is not enough to see that men speak without going to life facts, for on occasion the facts may be apparent, though not heeded.

The cliché of the therapeutists and mental hygienists, "adjust to reality," suggests that we should probably find in their patients' case histories evidence that many varieties of obsessions, antagonisms, compulsions, melancholias, etc., are rooted in the failure or refusal to be oriented extensionally.

There was once a man who went around saying, "You know, I think I'm dead." His friends finally persuaded him to consult a psychiatrist. When the patient told the psychiatrist that he thought he was dead, the psychiatrist told him to clench his fists, stand before a mirror, and say, "Dead men don't bleed." He told the man to repeat this motion six times a day for a month, each time saying, "Dead men don't bleed." He told the man to go home and carry out his instructions and return at the end of the month. The patient carried out the psychiatrist's instructions and at the end of the month he returned. The psychiatrist told him once again to go through the motions. The reason

[22] Reprinted from Joshua Rosett, *The Mechanism of Thought, Imagery, and Hallucination,* 1939, 212, by permission of Columbia University Press.

he had him tighten his fists was so the veins would come to the surface of the man's wrists. The man tightened his fists, and just as he said, "Dead men don't bleed," the psychiatrist jabbed a scalpel into the man's wrist. The blood gushed out and the man hollered, "By God, dead men do bleed!"[23]

Those who take refuge in private dream worlds, the man who believes he is forever conspired against by waiting enemies, those who suffer from delusions of grandeur, the chronically sick who find pleasure in the definitions of new illnesses, the temperamental who dodge responsibilities with hysterical attacks and nervous breakdowns, those overtaken with jealousy, etc.—in these the intensional orientation appears at its baldest.

However varying the details of these cases and the theories which account for their onset, and without regard for the host of measures and the special techniques of resolving the difficulties so that the individuals come to face the avoided life facts, our concern here is to suggest that deviations from extensional patterns may result in profoundly disturbed states. If so-called "normal" people have moments when their evaluations show them going by words rather than by life situations (and believing otherwise), we should understand that in those moments they move toward the "abnormal." Indeed, they may sometimes become ready for hospitalization.

The story is told of a college girl who sought to commit suicide because the results of a "personality test" had shown her to be a "manic-depressive type." Frightened by this report, she sought to read up on "insanity" and found, as might be expected, that she had the symptoms, along with additional information that led her to believe that in her family tree were other cases of what she defined as "mental diseases." Her worries increased as her symptoms became more marked. She then talked with a psychologist, who reported:

[23] From a speech delivered by Irving Fink, Northwestern University, Evanston, Illinois, reprinted in the *Daily Northwestern*, Feb. 18, 1941, 5.

It was not difficult to convince the patient that the test which started her into trouble was silly and that the doctrine of the inheritance of mental disorder, as she had learned it, was a myth; that her chances of going insane were no better than my own, or those of seven thousand of her fellow students. This treatment was effective.[24]

Of importance for us is the fact that this girl had proceeded to talk herself into an anxiety state on the basis of what she read. Whatever may have been her condition, study of it directly is not the same as applications to it of diagnoses from books. Notice, too, that she was seeing only the similarities and neglecting the differences.

4. *When men indulge in verbal "proofs," instead of going to life facts.*

A textbook in Euclidean geometry will explain that the square on the hypotenuse of a right-angled triangle is equal to the sum of the squares on the other two sides. However, assume that we have a triangular block of wood with each of the two sides measuring one inch. Then by definition (or words only) the hypotenuse must be equal to the square root of two inches. But that number must be numerically indefinite, for there may be an infinite number of places after the decimal, 1.4141. . . . Nevertheless, when one lays a measuring stick on the block, the size is something *very definite*. What can be found on observation differs from the result obtained by calculation and verbal proof.

One can argue verbally that the football team of the U. S. Marines in San Diego was superior to the Notre Dame team in 1940. Thus:

The Marines beat Montana, which beat Gonzaga, which licked Detroit, which beat Texas Christian, which whipped Arkansas, which beat Mississippi, which defeated Duquesne, which triumphed over St. Mary's, which trounced Fordham, which

---

[24] Knight Dunlap, "Antidotes for Superstitions Concerning Human Heredity," *The Scientific Monthly*, LI (Sept., 1940), 225. Reprinted by permission.

whaled Purdue, which cleaned up on Iowa, which beat Notre Dame.[25]

By facts, however, the Marines did not play Notre Dame, and what would have happened if they had played is something which would not be governed by any verbal deductions no matter how elaborate.

Debates on questions of moment in the halls of Congress or on public platforms often reveal such intensional procedures. To get public approval for a position while creating disapproval for others, men have found that it is not always necessary to speak extensionally with verifiable statements. Audiences are likely to applaud fervor in delivery, sharp turns of phrase, and pleasant diversions, and pay closer attention to devices which render an opponent's argument ridiculous and make him the butt of jokes. It is not these rhetorical effects which should be condemned but their substitution and acceptance as if they were statements descriptive of life facts.

If a public speaker can find ways of making his utterance more attractive and easier to listen to, while preserving his concern with life facts, we should hasten to welcome him. But in the heat of battle, in the effort to gain assent, that concern is too often put aside. In 1885 Gladstone began his debate with Huxley against the developing scientific investigations and the doctrines of evolution, carrying on the argument with high-powered eloquence. White has described some of his tactics in terms which reveal the intensional emphasis.

On the face of it, his effort seemed quixotic, for he confessed at the outset that in science he was "utterly destitute of that kind of knowledge which carries authority," and his argument soon showed that his confession was entirely true.

But he had some other qualities of which much might be expected: great skill in phrase making, great shrewdness in adapting the meanings of single words to conflicting necessities in discussion, wonderful power in erecting showy structures of

[25] Lloyd Lewis, "Voice from the Grandstand," the Chicago *Daily News,* Nov. 25, 1940, 21. Reprinted by permission.

argument upon the smallest basis of fact, and a facility almost preternatural in "explaining away" troublesome realities. So striking was his power in this last respect, that a humorous London chronicler once advised a bigamist, as his only hope, to induce Mr. Gladstone to explain away one of his wives.[26]

Argument by words only is apparent in the great good humor of Jonathan Swift's conclusive proof in *Predictions for the Year 1708* that Dr. Partridge, the almanac-maker, would "infallibly die upon the 29th day of March, about

THE INTENSIONAL METHOD

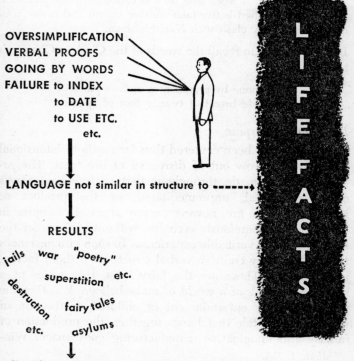

OVERSIMPLIFICATION
VERBAL PROOFS
GOING BY WORDS
FAILURE to INDEX
    to DATE
    to USE ETC.
    etc.

LANGUAGE not similar in structure to ------▶

L I F E   F A C T S

RESULTS

jails war "poetry"

superstition etc.

destruction fairy tales

etc. asylums

[26] Andrew D. White, *A History of the Warfare of Science with Theology in Christendom*, I, 243-244. Reprinted by permission.

eleven at night of a raging fever." However, on the 30th day of March Dr. Partridge published notice in the newspapers that he was very much alive. Nevertheless, in *A Vindication of Isaac Bickerstaff,* Swift again with relentless logic proved that the doctor had died just as predicted.

Sometimes documents are doctored to preserve the verbalism.

[In 1850] Sir J. G. Wilkinson, an eminent Egyptologist, modified the results he had obtained from Egyptian monuments, in order that his chronology might not interfere with the received date of the Deluge of Noah.[27]

A young biologist had just completed two years' intensive research on the problem of sex in the lower animals, and presented his report. A week later he was called in by his professor, who said: "You had better take another month and revise your conclusions. They clash with Nazi racialism."[28]

It is fitting here to recall the words of the Clerk in Chaucer's tale:

> Ye conne by argumentes make a place
> A myle brood of twenty foot of space.

Intension on Purpose

Attention has been centered thus far on those intensional habits which grow out of disregard of life facts. The assumption was made throughout that such behavior was either accidental, unpremeditated, or the product of ignorance. There are, however, many areas of discourse in which people consciously verbalize without concern for the facts of directly verifiable experience. In such circumstances they deliberately contrive verbal structures without factual underpinning. These are the fairy tales, the stories of a never-never-land, of a world of make-believe. Whether the purpose be the entertainment of children or the fun of spinning out a tale that hangs together, the production of fantasy and imaginative manufacturing goes apace. Win-

[27] *Ibid.*, I, 256.
[28] J. Emlyn Williams, "Nazi Nordicism Called Propaganda," *The Christian Science Monitor,* May 13, 1941, 4.

nie-the-Pooh, Br'er Rabbit, Pinocchio, Peter Pan, the Paul Bunyan tales, the Arabian Nights, Rip Van Winkle, the Pied Piper of Hamlin—these are the stock in trade of the storytellers. The comic strips, the Wild Westerns, the pulps, the patterned slick-paper magazine stories, etc., merely continue the tradition in modern dress. It is imperative that we understand here the lack of concern of the authors of this "literature" for reporting what they saw at some time and place. That they "told a story" which was interesting and pleasurable may be justification enough for their efforts. And if the stories fit no "real people and actions," we must understand that they were not intended to. For us to apply the life-facts criterion of criticism here is unnecessary. By definition, we expect fairy tales to deal with fairies and not living human beings.

Benjamino Bufano recently carved out a statue of a "bear" for the University of California. It had a beaver tail, a seallike body, a piglike snout, flattened ears, four fangs, and four flat feet. He explained the symbol to the students in these words: "Most people think of a bear only as a bear. I could make a bear that looked like a bear if I wanted to, but simplicity interests me more."[29] Which is but a manner of saying, "If I am not interested in making my statue resemble a lifelike bear, I don't have to." And we are satisfied if at the outset it is clear to all who look that the piece of sculpture was not meant to be bearlike. Likewise, it would help a great deal if speakers and writers were as frank and considerate as Bufano, for then we should not be in danger of mistaking fanciful utterings for statements of life facts. We should see the intensional creations for what they are intended to represent.

Little harm is done by mere verbalizing as long as one realizes what is happening. We should fear for the survival of the author of the following if he attempted to live by what he says:

[29] Excerpt from *PM*, March 2, 1941, 10, copyrighted by The Newspaper PM, Inc., N. Y. Reprinted by special permission of the copyright owners.

I'm not worrying over possible war shortages of the necessities of life. I can always find a fork in the road, a dipper in the sky, a bed in the stream, a shelf of rocks, a blanket of fog, a curtain of mist, and a carpet of leaves.—Maxellus

When Jimmy Savo sang *River, Stay 'Way from My Door* and with childlike gestures shooed the river away, vaudeville audiences laughed at his whimsy. And when in *Mum's the Word* "he performed a drunken surgical operation, pulling from his patient's insides a number of colored balloons, a string of sausages and a Punch and Judy show,"[30] his antics should not be analyzed in terms of what we know about human anatomy. His extravagance and caprice we take as such, and it is quite irrelevant to argue the legitimacy or accuracy of the performance. But it is not so easy to discover the fantastic character of much human speaking when the intent is less apparent or unconscious. The comedy of a Savo has a place and a function, and in a world beset with more somber happenings it may be that we need more of it. Nevertheless, too often do we listen to the verbalizing of men, far less entertaining, on the assumption that what they say is relevant to the here and now, when it, too, is conceived in the same never-never-land of illusion. And how often does our own serious speaking go unchecked and uncharted except in vain imaginings. How easy it is to speak "coherently" by word association which sounds "good" but which is entirely unrelated to life.

Fictional characterizations, even when labeled as such, sometimes make impressions so deep that they seem "real." Only the counselors and guidance experts know how the dramatizations of "love and romance" on the screen and in novels have colored and shaped the expectations of young men and women. Because Mary Jane felt and "came to know" screen stars who tempestuously or with vast abandon made love to bright young actresses, it seemed only natural that she should wait until that happened to her. The hard-working, dimly glamorous "good" men whom

[30] *Time,* Dec. 16, 1940, 72. Reprinted by permission.

she knew didn't fit the manufactured glosses, so that even though she married one of the flesh-and-blood kind, she expected him to behave otherwise. The long story of social relationships that have ended in conflict may have somewhere in the background a confusion of intensional verbalizations and extensional life facts.

It is all very well for a growing boy to enjoy the redoubtable figures of the comic strip and the robust exploits of his fictional heroes, but it is something else for him to assume that he should find the going in his own life as easy and completely satisfying. And if his expectations are shaped in terms of make-believe people, without realization of their intensional character, disappointments are in store for him.

Recent studies by Dr. Herta Herzog of the Office of Radio Research at Columbia University reveal that one-third of those who listen to radio serials believe that the characters and situations in the serials are "models of reality" and demonstrations of "what to do in a particular situation, or of how to get along with specific people." One subject when interviewed explained of her radio heroine, "She's just like me; she also doesn't want to be in her daughter's way." Dr. Herzog concluded that a great majority went to the radio stories to find ways of solving their own specific problems.[31]

The artificially engendered excitement of the night clubs, the stream of "escape" literature, the urge to get away, the efforts to speed up and multiply "thrills" may be a reflex of, and a clue to, the attempts of many to find for themselves the kind of world which the writers have fictionized about on paper. When men have drawn maps of territories conjured up inside their own skins and made them sufficiently attractive, then readers not carefully trained in the distinction between intension and extension may mistake them for the "real thing." And if the pursuit of the will-o'-the-wisp is ever accelerated so that disillusionment and frustration are inevitable, we cannot dismiss the

[31] See "Heard and Overheard," *PM*, May 20, 1941, 22.

necessity of becoming clear on the difference between fiction and life. Which is not to say that fantasy stuff should have no place in our reading or story telling. It is to say that the place of fiction must be recognized for what it is—verbalization not necessarily similar in structure to verifiable life facts.

When the Territory Is Inside-the-skin

We come now to language uses which represent what goes on inside-the-skin of the speaker. For example, the very first vocalization of a human infant, the birth cry, the gurglings, the expressions of pain seem to be responses to internal neuromuscular conditions. Our inner states can be considered one kind of territory, of life facts, even though others cannot become directly acquainted with them. The inner experience is felt only by the one person, and we can only guess what it was like. From the incoherent babbling of the child to the sophisticated utterances of our most sensitive and thoughtful adults are to be found evidences that speech maps what goes on within.

Perhaps the simplest way of describing this function of language is to see it in terms of a stimulus-response situation. Suppose Mr. A suddenly smacks Mr. B on the back of the head. "Ouch!" says Mr. B. What does the four-letter word represent? The word "Mr. A" serves to designate a non-verbal individual. The word "smacked" designates a non-verbal action. What, now, can the term "ouch" be taken to represent? Nothing, assuredly, that can be observed by others. It is true that Mr. B can be seen moving and his cry heard, but the inner state of affairs, which we assume prompted the exclamation, we cannot get to.

Consider another situation. In 1935 Marian spent two months in London, visiting the public buildings, churches, and stores. In the spring of 1941 she hears of the devastation caused by the hurtling bombs. The places she saw and walked in and lingered by, she learns, are reduced to rubble. She turns to people near by and says, "Oh, why do they do this!" The reports set something going inside, after which she spoke. And when Othello says,

> I do love thee! and when I love thee not,
> Chaos is come again.

he seems, in like manner, to be describing not happenings on the outside but stirrings on the inside.

From these examples a pattern emerges. Something happens, something is seen or heard or remembered, which produces effects on the nervous system of a human being. Something happens inside-his-skin. His talk then takes account of and represents it. We are familiar with the differences in a man's utterance when he is gay, sick, despondent, or in pain. From long association we can tell (though not always accurately) a cry of grief from the shout of delight. A shriek of victory conveys something different from the harsh tone of indignation. And the "Sig Heils" in the Berlin *Sportspalast* stand for inner perturbations far removed from the keenings at an Irish wake. Let us say, then, that there are vast areas of talk which can be characterized as variants

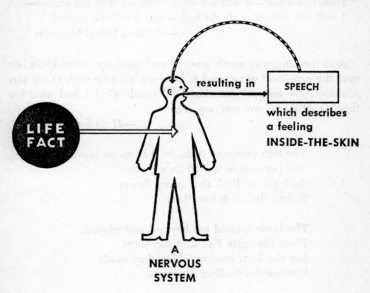

of the "ouch," that is, talk which results when we are moved or affected or when we respond or evaluate in terms that do not represent any *outside* objects, situations, people, etc., with which others can be acquainted.

We have come to be able to catalogue many of the frequently recurring patterns of language which represent the inner stirrings, such as fear, hate, hope, love, joy, sorrow, calm, apathy, wonder, amusement, indignation, righteousness, annoyance, worry, loneliness, sympathy, pity, *et al.* In terms of the kind of inner experiences the reader has had it is good exercise to try to "feel" silently and then to put into words what is represented by these lines:

> O for a lodge in some vast wilderness,
> Some boundless contiguity of shade,
> Where rumor of oppression and deceit,
> Of unsuccessful and successful war,
> Might never reach me more . . .
> —William Cowper

I am in earnest—I will not equivocate—I will not excuse— I will not retreat a single inch—and I will be heard!
—William Lloyd Garrison

And the king was much moved, and went up to the chamber over the gate, and wept: and as he went, thus he said, O my son Absalom, my son, my son Absalom! would God I had died for thee, O Absalom, my son, my son!
—*II Samuel* xviii:33

> Through primrose tufts, in that green bower,
> The periwinkle trailed its wreaths;
> And 'tis my faith that every flower
> Enjoys the air it breathes.
>
> The birds around me hopped and played,
> Their thoughts I cannot measure:
> But the least motion which they made
> It seemed a thrill of pleasure.

If this belief from heaven be sent,
If such be nature's holy plan,
Have I not reason to lament
What man has made of man?
                    —William Wordsworth

We should now be able to recognize the two levels involved in this analysis, (1) those affective states and disturbances that represent modes of evaluation which have an objective character and are on the silent level, and (2) the verbal expressions by which these non-verbal states are given representation.

Though we can distinguish in analysis between statements which point to objects, people, and happenings in the outside-of-the-skin-world and those which point to reactions inside-the-skin, the language habits of men in action do not make such clear distinctions. The two uses are most often to be found intertwined from sentence to sentence. A poem or argument which in one line maps verifiable situations may in the very next one be found to represent attitudes and feelings toward the situations. The task of extrication involves the sharpest and most acute consciousness of the differences between the two uses.

We have no intention here of urging that talk be limited to statements which represent what can be found outside-the-skin. Such a prohibition would be impossible even if urged. We are insisting, for proper evaluation, that statements be recognized for what they do represent. To confuse the forms is to open us to a congeries of misinterpretation. When Billy Sunday gives vent to the following:

Our country is filled with a socialistic, I.W.W., communistic, radical, lawless, anti-American, anti-church, anti-God, anti-marriage gang, and they are laying the eggs of rebellion and unrest in labor and capital and home; and we have some of them in the universities. I can take you through the universities and pick out a lot of black-hearted, communistic fellows who are teaching that to the boys and sending them out to undermine America. If this radical element could have their way, my friends, the laws of nature would be repealed, or they would reverse them; oil and water would mix; the turtledove would marry the turkey buzzard; the sun would rise in the west and set in the east; chickens would give milk and cows would lay eggs; the pigs would crow and roosters would squeal; cats would bark and dogs would mew; the least would be the greatest; a part would be greater than the whole; yesterday would be day after tomorrow, if that crowd were in control. . . .[32]

we must understand before reacting just what we are reacting to—sentences which describe what can be found in life, or sentences which represent the way the Reverend Mr. Sunday responds to what he talks about, or both. To do what he wants us to on the basis of his own inner perturbations is quite different from acting on the basis of what we should find on investigation of life facts.

In Short

To be oriented *extensionally* is to realize the primary importance of life facts, to emphasize the roles of observation and investigation, to go to the facts first and to abide by them. To be oriented *intensionally* is to order behavior in terms of definitions, arguments, verbal proofs, and theorizings, essentially disregarding the existence of verifiable life facts. Fairy tales, fiction, myths, etc., may be considered intension-with-a-purpose. Verbalization which represents what goes on inside-the-skin must be analyzed as such and not in terms of its correspondence with facts-outside-the-skin.

The basic attitude: "I don't know. Let's see."

studying the WORD

"APPLE"

instead of the FACT

For Further Study

1. For more generalized treatments of the orientations by extension and intension, read

1. Article on "Science" in the *Encyclopaedia of the Social Sciences*, Vol. XII.
2. Eve Curie, *Madame Curie, a Biography*. New York: Doubleday, Doran & Co., 1937.
3. Zsolt de Harsanyi, *The Star-Gazer*. New York: G. P. Putnam's Sons, 1939.
4. Paul De Kruif, *Microbe Hunters*, 1926; *Hunger Fighters*, 1928; *Men Against Death*, 1932. New York: Harcourt, Brace & Co.
5. Howard D. Roelofs, "In Search of Scientific Method," *The American Scholar*, Summer, 1940, 296-304.
6. Henshaw Ward, "Thobbing," in *Builders of Delusion*. Indianapolis: The Bobbs-Merrill Co., 1931.

2. Get a copy of *Science News-Letter*. What differences do you find between the content of its columns and that of, say, the Sunday supplement of any large-circulation newspaper?

3. Did you ever try writing something, every sentence of which came *after* the observation of life facts? And every sentence of which could be verified by another observer?

4. The next time you get into an argument with someone try to count the number of statements *you* make of whose extensional character you are uncertain. What would happen to discussions if they *had to be* rigorously extensional?

5. In what areas of your daily living are you most extensionalized? What about the others? What influences tend to prevent the spread of the habit in the other areas?

6. Are there any factors or influences in your community which interfere with the full application of extensional procedures in certain realms of thought and action?

7. In terms of our views and advice, how would you deal with a youngster whose "wild imagination" led him to even "wilder stories"? Do you think his imaginary flights should be curbed?

8. Suppose you were assigned the task of "popularizing" the principles given in this chapter; how would you go about it?

9. Have you ever read a poem that could be called "pure intension," i.e., its words in context representing nothing outside-the-skin of the author? A most useful exercise in developing your ability to recognize the two modes of orientation is to mark those phrases or lines of a poem which appear one or the other or both. Then check your analysis with that of someone else.

10. What man or woman in art, music, or literature would you consider most extensionalized, most thoroughly oriented by life facts? Is he or she considered "great" for that reason? What passages in Homer, what tales of Chaucer, what plays of Shakespeare (or anyone else) do you find governed by extensional methods? Should works of fiction be subject to such questioning?

11. What kinds of jobs, vocations, professions in our society require training in extensional habits? Are any organized to use intensional procedures?

12. The following quotation might well serve as a summary of differences between extension and intension as developed here. Read it carefully. Does it add a new factor?

"Here we need only point out that the problems of 'existence' are serious, and that any one who claims that something 'exists' outside of his skin must show it. Otherwise, the 'existence' is found only inside of his skin—a psycho-logical state of affairs which becomes pathological the moment he projects it on the outside world. If one should claim that the term 'unicorn' is a symbol, he must state what this symbol stands for. It might be said that 'unicorn,' as a symbol, stands for a *fanciful* animal in heraldry, a statement which happens to be true. In such a sense the term 'unicorn' becomes a symbol for a fancy, and rightly belongs to psycho-logics, which deals with human fancies, but does not belong to zoology, which deals with actual animals. But if one should believe firmly and intensely that the 'unicorn' represents an actual animal which has an external existence, he would be either mistaken or ignorant, and could be convinced or enlightened; or, if not, he would be seriously ill. (Alfred Korzybski, *Science and Sanity*, 80-81.)

13. "Winston Churchill ended with high fervor: 'Little did Hitler know when in June 1940 he received the total capitulation of France and expected to be master of Europe in a few weeks and of the world in a few years, that ten months later, in May 1941, he would be appealing to the much-tried German people to prepare themselves for war in 1942. When I look back on the perils which have been overcome, upon the great, mountainous waves through which our gallant ship has

been driven, when I remember all that has gone wrong and also all that has gone right, I feel sure we have no need to fear the tempest. Let it roar, let it rage! We shall come through!' " (*Time*, May 19, 1941, 26. Reprinted by permission.)

Analyze the sentences which represent facts outside and inside the speaker's skin.

14. "We find by our dictionaries that every word may be resolved into other words. Words often possess no signification but as representatives of other words. When an Englishman first learns the French word *oui*, its signification consists in its representing the English word yes. A portion of the words which every man uses is significant on the above principle only. . . .

"Decapitate signifies to me nothing but the phrase 'to cut off a head.' Should I unfortunately see a person guillotined, the word decapitate might thereafter signify the sight. To circumnavigate the globe, possesses with me no meaning but certain words and phrases; but with Anson or Cook, the meaning consisted of the revelations of their senses. The word gout, which to one man is significant of words only, is to another significant of excruciating feels, &c. . . .

"We possess words which never signify any thing but other words. Infinity, eternity, are of this class, and antediluvian, millennium, fairy, and Mahomet. When I read a treatise on eternity, the whole treatise becomes in a manner the signification of the word eternity. What I read in the Holy Scriptures in relation to it, becomes also a part of the meaning of the word. . . .

"God, heaven, hell, immortality, angels, and many other words of the most awful import, are principally significant of scriptural declarations, and of various other words, sentences, and treatises; except that they are significant of certain internal feelings also, which constitute a vivifying and essential part of their signification to persons who happily possess such feelings in association with the words. . . .

"Much errour occurs in our speculations from our not discriminating whether we allude to the verbal meaning of a word, to its sensible meaning, or to its meaning with reference to our internal feelings. The malignity of the errour is increased when the diversity of meaning is deemed an ambiguity of nature, instead of an ambiguity of language." (A. B. Johnson, *Treatise on Language: or the Relation Which Words Bear to Things.* New York: Harper & Brothers, 1836, 142-143.)

Observe that this adds to our intensional and extensional analysis a third type of "meaning." Has it been treated so far in this book?

15. "A fortnight after the fateful April 18th, Sarah Bernhardt came West. . . . Ashton Stevens of the *San Francisco Examiner* and I were the 'reception committee.' She asked us to have luncheon with her . . . and take her on a trip through the ruins. . . .

In scattered places fires were still smoldering, and there was some dynamiting where the firemen were razing dangerous walls and chimneys. Her reactions to the devastation were such that by the time we reached the Palace Hotel where she was to have stayed, it was apparent that she had taken the catastrophe to herself. . . .

"On our way back she wanted to send a cablegram to her son, Maurice. . . . 'Have just completed a tour through the ruins of this once so beautiful city. Sights are indescribable. In many sections the fire is still burning, walls collapsing dangerously near us. Thank God I'm safe.' The truth was that at no time were we within a quarter of a mile of the danger zone, which was under heavy military guard and no one was allowed inside. But such was the power of the divine Sarah's imagination that she projected herself, not as a mere spectator but as a sufferer into the very heart of the disaster. Often, years later when I saw her, she would talk about it, and what she really had seen was colorless by comparison with what she claimed to have been through. Once, in New York, when I was calling on her at her apartment in the Hotel Marie Antoinette and there were other visitors, she said, 'Do tell them, dear Doctor, how you saved my life when that wall collapsed. It was terrible.'" (Arnold Genthe, *As I Remember*. New York: Reynal & Hitchcock, 1936, 99-100. Reprinted by permission of The John Day Company.)

How would you describe Sarah Bernhardt's orientation? Is there any reason why she should not speak in that manner?

CHAPTER VIII

A SPELL OF WORDS

Thus, when crowds have come, as the result of political upheavals or changes of belief, to acquire a profound antipathy for the images evoked by certain words, the first duty of the true statesman is to change the words without, of course, laying hands on the things themselves, the latter being too intimately bound up with the inherited constitution to be transformed. The judicious Tocqueville long ago made the remark that the work of the consulate and the empire consisted more particularly in the clothing with new words of the greater part of the institutions of the past—that is to say, in replacing words evoking disagreeable images in the imagination of the crowd by other words of which the novelty prevented such evocations. The "taille" or tallage has become the land tax; the "gabelle," the tax on salt; the "aids," the indirect contributions and the consolidated duties; the tax on trade companies and guilds, the license, etc.

One of the most essential functions of statesmen consists, then, in baptizing with popular or, at any rate, indifferent words things the crowd cannot endure under their old names. The power of words is so great that it suffices to designate in well-chosen terms the most odious things to make them acceptable to crowds. Taine justly observes that it was by invoking liberty and fraternity—words very popular at the time—that the Jacobins were able "to install a despotism worthy of Dahomey, a tribunal similar to that of the Inquisition, and to accomplish human hecatombs akin to those of ancient Mexico." The art of those who govern, as is the case with the art of advocates, consists above all in the science of employing words. One of the greatest difficulties of this art is, that in one and the same society the same words most often have very different meanings for the different social classes, who employ in appearance the same words, but never speak the same language.

—G. LeBon[1]

✕✕✕◇✕✕✕

What is "wrong" with the facts described here? Ought people to respond thus to words? What should they do?

[1] From G. LeBon, *The Crowd*, 1922, 120-122. By permission of The Macmillan Company, publishers.

A SPELL OF WORDS

Strange Notions

There are at least two false-to-fact notions about language which children acquire as they grow up, and which, unless eliminated, persist in later years with hurtful consequences.

Sometime around the second year of a child's life a discovery is made—that along with colors, sizes, shapes, and other attributes, "things" have names. Observers report that during this period the child begins to point at objects, asking the equivalent of "What's that?" and when told the name of the object, appears to be quite satisfied that he has learned something about the object. As Koffka says, the name is considered to be an item in "the pattern of the thing," another attribute of it as significant, perhaps, as any other.[1] That is, when the child realizes that a name can be given to anything, that name may "become the most pronounced character of the thing." He may go on to assume unconsciously (1) that when he learns a name for anything, he somehow gets to know the important characteristic of whatever the name is associated with, (2) that the uniqueness of the "thing" is revealed by the name, and (3) that if a "thing" has no name, it is either nonexistent or inconceivable.

A conversation analyzed by Piaget makes a similar point.

Ar (6½) remarked during a building game: *"And when there weren't any names. . . ."*

Bo (6½) replied: *"If there weren't any words it would be very awkward. You couldn't make anything. How could things have been made (if there hadn't been names for them)?"* The

[1] Kurt Koffka, *The Growth of the Mind.* New York: Harcourt, Brace & Co., 1928, 320, 324.

name thus seems to be a part of the essence of the thing and is even a necessary condition of its being made.[2]

Piaget's findings lead him to suggest that the child does not regard the name "as being inscribed . . . on the thing," but that the word and thing are fused. "The name is . . . in the object, not as a label attached to it, but as an invisible quality of the object."[3]

If the view of these pages, that symbols are not inherent in what they are used to symbolize, is to be invalidated, then someone has the burden of showing precisely *where* the verbal attributes are to be found. Just as the existence of objects can be demonstrated, so should the existence of the "name-as-part-of-the-object." The futility and absurdity of such an enterprise will be apparent even before it is realized that words exist on a level quite different from that of direct experience. The beginnings of practical linguistic wisdom for us lie in recognizing in the words of Freeman,

. . . that the connection between an object and its name is purely external and arbitrary, and that the name is really not a property or attribute of the object but a symbol for it.[4]

When this fundamental fact is not explicitly realized and remembered, we find people who act as if words and what they represent have some inherent, inseparable, and perfectly natural connection. This leads to the implicit assumption that the "thing" *is* just what the word says it is, and, conversely, that words may even take the place of "things." In brief, the effect of the childish identification of verbal and non-verbal levels often leads people to substitute the language for the life facts. It is as if they said to themselves, "Since the two exist together, why not respond to one as if it *were* the other?" And when that happens, infantile behavior patterns appear inevitable.

The second false-to-fact notion arises from the child's

[2] Jean Piaget, *The Child's Conception of the World*. New York: Harcourt, Brace & Co., 1929, 62. Reprinted by permission.

[3] *Ibid.*, 70.

[4] Ellis Freeman, *Principles of General Psychology*. New York: Henry Holt & Co., 1939, 138.

relationship with other people. Youngsters quickly learn that words and certain kinds of expressions give them command over the environment. Prolonged wailing gets them what they want. To say "please" is often to have wishes fulfilled. A big smile and a "Mama" or "Dada" bring enthusiastic response. In short, merely to make sounds in a certain fashion is to produce results. It is no wonder that we come to "feel" that words have power, that there is something magical or mystical in language as such. And soon the child sees or learns the necessity of doing what he is told. Orders, directions, advice, encouragement, rewards, punishment—these come to him through the medium of words. When people talk, other people react. The child sees what happens when salesmen, preachers, orators, lawyers, judges, teachers, etc., go to work.

On occasion the child learns that disaster may follow in the train of words.

As an Ephraimite came up: . . . then said they unto him, Say now, Shibboleth: and he said Sibboleth: for he could not frame to pronounce *it* right. Then they took him, and slew him at the passages of Jordan: and there fell at that time of the Ephraimites forty and two thousand.—Judges xii:6

Sometimes men are healed after they are talked to.

In the 9th Century, the great physician Rhazes attended an emir who was so badly crippled that he could not walk. First Rhazes ordered the emir's best horse to be saddled and brought into the courtyard. Rhazes gave the emir hot showers and a stiff drink. Then, brandishing a knife, he cursed his patient, threatened to kill him. Furious, the crippled man sprang to his feet. With his patient hot on his trail, the doctor leaped on the horse and escaped.[5]

And the child may hear of the man, dying in a fit of hysteria, who cried out that his sister-in-law had put a curse on him and his family. When investigation was made, it was found that

. . . the man's son had been run over, his daughter died of

[5] *Time*, Nov. 22, 1940, 71. Reprinted by permission.

scarlet fever, and that his wife was lying on the point of death. All this had happened in two weeks. The family, poor folk who ran a small candy store in the Bronx, had actually been cursed by a wealthy sister. The sister had suspected one of them of stealing her diamond rings. She had come raging into the candy store and shrieked that they all would fall dead of horrible diseases unless the rings were returned to her. In the two weeks following, her witchcraft had practically wiped out the four people in the candy store.[6]

In short, from many areas we become exposed to the effect that words can have on human responses. By the time we have been sufficiently exposed to the workings of words, it will be easy to agree with Emerson, that "Speech is power: to persuade, to convert, to compel." So that if a man tried to be logical, he might move syllogistically in this wise: "I have seen that words have power over my actions. I have been told that the external world is made of the same stuff as I am. It follows, therefore, that words will have power over the external world." The argument on verbal levels is air-tight and can be destroyed only when one is conscious of the difference between the processes (1) outside- and (2) inside-of-human-skins, and (3) those *evaluation*-processes-in-our-heads. There is a difference between a man's blood vessels, muscles, bones, and nerves and his conscious and unconscious processes of evaluation and interpretation. Whereas words may affect the latter, we face new problems when we act as if words directly affect the former as well. That language affects human "meanings" is all too clear; and unless the bases of the "logic of their thinking" are exposed, we shall find people assuming that language affects the rest of the world, too.

Malinowski and the "Magical" Word

Cheering sections, fraternity initiation rites, and the performances of amateur magicians have probably introduced

[6] By permission of PM and The Viking Press, Inc., publishers of "1001 Afternoons in New York" by Ben Hecht, *PM*, April 23, 1941, 19.

the reader to the magical influence which unusual words are believed to exercise. We know better. But for some the verbalization of mystic refrains, the utterance of formulas of the *abracadabra, sesame, hocus pocus* type "are supposed to exercise a mystical effect *sui generis* on an aspect of reality."[7] There exists the belief among many primitive people that somehow these words (or their counterparts) possess certain miracle-working properties on those areas to which they are directed. Given a situation, along with possession of necessary knowledge concerning their use, and the "magician" is able to work his wonders.

According to Malinowski, "the main principle of magical belief is that words exercise power in virtue of their primeval mysterious connexion with some aspect of reality."[8] The authority of the spell-words is thought to have originated side by side "with animals and plants, with winds and waves, with human disease, human courage and frailty."[9] The mystery in the language of magic arises not because words are thought to be conventional symbols of non-verbal facts but because, removed from ordinary speech, they are able to work in devious ways. The power of the word derives from qualities which are believed to be specific and relevant aspects of the world, and capable of power over "things" when used by human beings who have the secret.

The operation of the magic may be seen in ceremonies designed among the Trobrianders to bring about the growth of plants. An accredited magician having received a sequence of words, i.e., a spell, uses it in well-organized ritualistic fashion. One example may suffice.

During the numerous rites of growth magic the voice is made to sweep the soil of each plot and thus to reach the tubers underground, the growing vine and its developing foliage. . . . In every act the magician's breath is regarded as the medium by which the magical force is carried. The voice—and let us remem-

[7] Bronislaw Malinowski, *Coral Gardens and Their Magic.* London: George Allen & Unwin, Ltd., 1935, II, 213, 219.
[8] *Ibid.,* 218.
[9] *Ibid.,* 218.

ber it must be the voice of the accredited and fully instructed magician, and that his voice must correctly utter the words of an absolutely authentic spell—"generates" the power of the magic. This force is either directly launched on the earth or the tuber or the growing plant, or else it is indirectly conveyed by the impregnation of a substance, usually herbs, which is then applied to the object to be affected: the earth, the saplings, the *kamkokola* or the harvested taro or yams.[10]

In this example Malinowski finds the gist of magical speech and its use. The verbal magic inspires the belief that the statement, the utterance is enough to influence situations. A man believed to possess the magic says something, and the effects are thought to follow in cause-effect sequence.

That physical conditions can be influenced by verbalization has been widely believed. Don't adults say *Unberufen* when "tempting providence" and "God bless you" after a sneeze to ward off spirits that might try to enter through the open passages? Haven't we worried about prayer chain-letters on the assumption that "misfortune" might come unless we followed the directions? This one bothered the author as a youth, because he disobeyed:

"O God, we beseech Thee to bless our soldiers and sailors. Keep them in the hollow of Thy hand. Protect them from all evil, and lead us to Thine eternal home. Amen." This prayer has been addressed and distributed throughout the world. Copy it out, and you will see what will happen. It has been asserted that all who copy it will be exempt from calamity, and that those who neglect this opportunity will be visited by misfortune. Copy it out and address it to seven persons, beginning the very day you received the prayer. On the seventh day you will meet with good fortune or will receive good news. Do not break this chain.

Isn't there someone in your experience who would break in upon stories of accidents and sickness to say: "Please don't talk of such things, or you'll make them happen." That Negro who worked in the camp of the astronomer studying an eclipse of the sun, harbored similar notions. The eclipse

[10] *Ibid.*, 216.

was predicted for a certain day, but the Negro left before the appointed hour, returning three days later when camp was broken, to bid the astronomer good-by. The latter asked pleasantly, "Samuel, how do your friends feel about the eclipse?" "Oh, Suh, no one's talkin' about it." "But why?" "Well, Suh, we's too afeared dat ef somebody talks, you'll go bringin' anudder."

The natives of Madagascar are reluctant to speak of lightning; the Baziba never mention earthquakes; rain is not mentioned by name in Samoa; fire is not named in China where there is a risk of conflagration; the ancient Scandinavians also observed the same precaution, and they did not use the ordinary word for water while making beer, lest the brew should turn out flat.[11]

Then there was the Chinese physician who prescribed for his sick patient a mixture of water and paper on which was written the formula for healing drugs. The words, he was certain, would do as well as the herbs. In a border war in India orders were given to have the name of the British general written on paper and covered with rice and turmeric. After the utterance of special incantations, the paper was to be burned. And with the flames would go, too, the life of the general.[12]

Unless we have been prepared somehow by the realization that language serves as a form of representation, we may even take Ko-ko, the executioner in the *Mikado*, at his word:

When your Majesty says, "Let a thing be done," it's as good as done,—practically, it IS done—because your Majesty's will is law. Your Majesty says, "Kill a gentleman," and a gentleman is told off to be killed. Consequently, that gentleman is as good as dead—practically he IS dead—and if he is dead, why not say so?

Euphemism

An understanding of the "magical" power of words as they are supposed to affect objects and the course of situa-

[11] From Robert Briffault, *The Mothers*, 1927, I, 15. By permission of The Macmillan Company, publishers.

[12] Joseph Jastrow, *Fact and Fable in Psychology*. Boston: Houghton Mifflin Company, 1900. 244-248.

tions may be obtained from a study of the rhetorical device known as *euphemism*.

> [This] is a form of circumlocution whose justification is that it states an unpleasant or delicate matter in softened terms. The impulse is very natural to use it of what, stated boldly, would shock the sensibilities or taste; as death and its accompaniments, crime, or vulgarity.[13]

This linguistic device is not limited in its application merely to "unpleasant or delicate" matters, but more generally, when the object of the speaker or writer is to put a "good face" on *any* matter. On the assumption that words can alter things, there is to be found the attempt to name them well. Somehow, it is felt that the ascription to life facts of the right kind of names may have something to do with "bettering" the facts. To call an object or situation by names which suggest desirable characteristics is thought to make that object or situation desirable in itself, apart from our changed attitude toward it. The mechanism takes this form: to say the word is to bring about a new condition, to change the make-up of the "thing." This magical change, widely sought in our society, may be seen as the attempt, in general, to replace the evil, the undesirable, the difficult, the useless, the dangerous, the negative, the painful, etc., by "good" words so that the statement will be assumed to make the thing better in itself as well as better in the attitudes of listeners or readers.

Euphemism should be understood as a classificatory device which, by renaming an object, situation, or feeling, acts to put it in a different category in so far as the renaming will evoke new or different attitudes. Thus, for example, it is more polite to say *expectorate* than *spit*, *inebriation* rather than *drunkenness*, *to pass away* rather than *to die*, to say that one has *veered from the truth* rather than *he is a liar*, etc. Note, however, that the life facts and the happenings

[13] J. F. Genung, *The Working Principles of Rhetoric*. Boston: Ginn & Co., 1901, 292. Reprinted by permission. The opposite of this process is to be found when one seeks to create negative attitudes about anything. The effort then is to give the thing "bad" names.

are not affected by the change in the language, though our interpretation or evaluation of them may be.

New Yorkers have long called those men who keep their streets clean "white wings," "scow trimmers," "garbage collectors," "G-man" (short for garbage-man), "gutter duster," etc. But in the attempt to establish the dignity and importance of the work of these men the title officially selected by the Sanitation Department of New York City is "Sanitation Men." If one would emphasize the menial character of this work, he would use the "gutter duster" classification, whereas the new official title seeks to establish a classification which gives a sense of social value. In any case, the change in name may affect human attitudes without affecting in any way the actual work done.

A United Press dispatch of April 5, 1940, tells of the efforts of one Georgia Sothern, a strip-tease artist, to find a "dignified word to describe the formal and rhythmic disrobing of the body in public." The story explained that she sought a word or designation which would "help the verbally underprivileged members of my profession," because, in her words, "I saw right away what was holding up the progress of strip-teasing: we just had the wrong word." Mr. Henry L. Mencken of Baltimore, according to later dispatches, came to the rescue. Said he, "The word 'moltician' comes to mind, but it must be rejected because of its likeness to 'mortician.'" However, he did discover that a "scientific" name for molting might be "ecdysiast." Presumably now the progress of the "fine art of undressing in public" will not be hampered by the "wrong" word. It might not be amiss to point out that the reclassification in all likelihood may not affect the performances.

In a brilliant series of pages Mencken has documented the attempt on the part of Americans to escape from feeling apologetic about the ways they earn their living.[14] He points out the rather widespread efforts to reclassify trades and crafts by "sonorous" names which will suggest a new sense

[14] H. L. Mencken, *The American Language.* New York: Alfred A. Knopf, 1937, fourth edition, 284-300.

of importance for the vocation. Some characteristic euphemisms include *mortician* for *undertaker*, *realtor* for *real estate agent*, *beautician* for *hairdresser*, *tonsorial parlor* for *barber shop*, *bootician* for *shoemaker*, etc. Nevertheless, the "sense of importance" might or might not affect the character of the work, but the terms are likely to affect the customers.

On February 11, 1941, in Hoboken, N. J., "The Fascio Arnaldo Mussolini Social Club" sought permission to call the organization "The Circolo Amerigo Vespucci." The officials insisted that the change had little to do "with events in Europe or Africa." It would be interesting to know whether the change in naming was accompanied by a change in the activities.

A restaurant menu once included the following:

Beautiful rosy red strawberries picked and specially selected are sent to us fresh each day from the sunny hills of Tennessee. These royal bits of juiciness have a superb flavor and when placed over an old-fashioned biscuit that is made with butter give you the perfect rhapsody of flavor for this ambrosia of tastiness.

If it is true that words can affect the character of things, then that shortcake will be utterly unique. But if the sentences are studied as an effort in magic, we begin to understand that for proper evaluation our primary concern must be directed at the food to be served, regardless of how it is talked about.

The fact that words are responded to with a feeling that what they represent is thereby affected is, according to Ruth McInerney, a factor in the sale of goods:

Name experts are important vertebrae of the business backbone. Companies handling everything from clocks to coal welcome them, for a good name facilitates sales.

Anybody can mark down a tableful of rubbers to 39 cents and dispose of them. It takes a sales intuition to name them *Rainbeaus* and watch them sell at a profit.

Recently a manufacturer called for help in concocting ideas

to sell pots in sets. "Hmm," mused a Name Expert. " 'Have You a Set of Quintuplets in Your Kitchen, Madam?' Pack them in sets of five and call them *Quintuplets*. They'll sell." They did.

Three times more men purchased a gray felt hat called *Tyrolia* than when unnamed. A piece of furniture becomes irresistible when called *Snuggle Sofa*. General Electric increased the sales saturation point for clocks with its *Morning Star*. Customers wishing cathedral-like doorbells ask for *Mello-Chimes*.

Ten times more women buy a shade of hosiery when it is called *Gala* than when it is offered as plain beige. A diplomatic hosiery company calls its short-legged lengths *Brev*, long-legged ones *Duchess*, while the stoutish lady unembarrassedly asks for *Classical* and feels understood. Doggy shades in hosiery, *Spaniel*, *Collie*, and so on, sell 10 to 20 times more than unnamed shades.[15]

Our response to the processes of euphemistic, magical naming probably ought to be that of the student who said, "The Greeks had a word for it, but was *it* any better or worse for being so called?" But that, you will remember, was Juliet's point:

> 'Tis but thy name that is my enemy;
> Thou art thyself though, not a Montague.
> What's Montague? It is nor hand, nor foot,
> Nor arm, nor face, nor any other part
> Belonging to a man. O! be some other name:
> What's in a name? that which we call a rose
> By any other name would smell as sweet;
> So Romeo would, were he not Romeo call'd,
> Retain that dear perfection which he owes
> Without that title. Romeo, doff thy name;
> And for that name, which is no part of thee,
> Take all myself.

No Power "in" Words

The notion that words have power over life facts is perhaps encouraged by the habit of those teachers and writers who have classified words as if there existed a kind of authority in the words themselves. Thus Quintilian, long ago,

[15] Ruth McInerney, "You've Got to Sell Glamour," *Nation's Business*, June, 1935, 38-40. Reprinted by permission.

wrote of obscene, offensive, exact, mean, proper, improper, obscure, and empty words. Similarly, Longinus said, "Sub limity is always an eminence and excellence in language. . . . The choice of the right words and of grand words wonderfully attracts and charms hearers. . . . It imparts to mere facts a soul which has speech. . . . [There are also] vulgar and expressive words to be avoided." More recently one finds John Addington Symonds writing, "Style is the right word used in the right place." In 1938 Stuart Chase wrote about "the tyranny of words" and Isaac Gold berg about "the wonder of words."

The assumption of this mystical attitude toward words is very apparent in a paragraph in Balzac's novel *Louis Lambert:*

The modern languages have divided up amongst themselves the remainder of the primitive folk-words—those majestic and splendid words whose radiance and majesty diminish to the de gree that society ages; . . . whose echo becomes forever weaker with the advance of civilization. . . . Is there not in the word "vrai" (true) a fantastic strength of honesty? Does one not find in the short sound which it commands a vague image of modest nakedness, of the inherence of the truth of everything? This syllable breathes forth an indefinable freshness. . . . And is it not so with all words? All bear the stamp of a living force invested in them by the soul which they give back through the mystery of wonderful action and reaction between word and thought. . . . Through their physiognomy alone words animate the ideas in our brain, the ideas which they clothe.[16]

Often, too, we find people responding to words as if they were something more than maps.

Ruskin tells how in his childhood the word "crocodile" with its long series of letters had for him something of the sinuous, jointed appearance of the real animal. For him the name of a Dr. Grant was always associated with a brown, gritty, bitter powder (rhubarb). This powder was "gr-i-ish" and "granty"

---

[16] Quoted by Heinz Werner, *Comparative Psychology of Mental Development.* New York: Harper & Brothers, 1940, 257-258, footnote. Reprinted by permission.

for him. Isolde Kurz, telling of her early childhood, says: "At that time words were not purely immaterial things. Clinging to them was that exquisite materiality which they described." She refused to eat anything when its name aroused her dislike. For example, the hitherto unfamiliar term "bonbon" (candy) displeased her greatly; in the nasal "on" and in the repeated syllable she discerned something lascivious and disgraceful.[17]

These attitudes and a suggestion of the misevaluation involved appear in Jespersen's note about the fear of an English child.

"I think it is the name that is so frightening, Moth; I don't like to say it, it is so terrible. Death," he shuddered as he lay in bed, "I wish it wasn't called that! I don't think I should mind it so much if it were called *Hig*." Here of course the child deceives himself. If he had belonged to a linguistic community in which *Hig* was the plain unadorned name for death, the three sounds would of course have produced the same horror in his mind as the three sounds which now in his native language make up the word *death*.[18]

Are we to infer from these examples (and there are countless others) that words (marks on paper, vibrations in the air, forms of representation) in some way possess attributes which may be the source of their control over "things"? We have already mentioned the infantile view which considered words as ingredients of life facts, and the impossibility of demonstrating that. It should now be observed that the above sophisticated literary analysis of words results in ascribing to them characteristics which we should have difficulty in finding *in* the words. The literary description seems to suggest that a power or force is invested in the words by some unexplained process, possessing which the words are able to have effects. It is a bit awkward, were this true, to try to account for the fact that to many people there are many different "most musical" or

---

[17] *Ibid.*, 260-261.
[18] Otto Jespersen, *Mankind, Nation and Individual from a Linguistic Point of View.* Oslo: H. Aschehoug & Co., 1925, 168. Reprinted by permission of the President and Fellows of Harvard College.

"ugly" or "strong" words. For if there existed a power *in* the words, should it not be manifested to all who look and listen?

The matter may be argued in many ways, but our view that language serves as a map, a means of representation, developed through cultural history and convention, leads to a different explanation. We should say that words exist, that the accidents of experience and usage result in different sorts of relationships between people and words, during which each learns to respond to individual words in specific ways. To a friend of mine "home" is the most beautiful word in English. To him the word "home" appears beautiful. He ascribes a quality to it. He responds to it and we should rather say that he evaluates the word as beautiful, which is much different from saying that "home" *is* a beautiful word. In this last sentence the word seems to have the characteristic in it, in the two other sentences the "appears" and "evaluates as" suggest that the characteristic results from a human nervous system making an interpretation. When the characteristics have been allocated in nervous systems, the words are shorn of the power which the literary men implied existed in them.

Having placed words back in their non-power-possessing role, our interest might well shift from efforts to describe and classify their power, to their use in representing objects, people, situations, feelings, judgments, values, etc. We should move to forget the "magic in them," to a concern with the life facts they consciously or unconsciously represent.

As further evidence that people uncritically assume a power in words we can turn to the vast area of what is tabooed or forbidden. People living in the United States in 1941 read and hear in public, in newspapers and books, many words and phrases reserved for private utterance twenty years ago. The vocabulary of anatomical functions, sexual activities, social diseases, etc., has for a variety of reasons long been subjected to the processes of circumlocution. Though perhaps known, these words are not and have not been, except for isolated instances, freely used in public. H. L. Mencken has given a most adequate and interesting account of the use and avoidance of these forbidden words, which should be "must" reading for students who would understand the scope of this phenomenon.[19] What concerns us is the fact that individuals, having canalized in their nervous systems a sense of propriety, should feel "peculiar" if they utter such words in places where the taboo holds. Let us realize that the reaction of shame and prudishness is to carbon patches on paper or to vibrations in the air, and not necessarily to the practices which the words represent. The activities of the body in sex, digestion, etc., have their customary restraints, but they go on.

Very recently a bachelor of my acquaintance whose life has not been especially distinguished by chastity, discussed with a tone of horror a book recently printed in which certain relationships between men and women were discussed in Anglo-Saxon terms. When he was asked if he cavilled at the *deeds* he said, "No"—he was offended at the *words*.[20]

Without regard for the usefulness of word prohibition, it is pertinent to inquire into the source of our sufferance of it. Certain words are reacted to, let us note, not at all because they are hurtful as marks or vibrations. The public-minded radio and movie censors who ban the use of *damn* and *hell* are not at all concerned with what could happen to audiences physically; that is, the sounds would probably not damage the eardrums.[21] But deep in our nervous systems we have learned to avoid such words (certainly these

[19] H. L. Mencken, *The American Language*, 300-318.

[20] Abraham Myerson, *Social Psychology*. New York: Prentice-Hall, Inc., 1934, 407. Reprinted by permission.

[21] In his most recent pronouncement, Will Hays, head of the Motion Picture Producers and Distributors of America, Inc., ordered the following words and phrases omitted from all pictures: Alley cat (applied to a woman), Broad (applied to a woman), God, Lord, Jesus, Christ (unless used reverently), "Fanny," "Fire"—cries of, Goose (in a vulgar sense), Hot (applied to a woman), "In your hat," Lousy, Nuts (except when meaning "crazy"), Razzberry (the sound), Tomcat (applied to a man), Buzzard (too similar in sound to bastard). (*Time*, June 16, 1941, 85.)

two are the feeblest of examples) because we have learned to evaluate them as forbidden. We are honoring in our reactions a power in the words. Just as the magician ascribes power to his words in influencing happenings, so too we seem to ascribe ill effects to the utterance of certain words. Profanity, obscenity, and blasphemy are the terms used to classify some of the expressions with which we have been concerned. That ours would be a better society if such expressions were completely expunged from use or if they were removed from the forbidden category is not the point at issue. It is the habit of assuming that language has in it sacrosanct or tabooed ingredients, that we respond as if the words had authority in themselves, as if they possessed magical equivalents—that we are emphasizing here.

When it is believed that there is some mystical power in language, then we are up against problems of misevaluation. To respond to a word as if it were more than a form of representation opens us to confusion and infantile behavior. It is the fur coat that is important for warmth, not the label. It is necessary to understand the social diseases, the sexual and digestive functions and their uses and abuses, for effective living, and a secondary matter how we choose to name them. The "magic" of the word is not an essential part of the non-verbal business of our actual direct experience of these "things." To respond to the word *as if* it were part of the unspeakable, first-order life facts is to pave the way to delusion.

Away from "Magic" and Back to Life

Once the unconscious belief in the mystical power in words has been ingrained in the nervous responses of individuals, it is but a short step to extend those responses to a wide variety of situations. In our society the power of the word is deeply ramified throughout the complex of human relations. Thus, for example, see the binding power of the marriage vows, the coercive force of legal business contracts, the formulas of devout observances and sacraments, the oaths of witnesses in court and of officials in public office.

That customary relationships are guided (and often disregarded) in terms of the phrases built around them bears witness to the deep belief in the authority of the words. We should agree with Malinowski, that "the sacredness of words and their socially sanctioned inviolability, are absolutely necessary to the existence of social order."[22] But that is not enough. That is, if the promises and contracts were not thought to be something more than mere words, the complex civilization that we know might well dissolve into anarchy. To which this must be added: Order in a society is achieved practically not by submission to the promises and contracts *as words*, but to the actions and relationships which those words represent. The life facts should be the focus of individual orientation rather than the words which we merely use to represent them. Human affairs will be coordinated and made productive to the degree that human beings are oriented to the intricate give-and-take of their public and private behavior far more than if they merely respond to the verbal definitions of that behavior. When men and women concentrate on the symbolized marriage vows while neglecting the reality of the behavior, the likes and dislikes, the peculiar abstracting, the ebb and flow of the temperaments of each, it is not surprising to find so many marriages ending in incompatibility and divorce.

Our public life is perhaps tragically transformed by this obeisance to words. Mention should be made of but one area. It is not strange that the terrible exhortations of our Hitlers and Mussolinis achieve acceptance by millions. People having been trained to respond to words will respond readily to the skillful manipulators too often without regard to the "realities" which those words represent. It is not surprising that the magician-like orators should be called *spellbinders*, men able to affect and unleash the forces of human beings in almost any direction by the hypnotism of their verbal rituals. All the savagery and brutality of which men are capable can be released once they

[22] Bronislaw Malinowski, *Coral Gardens and Their Magic*, II, 234.

believe in the word as spoken or written, without regard for what that word represents.

To the argument that spellbinders sometimes evoke action for "good" by their words, this should be said: Whenever we toy with human beings, seeking to get them to respond to words only without regard for the fact that they represent something else, we shall be breeding people ever at the mercy of those who would play with words—and with the people, too. Far better would it be to train men and women in proper evaluation, in the recognition of the duality of words and what they represent. Let us train our people in human responses to other people, in the methods of construction and achievement and analysis—and not in obedience to a non-existing "magic," no matter for what purpose it is used. When people have been trained to distinguish the living effects of what they do and think from the apparatus of verbal magic, then those who argue the good effects of word play will have what they want without the awful dangers that lurk in waiting.

In Short

Words do not exist in objects, situations, feelings, etc. Words can affect human evaluations, but not "things." Calling a spade a *shovel* does not change *it*. In spite of the experiments in euphemism, the ascription of magical properties to words, and the taboos of certain words, language serves as a form of representation. To respond to words as if they were more than symbols of something other is to revert to the primitive and the infantile.

The basic question: not, What was it called, but *What* was being so called?

For Further Study

1. Are there any words that "bother" you? Should you be so affected by ink-spots or noises? How do you account for your reactions?

2. For further examples of the magical effects of language, read

1. Isaac Goldberg, *The Wonder of Words*. New York: D. Appleton-Century Co., 1938.

2. H. R. Huse, *The Illiteracy of the Literate*. New York: D. Appleton-Century Co., 1933.

3. Aldous Huxley, *Words and Their Meanings*. Los Angeles: The Ward Ritchie Press, 1940. (Notice how Mr. Huxley implies in the title that words *have* meanings.)

4. Edward Jones Kilduff, *Words and Human Nature*. New York: Harper & Brothers, 1941.

5. H. L. Mencken, *The American Language*. New York: Alfred A. Knopf, 1936.

3. Suppose all writings were purged of euphemisms. Would it be easy to read them? Could all the euphemisms be purged?

4. The book by Elmer Wheeler, *Tested Sentences That Sell* (New York: Prentice-Hall, 1937), has as its goal the attempt to teach salesmen and advertisers methods of selling goods and services by focusing on the "effectiveness of words." Read the book and then analyze it in terms of language-fact relationships. What, from the point of view of this chapter, is Mr. Wheeler trying to do?

5. What is your attitude on the question raised on page 170? Do you think this would be a better world if tabooed words were entirely omitted from use?

6. Do you have the impression that the advice of this book is concerned with "defining your terms"? Let the fifty-ninth of Francis Bacon's "Aphorisms" suggest why such advice has plagued arguers through the centuries:

"But the *Idols of the Market-place* are the most troublesome of all: idols which have crept into the understanding through the alliances of words and names. For men believe that their reason governs words; but it is also true that words react on the understanding; and this it is that has rendered philosophy and the sciences sophistical and inactive. . . . The high and formal discussions of learned men end oftentimes in disputes about words and names; with which (according to the use and wisdom of the mathematicians) it would be more prudent to begin, and so by means of definitions reduce them to order. Yet even definitions cannot cure this evil in dealing with natural and material things; since the definitions themselves consist of words, and those words beget others: so that it is necessary to recur to individual instances."

7. What do you think of those medical students who upon reading the symptoms of strange diseases become suspicious that they suffer from the very illnesses they are reading about?

8. Analyze the evaluations in this paragraph:

"Superstition has interfered even in the *choice of names*, and this solemn folly has received the name of a science, called *Onomantia*; of which the superstitious ancients discovered a hundred foolish mysteries. They cast up the numeral letters of *names*, and Achilles was therefore fated to vanquish Hector, from the numeral letters in his name amounting to a higher number than his rival's. They made many whimsical divisions and subdivisions of names, to prove them lucky or unlucky. But these follies are not those that I am now treating on. Some names have been considered as more auspicious than others. Cicero informs us that when the Romans raised troops, they were anxious that the *name* of the first soldier who enlisted should be one of good augury. When the censors numbered the citizens, they always began by a fortunate name, such as *Salvius Valerius*. A person of the name of *Regillianus* was chosen emperor, merely from the royal sound of his name, and *Jovian* was elected because his name approached nearest to the beloved one of the philosophic *Julian*. This fanciful superstition was even carried so far that some were considered as auspicious, and others as unfortunate. The superstitious belief in *auspicious names* was so strong, that Caesar, in his African expedition, gave a command to an obscure and distant relative of the Scipios, to please the popular prejudice that the Scipios were invincible in Africa. Suetonius observes that all those of the family of Caesar who bore the surname of Caius perished by the sword. (Isaac Disraeli, "Influence of a Name," *Curiosities of Literature*, ed. by B. Disraeli. London: G. Routledge & Co., 1858, II, 72-73.)

9. "Magicians," John Cowper Powys has said, "have never been able to control their demons until they discovered their names. . . . A word is a magic incantation by which the self exercises power first over itself and then over other selves and then, for all we know, over the powers of nature." Do you believe that?

10. E. Haldeman-Julius published de Maupassant's *The Tallow Ball* and in 1925, 15,000 copies of it were sold. But when

he changed the title to *A French Prostitute's Sacrifice* in 1926,
54,700 copies were sold. How do you explain that?

11. Read E. R. Hunter and B. E. Gaines, "Verbal Taboo in a
College Community," *American Speech*, XIII (1938), 13-18.

12. An interesting area for study is to be found in the jargon,
argot, cant, and slang of special groups. Observe the specialized
vocabularies of special-interest groups. You should be able to discover the magical attitude at work.

13. "We employ words as though they possess, like specie,
an intrinsick and natural value; rather than as though they
possess, like bank notes, a merely conventional, artificial, and
representative value. We must convert our words into the
natural realities which the words represent, if we would understand accurately their value. Some banks, when you
present their notes for redemption, will pay you in other
bank notes; but we must not confound such a payment with
an actual liquidation in specie. We shall still possess, in the
new notes, nothing but the representatives of specie. In like
manner, when you seek the meaning of a word, you may obtain its conversion into other words, or into some verbal
thoughts; but you must not confound such a meaning with
the phenomena of nature. You will still possess in the new
words, nothing but the representatives of natural existences."
(A. B. Johnson, *Treatise on Language: or the Relation Which
Words Bear to Things*. New York: Harper & Brothers, 1836,
152.)

What has this to do with the "magic of words"?

CHAPTER IX

DESCRIPTIONS AND INFERENCES

※※※※※※※※※※※※※※※※※※※※※※※※※※※※※※※※※※

All the way from 23rd Street the little old lady on the Lexington Avenue bus had eyes for no one but the driver and his coin box. People got on and off, the bus weaved in and out of perilous traffic, a thousand distracting sights came into view outside, but this thin, frail thing kept fixing the man in gray with the same hard and purposeful look. Finally, as she prepared to get off at 86th Street, she stopped at the door and turned to the driver. "Young man," she shook a scolding finger, "you'll come to no good. I've been watching you for 20 minutes, and I saw you empty that box several times and put the money in your pocket."

—PM[1]

People who claim to know say that I smoke the worst cigars in the world. They bring their own cigars when they come to my house. They betray an unmanly terror when I offer them a cigar; they tell lies and hurry away to meet engagements which they have not made when they are threatened with the hospitalities of my box. Now then, observe what superstition, assisted by a man's reputation, can do. I was to have twelve personal friends to supper one night. One of them was as notorious for costly and elegant cigars as I was for cheap and devilish ones. I called at his house and when no one was looking borrowed a double handful of his very choicest; cigars which cost him forty cents apiece and bore red-and-gold labels in sign of their nobility. I removed the labels and put the cigars into a box with my favorite brand on it—a brand which those people all knew, and which cowed them as men are cowed by an epidemic. They took these cigars when offered at the end of the supper, and lit them and sternly struggled with them—in dreary silence, for hilarity died when the fell brand came into view and started around—but their fortitude held for a short time only; then they made excuses and filed out, treading on one another's heels with indecent eagerness; and in the morning when I went out to observe results the cigars lay all between the front door and the gate. All except one—that one lay in the plate of the man from whom I had cabbaged the lot. One or two whiffs was all he could stand. He told me afterward that some day I would get shot for giving people that kind of cigars to smoke.

—MARK TWAIN[2]

>⋙◇⋙

How would you explain the improper evaluation of the one lady and the twelve men? What proper habits would you suggest?

[1] Excerpt from *PM*, May 12, 1941, 8, copyrighted by The Newspaper PM, Inc., N. Y. Reprinted by special permission of the copyright owners.

[2] Mark Twain, "Concerning Tobacco," *What Is Man?* New York: Harper & Brothers, 1917, 275-276. Reprinted by permission.

DESCRIPTIONS AND INFERENCES

×××

The Natural Order of Evaluation

The burden of our analysis of the extensional method rests
on the consciousness that the non-verbal levels are of primary importance, with verbal levels coming after. To begin
with, "our lives are lived *entirely* on the *un-speakable*
level."[1] It is not easy to grasp the extent of what is involved
in that quotation. Human actions and reactions (muscular,
nervous, constructive, destructive, vocational, avocational,
recreational, biological, artistic, warlike, peaceful, etc.), the
specialized functions of the physician, dentist, bricklayer,
steel puddler, street cleaner, fireman, farmer, etc., the performances of the actor, writer, singer, pianist, dancer,
painter, composer, the feelings inside-the-skin of the girl
kissed for the first time, the man who has just lost his job,
the boy who makes the touchdown, the woman elected club
president, etc.—all these words represent silent, unspeakable processes which can be talked about.

Here the reader ought to do something (for example,

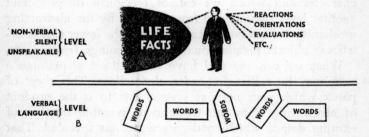

[1] Alfred Korzybski, *Science and Sanity, an Introduction to Non-
Aristotelian Systems and General Semantics.* Lancaster, Pa.: The Science Press Printing Co., 1933, 478.

walk around the room without talking), noting throughout that whatever happens is not on the verbal level. Without consciously recognizing that all direct experience is on this silent level, the point of this analysis may be missed. We now find ourselves living on two levels, as shown in the figure above.

It is necessary to show that this diagram conceals much, that A and B need to be further differentiated into kinds of silent and verbal levels. In Chapter V we explained the existence of unseen submicroscopic, physico-chemical processes at new depths. This event level, given by the most advanced findings of our physical scientists, constitutes the stimuli from which our nervous systems manufacture objects, the ordinary world of sense perception. That is, those electronic processes become registered by our receptors as "things" which we can see, etc., and become directly acquainted with. When you look at an electric fan or airplane propeller whirling about, your nervous system abstracts not blades, but a disk which you "see" as solid and unbroken. And when you are in a room lit by neon bulbs, wave your hand in an arc in front of your face. You will then see a series of five or six hands instead of the blur usually seen in daylight. There was but one hand moving; the nervous system manufactured more.

We have, then, one level, the scientific event, a dance of electrons, different all the time, with an infinite number of characteristics which we cannot recognize directly, and another level summarized from the first by the abstracting mechanisms of our nervous systems into the fewer characteristics of objects, people, situations, happenings, feelings, etc.

What we can see and have other direct acquaintance with may be called *first-order abstractions*. This sheet of paper which your nervous system gets to is the product of abstracting from the tremendous possible number of existing details which modern science has revealed. That you do not get to "all" of them at any moment is quickly demonstrable (see Chapter IV). If this sheet could be covered with the chemical phenylthiocarbimide and tasted by several individuals in succession, we would see the abstracting quickly, for to some it would be bitter, to others either salty, sweetish, or sour. Such a phenomenon becomes understandable as soon as we have defined the silent world as made up of (1) the level of events in process, (2) the objective level, an abstraction of first order from the event. The diagram now looks like this:

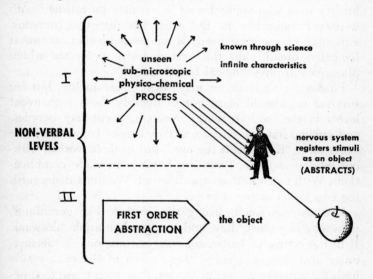

Just as the two orders are numbered with the abstracted objective level coming second, so in our daily evaluation the event is more important for human adjustment and survival. Advertisements have said, "Bread is the staff of life. Eat more of it." In a recent issue of *Life* there was a picture of two loaves concerning which this was written:

The heavy, coarse-grained loaf of black bread at left is made of the whole wheat kernel, crudely milled. It was the staff of life a century ago because [unknown to the eater] it was a rich source of vitamins and minerals. The white bread at right is the product of more refined public taste and milling methods, which have reduced its nutritive values to a minimum.[2]

[2] *Life,* April 21, 1941, 65. Reprinted by permission.

Most significant is the report of doctors that "U. S. citizens suffer generally from deficiency of some of the essential vitamins."[3] In short, what the human organism needs for healthy functioning is not the ordinary object labeled "bread" which bakers have been selling, but the physico-chemical processes, the vitamins, the ingredients of a scientific object which we have not been getting. The untrained hungry man who wants bread to eat may be satisfied with whatever looks like it. But what his digestive, nervous, muscular, etc., system needs is not what he sees, nor what he calls "bread," but the unseen active processes which play roles in physiological functioning.

First-order abstractions may seem closer to life, but for survival we should learn not to identify them with event levels in the modern world. Animals, preliterate peoples, and savages have no science, so they cannot know that there exists more "than meets the eye." But in their worlds, without modern science, there are fewer man-made complications. With us conditions are different. We must distinguish the two levels or pay a price.

Mustard gas smells like garlic, lewisite like geraniums, phosgene like musty hay, and tear gas like apple blossoms. If in the course of battle, soldiers, unconscious of the first-order abstractions, identify these odors of the countryside with the submicroscopic processes, they soon cease to function. Customers who buy Alaska seal fur coats without awareness that for warmth they need the event characteristics of that fur, may buy what merely appears so but which has the event characteristics of muskrat skins. Techniques of dyeing, blending, and simulating have been so skillfully developed that we must distinguish the levels lest we be fooled too easily in all areas of purchase. Buyers equipped with the question, "It looks like (Alaska seal, genuine walnut, leather, steel, fresh meat, rubber, mushrooms, etc.), but how about the unseen physico-chemical processes?" take the first step in proper evaluation. For adequate adjustment, then, the natural order of evaluation

[3] *Ibid.*

must be the submicroscopic level of events first, and next the abstracted objective level. Let Korzybski clinch the argument.

It should be stressed that the "object" of daily experience, in human life, is by far not so reliable as that in the life of animals entirely without human interference. Thus, a high-tension wire, or a third rail, or high explosives are not found in unaided nature and do not forewarn us as ordinary objects do. These "objects" possess characteristics concealed or not obvious on the objective level of our ordinary inspection of, let us say, sight, hearing, or smell; yet these characteristics appear just as "real" and dangerous as ever. It appears, then, that the "scientific object," or the event, in contradistinction to the ordinary object, is more important than the daily object, no matter how important the latter might be. In fact, the only macroscopic importance of objects, outside of aesthetic and symbolic values, may be found in those not obvious physico-chemical, microscopic, and submicroscopic characteristics. Thus the importance of food, or air, or a chair is found precisely in these physico-chemical effects which result from eating, from breathing, and from resting on a chair, and so again these hidden characteristics, revealed *only* by science, appear much more important than the gross characteristics manufactured by our nervous systems which we recognize as an object.[4]

Verbal Levels

At least two verbal levels must now be distinguished. Observe this sheet of paper, an abstraction from the myriad subatomic phenomena we do not see. We can talk about it. It can be verbally named or described variously, "a piece of paper," "a 5″ by 7″ sheet," "a page in a book," "½ ounce of paper," etc. What do these terms represent? They are names for *abstractions of first order*. Each term shows that someone has abstracted some from the many characteristics of the object. Each says something different about it. These descriptions can thus be called *second-order abstractions*. Our nervous systems have now abstracted twice, once from the event, and once from the object.

[4] Alfred Korzybski, *Science and Sanity*, 479.

Animals may stop here, but we can go on to talk about these descriptions, i.e., abstract further in higher orders. Thus, "Paper is an index of man's achievement and we couldn't get along without it," or "This paper will probably last longer than if it were lighter in weight," or "This is one of the most important pages in the book." Now, what do these sentences represent? *Abstractions of higher order.* From the vast number of statements that could have been made about the *second-order abstractions* these three have been abstracted. Something was said about the first verbal level to give a new verbal level, for a statement is not the same as a statement about it. And we need not stop here, for we could go on making statements about statements about statements, etc., in self-reflexive fashion, just as we can make a map of a map of a map of a map, etc. Thus, one could say of "this achievement of man, that it was an aspect of his work which should have made it possible to liberate his time-binding creativeness, whereas it often carries on it the seeds of lies, hate, and fanaticism." In this sentence we have gone to make a higher-order abstraction different from the first statements.

This abstracting in different orders may be shown by a visual example. Pick out some corner of your room. Suppose a painting is made of it. The non-verbal scene will then be represented by means of colors, shading, lights corresponding to it, etc., with, of course, many details left out. Now suppose a photograph is made of the painting. The colorings will now be left out. And a painter could then do that photograph, and a photographer that painting, etc., endlessly. It should be clear that each successive reproduction was an abstraction of higher order. In this process three results would be inevitable: (1) the greater the number of paintings, the further we get from the corner of the room as we see it, and the more details will be omitted; (2) the later paintings especially will show characteristics added by the impressions, judgments, preferences of the painter, not verifiable by observers of the extensional corner; (3) fewer and fewer unique details of the corner would be shown, so that the painted corners would begin to look like corners of other rooms, similarities now being emphasized; or at the very least the later pictures would show less and less correspondence with the original.

Reread the preceding paragraphs on the abstracting from the sheet of paper and see how these results apply there also: details omitted, similarities emphasized, judgments entering.

To return to language. Here, too, the going-away-from-the-object mechanism is ever at work. On a desk in a vase is an unspeakable object, unique and in process. It has been called a "Talisman rose." There is talk about it.

He: This was a good year for *roses*, more on the market than last year.

She: *Talisman roses* have been especially colorful, too. But do you suppose they'll ever get hot-house *flowers* as sturdy and fragrant as those which grow wild?

He: I don't know. There have been tremendous advances in the study and cultivation of *plants* in the last few years. The florists have gone in for national advertising. Your little flower is a very flourishing item in American *business*.

She: Well, whatever happens in the market place, these fragile things are still *moments of beauty* in a very unbeautiful world.

He: Yes, but even beauty seems less beautiful when thirty-ton tanks go ripping up the countryside.

Not especially stimulating conversation, but revealing, because the talk about the object moves from lower- to higher-order abstractions as statements are made of statements, (1) giving fewer and fewer details of the particular object, (2) lumping it together with other objects similar only in some respects, (3) going beyond the object to conclusions and judgments about it. (1) and (2) can be shown by listing the terms in order—Talisman rose, roses, flowers, items of business, moments of beauty. Each term classifies more and more objects while neglecting the unique object in the vase, about which less and less is being said. See, too, how the words "colorful" and "moments of beauty" represent judgments of the observer, and not outside aspects directly verifiable.

One more example[5] of the mechanism of abstracting in various orders. In 1691 in Salem Village, Mass., the Reverend Mr. Samuel Parris had a West Indian servant, a woman named Tituba, who used to amuse a group of girls at the parsonage by telling fortunes. As the winter went on, she told them of voodoo and magic, of black dogs and red cats, of women with legs and wings, etc. After that the members of the group began acting in unaccustomed ways, crawling under tables, shrieking, moaning, trembling, and shaking. Villagers became concerned. The goings-on were described in detail. "Normal" girls never behaved like that. A Dr. Gregg delivered a judgment that the children were afflicted, that this was witchcraft! On February 29, 1692, Tituba and others were arrested on the charge of "bewitching the children." And at the trial Justice Hathorne asked the first defendant, "What evil spirit have you familiarity with?" and after the hearings one man wondered at "the fearful workings of God's providence." The intolerant fanaticism which soon became manifested in the community had very specific results—at least nineteen men and women were hanged.

Let us list the abstractions as they moved to higher and higher orders from the non-verbal happenings.

A woman talked with girls.
The girls reacted, and then acted differently from before.
People then began to speak: "These goings-on are not normal."
"The girls are 'afflicted, tormented, and possessed.'"
"This is witchcraft."
"The girls were 'bewitched' by a woman who knew evil spirits."
"The fearful workings of God's providence."

Note (1) how the attention went from a study of the behavior of the girls to factors beyond them, (2) that conclusions and assumptions entered to account for the be-

[5] Stephen Vincent Benét, "Witchcraft Days in Salem," *Esquire,* May, 1937. See also, *Reader's Digest,* June, 1937, 83-86.

havior of the girls, and (3) that the punishment grew out of the witchcraft judgment and was not based on the description of what the girls did.

Descriptive and Inferential Terms

If the making of a hierarchy of abstractions is understood as a basic mechanism of the working of the nervous system, we can move on to analyze the kinds of terms which characterize the verbal levels. Two categories have been implicit in the above examples: (1) *descriptive* words, those which are functional, applying directly to what we have been acquainted with, and (2) *inferential* words which involve generalizations, judgments, conclusions, which enter when statements are made about descriptions of non-verbal life facts. Such a distinction, though enormously important for proper evaluation, is by no means absolute. We cannot label words as one or the other apart from their use in a context at a date.[6]

We shall call *descriptive* those words which represent observed life facts. When walking down the street, it would be descriptive to say, "An automobile with a physician's insignia on the radiator is parked in front of the Smiths' house." But the statement, "Somebody must be sick in the Smith family," we shall call *inferential*, for it goes beyond what is observed, being based on supposition, conjecture, guess, opinion, on a certain similarity with other occasions, on what may be the case. From the one set of abstracted silent-level life facts, many inferential sentences are possible. The physician's wife may be using the car; the physician may have come to play bridge; he may be visiting people next door, etc. In the second kind of sentence, the speaker abstracted details from the lower level of abstraction and associated them with other experiences. He made a statement about the descriptive level, which is no longer a descriptive statement. Were a third person to comment about the first inference, "What a silly thing to say when you don't know why the car is there!" the state-

[6] Alfred Korzybski, *Science and Sanity*, 470.

ment would be of a different order on a higher level, that is, a judgment about a judgment. There is no end to this ordering process.

In December, 1940, earthquakes shook some areas in northeastern United States. "They were the most violent ever recorded with modern instruments in solid old New England. Chimneys tumbled, dishes and canned goods fell from shelves, walls cracked, furniture slid." Let this be taken as a descriptive statement of what happened.

In Milton, Mass., a woman telephoned to police to find out whether the Navy ammunition depot at Hingham had blown up. In White Plains, N. Y., a filling-station attendant yelled that the Kensico dam had burst.[7]

We should classify the reactions and statements of the woman and the filling-station attendant as inferential, as involving assumptions and conclusions about what went on. It is as if they heard the numbers 1, 2, 3, and then added 4 and 5 themselves. Each moved to fill out the situation with personal notions added to what was heard or seen.

A humorous illustration (judgment by I. J. L.) of the inferential process comes from Arnold Genthe's *As I Remember.*

I could appreciate the story Ethel Watts Mumford once told me. On a Mediterranean cruise she had heard enough on the voyage between New York and Athens to make her decide to visit the Acropolis alone. With this in mind she had waited patiently for the cruise taxis to depart before setting out by herself. It was a hot day and she had taken the climb slowly. When she caught her first view of the Parthenon she was so overcome by its incredible beauty that she slumped onto a rock by the roadside and actually cried. Just then around the bend came the returning cruise party headed by Ethel's pet aversion, a school teacher from the Middle West, who called out, "I know just how you feel, dearie, my feet hurt, too."[8]

[7] *Time,* Jan. 6, 1941, 45. Reprinted by permission.
[8] Arnold Genthe, *As I Remember.* New York: Reynal & Hitchcock, 1936, 236. Reprinted by permission of The John Day Company.

Let us admit that the teacher's feet hurt. Her last four words, then, could be considered directly descriptive. But the first six words become inferential, a higher-order abstraction as soon as she *ascribed* her pain to Ethel Watts Mumford. What she saw was different from what she felt, and to suppose that another felt as she did was to theorize and speculate on what might be. Verification by asking could reveal the inferential character of those first six words.

An experienced and exacting social worker was visiting a third grade in a school in one of Chicago's slum areas. The teacher said, "See how clean the pupils are." The visitor looked about and answered, "Clean on the outside, anyway," refusing, perhaps unkindly, to make the inference about what she didn't see.

A midwestern newspaper in 1940 named Steve Gergeni, end of St. Benedict's College, to an All-Italian-American football team, and the Ohio State end, Charlie Anderson, was picked for the All-Swedish-American team. However, Gergeni's parents are of German descent, and Anderson is a Negro. The statements made about the names represent abstractions of high order and illegitimate inferences based on ignorance of the life facts. We might note here that inferences which result without verification may be most unreliable. This conclusion becomes apparent in this telegram with a New York address sent to the editors of *Life*.

YOUR COVER ON NAVY ISSUE TYPICALLY ILLUSTRATES REARMAMENT PROGRAM UNDER THE NEW DEAL. PLEASE NOTE THAT THE RIFLE CARRIED BY THE GOB ON DRILL IS NOT IN SHOOTING CONDITION DUE TO REAR SIGHT HAVING BEEN BROKEN.

Two inferences are discernible here: first, a judgment about the New Deal, and second, in connection with the word "broken," for in the picture one merely sees that the rear sight is not in place. Many inferences can be drawn to account for that. The Editor's answer is most revealing.

At naval training stations the rear sight leaf is taken off the rifles. Otherwise trainees might break them.[9]

[9] *Life*, Nov. 18, 1940, 4. Reprinted by permission.

These illustrations of the difference between descriptions and inferences may be epitomized in a typical extract from the *Tales of Sherlock Holmes*.

"Wedlock suits you," Holmes remarked. "I think, Watson, that you have put on seven and a half pounds since I saw you."

"Seven," I answered.

"Indeed, I should have thought a little more. Just a trifle more, I fancy, Watson. And in practice again, I observe. You did not tell me that you intended to go into harness."

"Then how do you know?"

"I see it, I deduce it. How do I know that you have been getting yourself very wet lately, and that you have a most clumsy and careless servant girl?"

"My dear Holmes," said I, "this is too much. . . . It is true that I had a country walk on Thursday and came home in a dreadful mess; but as I have changed my clothes, I can't imagine how you deduce it. As to Mary Jones, she is incorrigible, and my wife has given her notice; but there again I fail to see how you work it out."

He chuckled to himself and rubbed his long nervous hands together.

"It is simplicity itself," said he; "my eyes tell me that on the inside of your left shoe, just where the firelight strikes it, the leather is scored by six almost parallel cuts. Obviously they have been caused by someone who has very carelessly scraped round the edges of the sole in order to remove crusted mud from it. Hence, you see, my double deduction that you had been out in vile weather, and that you had a particularly malignant bootslicking specimen of the London Slavey. As to your practice, if a gentleman walks into my rooms, smelling of iodoform, with a black mark of nitrate of silver upon his right forefinger, and a bulge on the side of his top hat to show where he has secreted his stethoscope, I must be dull indeed if I do not pronounce him to be an active member of the medical profession."[10]

It should not be difficult to pick out the statements which embody Holmes' observations from those in which he makes deductions and inferences. The example should, moreover,

[10] A. Conan Doyle, *Tales of Sherlock Holmes*. Washington: National Home Library Foundation, 1932, 236.

serve to indicate that inferences can have close connection with extensional facts.

Lawyers who must deal with witnesses untrained in the differences between descriptions and inferences know well how these are confused. One important problem of the lawyer arises when he must get descriptive statements from the witnesses to the judge or jury. Theirs is the task of passing judgments and of concluding on matters of guilt and innocence from descriptions of the life facts which bear on the case. That these are matters which are sensed appears in a decision handed down in *Pickham* vs. *Illinois, Iowa & M. Ry. Co.*

. . . It is true that McSwiney when asked by leading questions, two or three times, whether he "authorized" any extra repairs, answered that he did not. However, those questions were not only incompetent, because calling for conclusions and conclusions of law at that. . . . "A witness can only testify to facts, not inferences deducible from facts." . . . Nothing could be more erroneous and dangerous than to permit a witness to determine the law upon questions involved in a case on trial, through failure to require the witness to testify to facts instead of giving his conclusions involving propositions of law as well as of fact.[11]

The order of the court in the last sentence contains an admonition to one set of attorneys who permitted (evidently without objection) inferences to pass as description. It would seem here that training in the awareness of the distinction between the two sets of terms would constitute a basic discipline in legal training—as well as elsewhere.

Some Conclusions About Inferential Levels of Abstraction

We begin by what should be evident, that "the reliability of inferences depends on the reliability of the descriptive premises, and description is more reliable than inference."[12] A rereading of each of the examples in the previous section

[11] *Pickham* v. *Illinois, Iowa & M. Ry. Co.*, 153 Ill. App. 281 (March, 1910), 292.
[12] Alfred Korzybski, *Science and Sanity*, 479.

should bear this out. Since inferences are on levels removed from the infinity of details of the non-verbal life facts, they must be considered, at best, as merely probable, not "certain." When inferences are made without prior checking of observed conditions, they may turn out to be irrelevant, fantastic, or just silly. And in so far as we can make an unending number of inferences from any observation or description, it follows that any one inference may have only remote connection with the particular life facts.

This is not to say that inferential statements should be avoided. That is impossible. As you sit and read this, you are silently or unconsciously making many assumptions and inferences, "that the room is not going to cave in upon you," "that what you read does or does not make 'sense,' " "that what you ate at the last meal will not poison you," etc. Without high-order abstractions, we should be unable to see similarities, to generalize, give advice, develop theories, and participate in any scientific advances whatsoever. If researchers did nothing but describe what they found, there would be no science. The hypotheses, generalizations, and laws, developed after inspection of data, constitute the body of our knowledge. What is being emphasized here is this: that inferences represent a different order of abstraction from descriptions; that inferences made before descriptions and without checking with life facts may lead to misevaluation; that when we observe the natural order of evaluation—descriptions first and then inferences—we shall be in less danger of acting foolishly; that descriptions without inferences are futile for time-binding achievements, while inferences unconfirmed and unverified may well end in folly.

We seek a consciousness of the difference between the two, so thorough that abstractions of high order will not be identified with those of lower order. When a man infers, he is not describing, and a consciousness of that may prevent behavior set off by inferences on the assumption that they are descriptions of fact.

We should caution against an unintelligent skepticism of

high-order abstractions because, being removed from descriptive levels, they appear vague and unspecific. To deny them a place is with one uncritical gesture to wipe out the achievement, the poetry and sublimity of so much human utterance. It is easy to condemn a man by showing that his speech is a tissue of judgments and inferences, but that labeling fails to point to the more important concern: Does that utterance come after and can it be checked with descriptions of life facts? Does it take cognizance of the complexity, process, and uniqueness of lower levels? Inferences may lead to improper evaluations when we fail or are unable to go from them down to descriptions of happenings on unspeakable levels. Inferences as inferences cause us little trouble; it is only when we act as if they were descriptions of facts that we are lead astray. It is no great feat to recognize the high-order abstractions in these opening sentences of *The Crisis* by Thomas Paine:

These are the times that try men's souls. The summer soldier and the sunshine patriot will, in this crisis, shrink from the service of their country; but he that stands it now, deserves the love and thanks of man and woman. Tyranny, like hell, is not easily conquered; yet we have this consolation with us, that the harder the conflict, the more glorious the triumph. What we obtain too cheap, we esteem too lightly; it is dearness only that gives every thing its value. Heaven knows how to put a proper price upon its goods; and it would be strange indeed if so celestial an article as FREEDOM should not be highly rated.

Having recognized the level of these sentences, does it follow that we sneer at them? With equal logic we should turn away from the finished chocolate cake because we do not see the subatomic process levels. But just as we are interested in the deeper levels for survival, so, too, should we check, when possible, with the lower orders of verbal and non-verbal abstractions. We live in a period in the world's history when demagogues and dictators find it expedient to speak on high levels with conclusions and inferences that may or may not grow out of descriptions of what takes place. With this notion uppermost, read this paragraph from a speech "The Position of Germany Today" given in 1939 by Adolf Hitler.

Germany has no territorial demand against England and France, apart from that for the return of our colonies. While the solution of this question would contribute greatly to the pacification of the world, it is in no sense a problem which could cause a war. If there is any tension in Europe today it is primarily due to the irresponsible activity of an unscrupulous press, which scarcely permits a day to go by without disturbing the peace of mankind with alarming news which is as stupid as it is mendacious. The efforts of various organs to poison the mind of the world in this connection must be regarded as nothing short of criminal. . . .

Is it easy for us to go back from such utterances to lower levels? Not at all. But considerations of difficulty are not enough to make us deny that "meaning" is to be found here. Going back to life facts may indeed be impossible now; but when the conclusions and assumptions of this paragraph are accepted *as if* they were descriptive and verifiable, then do we understand how unchecked high-order abstractions can leave a blight wherever they are accepted.

When men overwhelm us with inferential statements, we are hardly intelligent if we dismiss them. Wiser is it to consider them invitations to more study. Thus when we hear of acts considered honorable, tragic, or just, we do well to ask what was seen or heard at lower descriptive levels. When teachers talk of "dumb students," listeners of "stupid speeches," critics of "arresting books," salesmen of "efficient operation," and druggists of "health-giving remedies," we ought to pause to ask: What actions, performances, processes are observable or verifiable? What is the basis in descriptive statements for these judgments? Bringing the high-order abstractions down to lower levels lets us "see." And when that happens, we begin to know how hard-won and precious is exact knowledge and understanding of anything. We may then, too, understand what d'Alembert has said: "Philosophers tell us that we owe our errors

chiefly to the abuse of words. To this abuse we may owe
our axioms, too."

Signal and Symbol Reactions

Abstracting, it has been shown, takes place at different
levels. We manufacture objective levels from subatomic
processes (events). We abstract some descriptive statements from the many possible, and we make some inferences from these descriptions. Because these levels are
different, we misevaluate when they are confused. To act as
if one level is the same as another is to make for faulty
responses. When different phenomena are treated as "identical," we behave delusionally.

Let us call the mechanism of such maladjustment *identification.* It occurs whenever the natural order of evaluation
is reversed, when, for example, an object is taken for the
event or when inferences are taken for non-verbal levels.
We should not be disturbed if identifications (i.e., non-
differentiating behavior) are to be found in the lower scale
of animal existence. The behavior of the flatworm, *Con-
voluta roscoffensis,* may be illustrative.

As the water rises, and the waves begin to beat on the sand
near them, they go downward into the sand, where they are
protected. As the water sinks, the animals creep upward and
appear again on the surface. . . . If the worms are removed to
an aquarium . . . they continue to go downward at the period
of high tide, upward at the period of low tide . . . for about
two weeks, so that the worms may be . . . used for a time as
tide indicators. But under such conditions the periodicity after
a time disappears.[13]

During the two weeks the flatworm may be said to identify
water in the sea with water in the aquarium.

A neat example of bird behavior which shows the identification occurring for a time, then being replaced by more
discriminating responses, is given by Carpenter.

[13] Reprinted from H. S. Jennings, *Behavior of the Lower Organ-
isms,* 1931, 254-255, by permission of Columbia University Press.

A wren, having built her nest in a rather dangerous situation in the slate-quarries at Penrhyn, was liable to great disturbance from the occasional explosions. She soon learned, however, to take warning by the sound of the bell, which was rung to give notice to the workmen when a blast was about to be made; and would then quit her nest and fly to a little distance, remaining there until the shock of the explosion had passed off. This was noticed by the workmen; and . . . was made the subject of exhibition to the visitors at the quarry, the bell being frequently rung for the mere purpose of causing her to quit the nest. After a time, however, it was observed that the bird no longer flew away upon the ringing of the bell, but that she remained until she saw whether or no the workmen began to move; if they drew off, she would go too; but if they remained in their places, she would not stir.[14]

Michael gives an example of identification by animals in a man-made situation.

Dogs were placed upon a platform which was caused to move simulating the movement of a ship. The animals soon became sick. . . . The next day the dogs were again put on the platform, but the machine moving the platform would not function. Nevertheless the dogs became sick. . . . They remembered what had happened the previous day.[15]

It may be natural for a dog to get sick when a platform moves, but when the sickness comes on a non-moving platform, then the nervous-organismal identification of the two situations produces behavior that does not make for adequate adjustment.

This kind of response happens with human beings, too. There is the experience of the man who went to sleep in a hotel room. Waking during the night, he felt warm and in need of fresh air. In the strange surroundings, because he was unable to find the light, he sought the window, and

---

[14] William B. Carpenter, *Principles of Mental Physiology*. New York: D. Appleton & Co., 1874, 86-87; quoted by Joshua Rosett, *The Mechanism of Thought, Imagery, and Hallucination.* New York: Columbia University Press, 1939, 143.

[15] W. H. Michael, "Seasickness," *Harper's Magazine,* Nov., 1940, 618. Reprinted by permission.

after some fumbling, found a glass but could not get it to open. His patience worn, he broke the glass, took a deep breath, felt instantly better, returned to bed, and slept soundly. Upon waking in the morning, he discovered the window closed tightly and the glass in a bookcase across the room broken to bits. The facts of temperature and humidity, though unaffected, were as nothing to one who is relieved by making inferences about them.

These characteristic types of reaction, automatic and undiscriminating, may on occasion provide the means of survival in the conditions of animal habitat where recurrences are more highly predictable. For us to *copy* in our nervous responses similar patterns is to open up and increase the possibilities of non-adaptive behavior, especially since the changing and varied conditions in which we live require more discrimination. The flatworm and the wren became adjusted to the new situations, but only after some time had passed during which they behaved stupidly. If in the hurly-burly of modern life, we act like animals, the consequences will not wait. We get the effects of stupidity more quickly, and sometimes so devastatingly that there is no later occasion for applying intelligence. For our survival it may be necessary to delay and discriminate first, before reacting.

Two types of reaction may now be distinguished: *signal reactions*, which are undelayed, over-quick, automatic, less observing, impulsive, seeing similarities only, undifferentiating—in short, those which go on the assumption that what is seen is "all" there is to be seen and known; *symbol reactions,* which are delayed (if only for an instant), taking into account more factors in the situation, going to the present facts rather than to prior-held judgments of them—in short, those which accompany a consciousness of the partial character of acquaintance and attend to differences as well as similarities.

No matter how it may be explained—as a national "speed psychosis," or as the result of an attitude that "life is short, so we mustn't delay," or because we separate in our talk-

As his new false teeth popped out of his mouth and skidded across the floor, two stenographers took the plate for a mouse, jumped up on their chairs and screamed.[17]

Jacob Epstein made

. . . an appealing, life-size bust of a child, arms outstretched, modeled after [his] infant granddaughter, Leda. It was to be put on sale for the benefit of British war relief. . . . As Miss Edith Lutyens was on the point of leaving London Sculptor Epstein impulsively put it in her care. It was not even wrapped. Before she got to the boat train air-raid alarms sounded. . . . When Miss Lutyens and her bronze baby took to the London subways, sleepy air-raid refugees rubbed their eyes in horror. On the blacked-out train ride to Liverpool a flashlight suddenly revealed Miss Lutyens and her infantile fragment to a woman seated opposite. The woman fainted.[18]

That faint might never have occurred if momentary delay had been accompanied by more looking.

The newspapers are a mine of cases in which more than fun results from failure to delay evaluation. Here are two with tragic outcomes:

For slashing the throat of a Roosevelt supporter who ribbed him about Willkie's defeat, a 56-year-old Omaha Republican was sentenced to two years in prison on a manslaughter charge. The judge said the defendant had done it in a sudden rage because of "ill-timed" amusement.[19]

In Pittsburgh, Saloonkeeper Carlo Colombo, 45, looked up from his bar, was frightened to death by a man who entered wearing a mask of Adolf Hitler.[20]

The strategists of warfare sometimes take advantage of the all-too-prevalent identification of judgments with facts by unsuspecting men. General Baden-Powell, with a small force, was able to defend Mafeking against the Boers for

---

[17] *Time,* Oct. 7, 1940, 81. Reprinted by permission.

[18] *Time,* March 3, 1941, 62. Reprinted by permission.

[19] Excerpt from *PM,* March 2, 1941, 10, copyrighted by The Newspaper PM, Inc., N. Y. Reprinted by special permission of the copyright owners.

[20] *Time,* April 14, 1941, 48. Reprinted by permission.

217 days by erecting imitation cannon and breastworks around the outpost. A further part of his *coup* consisted of the dispatch of a few scouts dressed in uniforms new to the Boers, leading them to make inferences about the make-up of the defending army. Notice that the delay and inaction of the Boers was not accompanied by looking to the facts. More recently, Deuel told the story of the effectiveness of Nazi propaganda tactics in preparing the expectations of enemy soldiers so that their responses would be shunted away from the life facts.

German troops storming one sector of the Allied lines last May put the defenders to flight by simply firing signal rockets at them. The Allied troops thought the Nazis were using some new and deadly secret weapon, and ran for their lives.[21]

Now and then there comes a story in which one unconsidered signal reaction breeds another:

Any doctor would have been glad to be called to this house, one of the most beautiful old homes in the city. I felt that my standing in the community was at stake and that it was an important moment.

At the conclusion of the examination I wanted to talk privately with the stiffly starched and immaculate nurse who was in attendance, who, too, was apparently making every effort to be perfect in her professional attitude. I wanted to give some instructions to the nurse and asked the family to excuse us for a moment while I talked to her privately. The nearest and most obvious place was the old-fashioned bathroom adjoining and I asked her to go in. I closed the door.

"Sit down," I said pointing to the bathroom stool, and then, as she took it, I noticed that the only place left for me was the indispensable one in any bathroom, which was covered by a gold and white lid.

I seated myself and talked for several minutes while the family waited anxiously outside for the verdict. Finally she rose and as I, too, rose, my hand automatically grasped the ornate pear-shaped knob at the end of the chain hanging beside me— and I pulled.

[21] Wallace R. Deuel, the Chicago *Daily News*, Jan. 10, 1941, 1. Reprinted by permission. .

Why I pulled the cursed thing I'll never know except, of course, from force of habit. Instantly the place resounded with the familiar screeches and hisses of flushing water.

"Oh, doctor!" she gasped, "what will they think?—And the door shut!—What can I do?"

"Hell, woman," I said, my dignity ruined, "Don't ask me what you can do. I don't even know what I can do!"

I was never asked to return.[22]

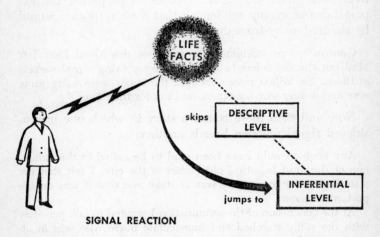

LIFE FACTS

skips   **DESCRIPTIVE LEVEL**

jumps to   **INFERENTIAL LEVEL**

SIGNAL REACTION

The possibilities of misinterpretation that stem from the confusion of inferences and life facts provide abundant opportunities for dramatic conflict. The development of such identifications gives the dramatist or novelist an almost endless source of typed reactions which can be utilized either in the course of the story or as its central theme. Examples are numerous. Two from Shakespeare are sufficient to describe the mechanism. In Act III, Scene 4, Hamlet's signal reaction is followed by the death of Polonius. The staccato character of the dialogue seems in harmony with the impulsive pattern of the action.

Queen: What wilt thou do? Thou wilt not murder me? Help, help, ho!

[22] Frederic Loomis, M.D., *Consultation Room*. New York: Alfred A. Knopf, 1939, 38 ff. Reprinted by permission.

Polonius: (*Behind the arras, hiding*) What ho! Help, help, help.
Hamlet: (*Drawing*) How now! a rat? Dead, for a ducat.
Polonius: (*Behind*) O, I am slain! (*Falls and dies*)

In the tragedy of *Othello* the mechanism of identification appears magnificently documented. In Act III Iago has begun to raise questions about Desdemona's relationship with Michael Cassio, and in the course of conversation Othello insists, as if mindful of the natural order of evaluation, "No, Iago; I'll see, before I doubt; when I doubt, prove." But it is not very long before these high intentions are forgotten and his suspicions are heightened by Iago's subtleties. However, after some private reflection, he concludes,

> If she be false, O then Heaven mocks itself—
> I'll not believe it.

But he does, and by Act IV his jealousy is so apparent that Iago can say,

> Work on,
> My medicine, work! Thus credulous fools are caught
> And many worthy and chaste dames, even thus,
> All guiltless meet reproach.

And so "caught" was Othello that in the climax of the play he smothers Desdemona in her bed.

What were the descriptive facts about which Othello formed his judgments of the infidelity of his wife? The most important may be mentioned. (1) He sees Desdemona with Cassio. (2) He hears Iago say that Cassio talked in his sleep about Desdemona. (3) He hears from Iago that Cassio wiped his beard with a handkerchief originally given by Othello to Desdemona. (4) He learns that Desdemona does not have the handkerchief. (5) He hears Cassio speak derisively of a woman. (6) He sees a handkerchief pass between Cassio and Bianca. Etc. At one point Iago says,

> I told him what I thought; and told no more
> Than what he found himself was apt and true.

It was, however, not what Othello saw and heard that led

to misevaluation, but his behavior based on conclusions that went beyond the life facts. The tragedy was compounded by the completeness of Othello's faith in (or inferences about) Iago, and his failure to check his judgments for possible identifications.

As a way of summarizing what is involved in signal reactions and the advice given for their elimination, the words of Mrs. Poyser in *Adam Bede* may serve well.

I tell you now, as I told you ten years ago, when you pommelled young Mike Holdsworth for wanting to pass a bad shilling, before you knew whether he was in jest or earnest—you're over-hasty. . . .

In Short

Event, Objective, Descriptive, Inferential—these constitute different levels of abstracting, and in that progression the natural order of human evaluation. Descriptive terms, because closer to life facts, actional and functional, make verification and agreement possible. Inferential terms add to the products of direct experience, introducing judgments, conclusions, creeds, theories, etc. Life is impossible without inferences, which, nevertheless, must be differentiated from descriptions. Confusion of the orders of abstraction leads to non-adaptive signal reactions, automatic, unconsidered behavior, copying animals in our responses. Delay of reaction gives time for observation and more human symbol reactions.

New habits to be acquired: (1) Consciousness of abstracting in different orders, (2) Recognition that descriptive statements are not inferential statements, (3) Delay for an instant while looking.

"beauty"   "luscious"

"forbidden fruit"

"3 inches in circumference"

ETC.

For Further Study

1. The next time you go to the movies or the theater watch for the places in the development of the plot where individual characters create "situations" by their confusion of descriptive and inferential levels.

2. "As most of our observations are accomplished by the aid of the eye, we should expect auditory types to be *poor observers*, and so racially, in the long run, not so well adjusted semantically. Observation shows that the auditory types often have infantile reactions—a serious handicap. From an adaptive point of view the 'normal,' non-infantile, best-adjusted individual ought to be a visual type. Auditory types must also be further detached from actualities than the visual types, as auditory stimuli involve more inferences than descriptions, which is the opposite of the functioning of the visual types . . .

"Even to common sense it seems clear that there is a significant difference between 'knowing' this world by hearing and 'knowing' it by seeing. There is, likewise, a difference between the translation of higher abstractions into lower terms by the visual path, and the corresponding translation by the auditory path. In daily life we never say 'I hear' when we wish to convey that we understand; but we say 'I see.' When we say 'I hear,' we usually wish to convey that we have heard something which we did not fully grasp or approve." (Alfred Korzybski, *Science and Sanity*, 460-461.)

What fundamental suggestion indicated in this paragraph will help you distinguish between descriptive and inferential terms?

3. What advice was given about inferences? Do you understand this chapter to say that we ought to eliminate the making of inferences and judgments?

4. Try writing a letter or essay in which you use only descriptive terms. Will this be easy? What problems are you likely to face?

5. Read a detective story (the cheaper the pulp magazine, the better). As you go through it, check the sentences which to you are predominantly descriptive or inferential (or both). This will not be easy, for the influence of judgment-making is widespread.

6. Read the paragraph which follows as an explanation of the role of descriptive statements in arguments.

"An important aspect of the problem of existence can be made clear by some examples. Let us recall that a noise or written sign, to become a symbol, must stand for *something*. Let us imagine that you, my reader, and myself are engaged in an argument. Before us, on the table, lies something which we usually call a box of matches: you argue that there are matches in this box; I say that there are no matches in it. Our argument can be settled. We open the box and look, and both become convinced. It must be noticed that in our argument we used *words*, because they stood for something; so when we began to argue, the argument could be solved to our mutual satisfaction, since there was a *third* factor, the object, which corresponded to the symbol used, and this settled the dispute. A third factor was present, and agreement became possible. Let us take another example. Let us try to settle the problem: 'Is blah-blah a case of tra-tra?' Let us assume that you say 'yes,' and that I say 'no.' Can we reach any agreement? It is a real tragedy, of which life is full, that such an argument cannot be solved at all. We used noises, not words. There was *no third* factor for which these noises stood as symbols, and so we could argue endlessly without any possibility of agreement. That the noises may have stood for some *semantic disturbance* is quite a different problem, and in such a case a psycho-pathologist should be consulted, but arguments should stop." (*Science and Sanity*, 81-82.)

7. Make a note of the number of the little signal reactions you commit during the course of any one day. What is the remedy for such reactions?

8. Does the analysis of delay of reaction in this chapter seem to you to advocate a stoppage of action?

9. Are there any situations where split-second responses are needed? Is there a place for them in the present analysis?

10. The unconscious making of inferences is so basic a part of our daily responses that we become easy game for the skillful magician. His use of the techniques of misdirection seems an attempt to lure an onlooker by irrelevant distractions into deductions and inferences and away from direct observations. Read any book on magic and prestidigitation for details.

11. "Matters of Opinion, not being disputed questions of fact, are general propositions or theorems relating to laws of nature or mind, principles and rules of human conduct, future

probabilities, deductions from hypotheses, and the like, about which a doubt may reasonably exist. All doubtful questions, whether of speculation or practice, are matters of opinion. With regard to these, the ultimate source of our belief is always a process of reasoning. . . . 'I remember it was with extreme difficulty that I could bring my master to understand the meaning of the word *opinion*, or how a point could be disputable; because reason taught us to affirm or deny only where we are certain, and beyond our knowledge we cannot do either. So that controversies, wranglings, disputes, and positiveness in false or dubious propositions, are evils unknown among the Houyhnhnms.'—Swift.

"The essential idea of *opinion* seems to be that it is a matter about which doubt can reasonably exist, as to which two persons can without absurdity think differently. The existence of an object before the eyes of two persons would not be a matter of opinion, nor would it be a matter of opinion that twice two are four. But when testimony is divided, or uncertain, the existence of a fact may become doubtful, and, therefore, a matter of opinion. For example, it may be a matter of opinion whether there was a war of Troy, whether Romulus lived, who was the man in the iron mask, who wrote Junius, &c. So the tendency of a law or form of government, or social institution, the probability of a future event, the quality of an action or the character of an historical personage, may be a matter of opinion.

"Any proposition, the contradictory of which can be maintained with probability, is a matter of opinion." (George Cornewall Lewis, Esq., *An Essay on the Influence of Authority in Matters of Opinion*. London: Longmans, Green & Co., 1875, 1-2.)

Is Lewis here saying anything about "opinions" that was not said about judgments and inferences in this chapter?

12. "Every writer who treats of physicks, seems to carry on a game of bo-peep between nature and language. The verbal meaning of a word, and its sensible meaning, are so confounded, (the writer referring at one moment to the verbal meaning, and at the next to the sensible meaning), that a reader usually acquires by his study, a knowledge of the verbal ingenuity of man, but not a knowledge of the sensible realities of the universe. I wish not to depreciate verbal learn-

ing, but to mark distinctly the boundaries between what is verbal and what is sensible. Our senses alone can reveal to us sensible realities; and the moment words attempt to express more than our senses discover, the words lose all sensible signification, how much soever they may retain a verbal signification." (A. B. Johnson, *Treatise on Language: or the Relation Which Words Bear to Things.* New York: Harper & Brothers, 1836, 152-153.)

Does this adequately mark off the orders of abstracting?

CHAPTER X

WHEN TO "KEEP STILL"

✕✕✕✕✕✕✕✕✕✕✕✕✕✕✕✕✕✕✕✕✕✕✕✕✕✕✕✕✕✕✕✕✕✕✕✕

Language is but a poor bull's eye lantern wherewith to show off the vast cathedral of the world.

—ROBERT LOUIS STEVENSON

When 'I heard the learn'd astronomer;
When the proofs, the figures were ranged in columns before me;
When I was shown the charts and the diagrams, to add, divide, and
    measure them;
When I, sitting, heard the astronomer, where he lectured with much
    applause in the lecture-room,
How, soon, unaccountable, I became tired and sick;
Till rising and gliding out, I wander'd off by myself,
In the mystical moist night-air, and from time to time,
Look'd up in perfect silence to the stars.

—WALT WHITMAN

I never presumed to speak except in answer to a question, and then I did it with inward regret, because it was a loss of so much time for improving myself. But I was infinitely delighted with the station of a humbler auditor in such conversations, where nothing passed but what was useful, expressed in the fewest and most significant words; where the greatest decency was observed without the least degree of ceremony; where no person spoke without being pleased himself and pleasing his companions; where there was no interruption, tediousness, heat, or difference of sentiments. They have a notion that when people are met together a short silence doth much improve conversation. This I found to be true, for during those little intermissions of talk new ideas would arise in the thoughts, which very much enlivened their discourse.

—JONATHAN SWIFT[1]

✕✕✕◇✕✕✕

There are times when talk is hurtful and when silence is the beginning of wisdom. Do you know when?

[1] Jonathan Swift, "A Voyage to the Houyhnhnms," *Gulliver's Travels.*

WHEN TO "KEEP STILL"

On Silence

If the reader will do what he is told here, he will gain immeasurably the sense of what this chapter is about. What is asked may seem pointless, but the experience of many students of language in its relation to life facts indicates that the procedure is effective. This is a plea for participation.

Pinch your finger. Say no words. Notice the experience. Do it again. Notice that something happened on the silent level. You had a direct experience which may be described verbally in many ways. But whatever might be said in words would not be what you felt by the pressure of the pinch. You should continue to remain silent so that you may become more aware of what goes on inside-your-skin. The nature of that inside feeling, of whatever happens, of whatever comes to awareness is not an affair of language, but is in its entirety an un-speakable matter. This may seem obvious, but unless it is sharply realized that what was felt belongs to the realm of silence, that it is quite different from what may be said in the realm of discourse, we shall miss a most important factor in the process of proper evaluation.

Pick up an object, a pencil or a book. Turn it over in your hands. Handle it. Drop it to the floor. Say nothing as you go through these operations. Look at the object. Now say the word "book." Notice that what you said was not the object itself. What you handled is not words. You might write with the pencil, but you could not write with the word "pencil." You could drop the book to the floor, but you could not drop the word "book" unless the word was objec-

211

tified by being written on paper. You must see that you are dealing with two distinct levels, one verbal, one silent.

Stand up and walk the length of your room. Notice the movements of your feet. Say nothing about what you are doing. Don't even talk to yourself "inside." Merely realize that you are engaging in a form of physical action. After walking, sit down. The action is now ended. Is it clear that the walking took place on a level that was non-verbal, that you merely did something? Now you might try to describe the process of walking, the way your legs move, the shifting positions of your body, the character of the action as you felt it. Regardless of the clarity or complexity of what you have just said, that description will not be on the silent level of the actual walking. No matter how you walked, that action will not be on the level of what you said. Whatever you may say about your behavior, the behavior itself will be different.

In short, the "feeling" of the pinch, the objective pencil or book, the action of walking and sitting belong to a *silent* universe, while anything said belongs to a *verbal* universe. It must be clearly understood that what was called "a pinch," "a pencil," and "walking" are matters which exist on un-speakable levels, very much different from whatever exists on speech levels. Students who are in any doubt about this point should reread the preceding paragraphs and follow the directions before going on.

What is the importance of this emphasis on the difference between the silent and the verbal?

In the first place, it must be realized that our lives are lived on the silent, objective levels, that whatever we "think," "feel," and "do" happens as such silently, and that only as a secondary matter does talk come in. Actual living happens silently and is first in importance before speech. When you sit down to dinner hungry, you are primarily interested in the silent food before you. The digestive system, blood stream, etc., could not be nourished by words, but only by life facts capable of being digested. As Emerson says in "New England Reformers,"

The sight of a planet through a telescope is worth all the course in astronomy; the shock of the electric spark in the elbow outvalues all the theories; the taste of the nitrous oxide, the firing of an artificial volcano are better than volumes of chemistry.

Language enters to serve auxiliary functions as a convenience at a different level of life. Whatever use that language serves will be a use quite different from the use to which the food is put in the stomach. Experiences of anything are primary in human living. And whatever may be said of them does not appear as a part of that silent living.

Secondly, objective levels, objects, feelings, happenings, actions, etc., are infinitely diverse and complex in their characteristics. So full of particulars are they that their fullness can never be reached by words. The classic example of the inadequate coverage of speech appears in the futile attempt to describe the taste or color of something to one who has never had a similar direct experience. To know a taste or color it is necessary to go beyond the words to the experience itself. Though the tasting or the seeing may be immediate and seemingly simple, the full perception is so inconceivably complex that one cannot get to it by words alone. It can be reached only as a first-order direct effect of the experience. The same may be said of objects. One may pick up an object and say "This is a book" without recognizing the false-to-fact character of what was said. The object appears as an absolute individual full of countless characteristics and it is not words and never can be; to speak as if they are "identical" may be described as delusion. Further, to say that it is a "book" is to say something that does not correspond to the totality of the object. Whatever is said is not "all" that can be said. The manifold uses, interpretations, characteristics of the silent objects and first-order experiences with which we become acquainted are ever so infinitely complex and diverse that talk cannot exhaust them. A feeling of this may be at the bottom of Maeterlinck's view in *Treasure of the Humble*:

It is idle to think that by means of words, any real communication can ever pass from one man to another. From the moment we have something to say to each other, we are compelled to hold our peace.

And in the Book of Job (ii:13):

So they sat down with him upon the ground seven days and seven nights and none spoke a word unto him: for they saw that his grief was very great.

For us, even more important is this: an understanding of this silent universe will help dissolve the false-to-fact character of our limited, too-often dogmatic talk.

In the third place, when you realize the complexity of un-speakable levels, you may not be so eager to "burst into speech." It is easy to say something about anything. It is not so easy to be conscious of the limited, partial character of what is said. Verbal levels represent abstractions of some details from the fullness of the silent objects, actions, and experiences. This *consciousness of abstracting* whenever one talks will be more readily acquired when one stops to notice the silent levels. The acquisition of this habit is most difficult. Existing educational procedures somehow generate habits of speaking as the primary human function, so that students too readily speak without awareness that the first-order experiences about which they speak are unreachable by words. To train students to be silent, to know they live on a level comparable to the level of "things" goes contrary to conventional training. And yet training in silence seems to be the most practical means by which to become aware that there are un-speakable realms in actual living. One must learn to be silent outwardly as well as inwardly. Students should learn to look at objects and actions while closing their lips with one hand. To see what is going on and to evaluate it properly without identification *we must be silent*. There must come a consciousness that as soon as we speak we shall be leaving out differences and emphasizing similarities. Learning to point with a finger will keep the silence. Looking and pointing are silent means of expression, analogues of the silent world. *Silence on the objective levels* may well be the first step to the achievement of a consciousness of abstracting and of the realization that there is much more in our world than we normally take cognizance of.

In the fourth place, one of the more immediate beneficial results of acquiring the habit of silence is the development of an awareness that study and analysis are on-going, never finished. When once this is understood, the student develops a *creative* outlook; more and more of the limitless content of the world about him comes into view. Silence gives opportunity for observation. There is time to see what there is to be seen. Arguments, debates, conflicts are quickly generated when the objects, situations, people are known only in part but thought and talked about otherwise. The habit of silence gives one time to look first before speaking. And that looking is, after all, the creative source of what we know as science, art, technology, etc.

The experience of those who have learned silence on the objective level reveals a heightened development of critical attitude. Constant and continuing use of silence when writing or speaking may develop sharply the memory of characteristics left out, no matter what the subject under consideration. Statements are not the un-speakable world; the demarcation of the two levels automatically suggests that statements will leave some things unsaid, some characteristics omitted. Inquiry, investigation, further searching —these are the hallmarks of useful criticism. Students will learn, once silence is fundamental in their reactions, to ask questions: "What do you mean?" "Does that statement cover all?" "Where was the abstracting?" Questions inevitably lead to further search and more talk and an understanding of the limited reasons for whatever conflicts arise.

Our eagerness to make statements on matters which may be foreign to our experience or knowledge may well be a major source of the superficiality of so much speech-making and writing. Students too readily take what they hear and see as the full expression and the complete experience, instead of sharply realizing that too often those statements are merely introductory to the matter in question. As Lippmann has said, "For the most part we do not first see, and then define, *we define first and then see*."[1] The achievement of silence should reverse this unnatural pattern. Looking at the silent world, we must first be silent. For unless we have learned to observe the vast panorama, "the great blooming, buzzing confusion of the outer world," we shall pass over too much that we might know about.

It is important to point out that "we *do not* repress or suppress . . . the bursting into speech; a gesture of the hand to the labels reminds us that words are *not* objects, or actions, or happenings, or feelings."[2] Lapsing into silence will have a jarring effect, which is not to repress but to make for the realization of an important evaluation mechanism in which we must be trained, if we would avoid the harmful effects of speech which becomes false-to-fact when too little is considered.[3]

Phatic Communion

Silence must be regarded as a methodological device of first importance when it functions to induce delay, to aid the inspection of life facts, and to achieve a non-allness orientation. But there are, as Jespersen says, occasions when we do not wish to keep still, when we talk for the sheer joy of talking.

There are people everywhere who are equally capable of being intoxicated with their language and revelling in the enjoyment of their own voices, or who at any rate do not wait to open their lips till they have something to say which is worth hearing. In what I have written about the language of children, I have pointed out that children would never learn to talk at all

---

[1] Walter Lippmann, *Public Opinion*. New York: Harcourt, Brace & Co., 1922, 81.

[2] Alfred Korzybski, *Science and Sanity, an Introduction to Non-Aristotelian Systems and General Semantics*. Lancaster, Pa.: The Science Press Printing Co., 1933, 481.

[3] For the substance of the material on "silence," see *ibid.*, 34-35, 399-400, 416-417, 476-477, 481-485.

if they were surrounded exclusively by thinkers who only used language as a means of . . . [describing and inferring]. Luckily for them in their earliest years they have the chance of hearing those about them, especially mother and nurse and other women, talk on end with everlasting repetitions even when they are absolutely certain that the dear baby does not understand a syllable of what they say. Notice again how people who are fond of animals will talk at length to their dog or cat or horse. We shall have a later opportunity of drawing attention to all that meaningless jingle which in more or less metrical form makes up a great deal of what men say or sing. We must then never forget that the organs of speech besides serving for . . . [description and inference], and before they begin to be used for that purpose, are one of mankind's most treasured toys, and that not only children but also grown people, in civilized as well as in savage communities, find amusement in letting their vocal chords and tongue and lips play all sorts of games.[4]

There are, in addition, situations when silence takes on asocial characteristics. The necessity of working with and meeting people in the affairs of the day amidst the folkways of group life often have the effect of suggesting, as Malinowski has said, that "another man's silence is not a reassuring factor, but, on the contrary, something alarming and dangerous"; and furthermore, "taciturnity means not only unfriendliness but directly a bad character."[5] To preserve silence and not to engage in talk with others carries the marks of ill will. Conversation ceases when friendliness is no more.

We should see that our key word here represents at least two different states of affairs.

Silence$_1$ should be taken as a mode of delay preliminary to talk. Refraining from impulsive commenting, even momentarily, provides occasion for further observation and the

[4] Otto Jespersen, *Mankind, Nation and Individual from a Linguistic Point of View.* Oslo: H. Aschehoug & Co., 1925, 8. Reprinted by permission of the President and Fellows of Harvard College.

[5] Bronislaw Malinowski, "The Problem of Meaning in Primitive Languages," Supplement I in *The Meaning of Meaning* by C. K. Ogden and I. A. Richards. New York: Harcourt, Brace & Co., 1930, 314.

recognition that abstracting goes on. This kind of silence does not do away with speech, it merely paves the way for speech that is a better representation of the life facts.

Silence$_2$, on the other hand, is the sort to which Malinowski seems to refer. It has to do with the failure or refusal or unwillingness to speak. The purpose of this silence may be variously described, but it will most likely not suggest that the individual is preparing for talk to come later. This non-communicative state will have in it the suggestion of strangeness and uncertainty, especially where others expect talk to flow freely. Silence$_2$ goes counter to fellowship and acquaintance. It makes for "strange and unpleasant tension" whenever people face each other. In short, there are social situations when silence$_1$ might breed intelligence, whereas silence$_2$ might breed unpleasantness.

The affairs of the day are not all serious. There are occasions when we don't have to "think," when productive work can be set aside, when problems of adjustment are not involved. Such occasions are not dependent upon solving problems, but they do have purposes. They provide a means of relaxation, ways of reducing tension. Such restful functions may even take place in the course of practical work. The work songs, the gossip around work tables, the verbal play of road gangs and loggers, the pleasantries that accompany group efforts are to be understood as the use of speech which may not only ease the effort but also establish rapport between individuals. Free, easy, aimless give-and-take between men makes for co-operation in their communal undertakings.

The list of occasions in our society in which talk seems to have primarily social purposes is by no means a small one. Consider only the teas, smokers, dinners, dances, club meetings, dates, reunions, celebrations, commemorative gatherings, etc.

Such conversation as is here referred to exists in general for the mutual exchange of non-practical talk. In its simplest stage we know it as "weather talk," where there is a sharing of views and attitudes in which none of the parties expects

"real information." Small talk and polite give-and-take provide a form of social communication which breaks down
the barriers of strangeness and establishes the participants
on a plane of more intimate relationships. What is said is by
no means as important as the fact that the talk establishes
friendly feelings. Stereotyped comments on the state of the
weather, pleasant inquiries about the health of the one
spoken to, generalized references to affairs of the moment
act as lubricants to the establishment of mutuality between
people. The complex routines and specialized activities
which prevent individuals from speaking the language of
others seem to make necessary the existence of methods of
approach which will break through the barriers. These simple exchanges serve to set up avenues for further communication.

Common sentiments, an atmosphere of sociability, the
production of companionship—these may be the concomit-
ants of "the breaking of silence, the communion of words"
which establishes those links of fellowship, "which is con-
summated only by the breaking of bread and the communion
of food."[6] Our alumni gatherings, women's clubs, business
men's luncheons, lodge meetings, etc., are some of the situations in which there exists that "type of speech in which
ties of union are created by a mere exchange of words,"[7]
called by Malinowski *phatic communion.*

One frequently hears cynical comments about the "low
state of intelligence" exhibited when people get together for
an evening. One may also hear derisive references to the need
which people seem to have for card games, bridge clubs,
and visits to the movies so that they will not have to endure
the rigors of thinking and talking. Such comments are relevant only if the social nature of our non-reflective group
life is disregarded. Talk built around polite nothings breaks
the tensions of existence, and it may not be designed to be
reflective and intelligent. The achievement of this relaxation
and bonds of friendship between people need not necessarily

[6] Bronislaw Malinowski, "The Problem of Meaning," 314.
[7] *Ibid.,* 315.

occur as a by-product of talk; they may arise just as well as a by-product of group action, i.e., games, visits to see things, etc. The important point to be grasped is this: The manifestations of good will do have a role in our society, and the purpose of social speech must not be confused with the purposes of an anthropologist on a field trip or a chemist making observations in his laboratory or a man trying to decide where to go on a vacation. The use of language which results from these latter activities has an important place in the efficient functioning of our lives, but it must be seen that they are not the purposes of that social intercourse called *phatic communion*. The aims of a hostess at dinner should not be confused with the aims of a chairman of a group deliberating the problems of national defense.

We shall be properly evaluating speech situations when we distinguish between talk supposed to do work and talk supposed to bring release from work. Confusion arises and analysis often goes askew because these two forms are identified rather than differentiated.

Recognition of abstracting may help avoid the identification. People who talk about trivial matters and subjects which provoke no antipathy but which do make for pleasant interchange are simply abstracting those particular features from the complex of possible relationships while neglecting others. The scientist, on the other hand, might proceed to abstract a set of particulars in his work, which features are relevant because of the peculiar context in which he operates. The selective character of the interests which motivate non-practical talk has been well described by Znaniecki.

The first requirement of the art of "polite" conversation is that subjects be chosen and treated in such a way as to make the process of social communication easy and interesting, without ever stimulating active tendencies or suggesting the possibility of any practical use for the data communicated. Everything told should be sufficiently new to be a real addition to the realm of experiences already shared by the talker and the listener; and yet not too new, for the listener must share with-

out difficulty the experience of the talker. The subjects should
be many and varied, particularly in general conversation, so
that the common field will extend rapidly in several directions;
and yet not too many or varied, lest the extension be superficial,
and no single experience truly shared. Every subject ought to
be sufficiently interesting in itself to stimulate a desire to share
it, and yet none so interesting as to absorb attention and dis-
tract it from the conversation as a social activity and the conversing people themselves. Vital subjects are not altogether
avoided, as in periods of spontaneous relaxation on lower stages,
but must be handled lightly and carefully, viewed in their non-
exciting aspects: this is where the "leader in conversation"
needs the most consummate refinement. In short, the art of
polite conversation imposes actions dominated by the specifically
social tendency to share experiences rather than data as a duty
on every participant, and demands that this duty be performed
in spite of all temptations to subordinate the conversation to
any utilitarian tendencies.[8]

One point of view taken toward idle conversation says
that merely to talk for talk's sake is to talk "nonsense." Even
though a certain innocent pleasure results, nevertheless the
"nonsensical" character of the speech act is what is ridiculed.
The defenders of this view might admit the impossibility of
eliminating such talk because it is so often satisfying. They
would, however, insist upon putting such talk in its unintelligent place.

If nonsense$_1$ be taken to represent "foolishness" and non-
sense$_2$ be taken to represent "absence of purpose," then it
must be argued here that *phatic communion* is neither
(though it might be either in individual cases), for it may
be not foolish but pleasant, and not "meaningless" but
designed for relaxation. Nonsense$_3$ may be taken to represent talk which is supposed to correspond to life facts but
does not. One may find few productive, demonstrable results from sessions of *phatic communion,* if "results" are
measured in terms of new findings and the charting of new

---

[8] Florian Znaniecki, *Social Actions.* New York: Farrar & Rinehart,
Inc., 1936, 527-528. Reprinted by permission.

relationships. That there are observable effects of social talk must be admitted. We get mired in new confusions if the subtle variants of "nonsense" are unrealized. There is danger in the wholesale ascription of the term "nonsense" to everything that is not scientifically descriptive and verifiable. It is far better in terms of proper evaluation if we are conscious that the peculiar manifestations of *phatic communion* are something different from the abstracting procedures of those bent on charting the universe, and if we refuse to permit one to happen as if it were the other.

In Short

Silence on the objective levels is paralleled by silence in human responses. To get to silent levels, we must keep still. Silence$_1$ makes possible consciousness of many details and the abstracting therefrom, gives time for more looking, develops a more critical attitude, and helps to induce delay-of-reaction. Silence$_2$ in the play of social situations may breed antagonism and ill will, for the conventions of group life encourage idle conversation and *phatic communion*.

New habit to be acquired: Get to silent levels by learning silence.

For Further Study

1. Are you acquainted with the following books? David Grayson, *Adventures in Contentment* (New York: Grosset & Dunlap, 1907); William Henry Hudson, *Far Away and Long Ago* (New York: E. P. Dutton & Co., 1926); and Henry David

Thoreau, *Walden* (New York: E. P. Dutton & Co., 1910). Is silence₁ the kind of silence discussed in those pages?

2. If you thought the advice at the opening of the chapter on the value of feeling the silent levels "funny" and childish, do what you were told now. The experience of many teachers says that the notion of silent levels cannot really be understood by merely reading about it. It must be experienced.

3. How would you classify the two-minute silence practiced on Armistice Day in the scheme set out in this chapter?

4. What is the purpose of these "Instructions to Graduates" taken from the Commencement Register and Programme of the University of Wisconsin, in terms of the analysis of "silence"?

"When the Governor steps forward to extend greetings from the State, members of the class should rise and sing 'On Wisconsin' as a salutation. When the President comes forward to give his charge to the Class, the members should rise and sing the Varsity Toast. Give the 'locomotive' also, and then be seated.

"It is good University tradition to give a 'skyrocket' *after* the conferring of each *honorary* degree—*i.e.*, immediately *after* the hood has been placed on the recipient. There are only seven candidates for honorary degrees. Do *not* give the 'skyrocket' for the Doctors of Medicine or Philosophy. There are too many of them.

"But put *pep* and more *pep* into your 'skyrockets!' It will please your parents and astonish the honorary degree men."
(*The American Mercury*, Sept., 1928, 32. Reprinted by permission.)

5. Have you ever noticed that when people know each other well, they do not find it necessary to fill in the silences with "nervous chatter"? Do you believe that courses in conversation ought to be given in our schools as a way of promoting the exchange of good will between people?

6. Put in your own words what Walt Whitman is trying to say in "When I Heard the Learned Astronomer," given at the beginning of this chapter.

7. Jonathan Swift's "Hints Toward an Essay on Conversation" suggests that "social talking" also has its difficulties. It is worth reading, as is George Boas' "The Complete Scandalmonger," *Harper's Magazine*, August, 1937, 270-274.

8. "I cannot teach you the relation that words bear to created

existences, till you can contemplate the existences apart from words. . . .

"Our almost incessant employment of words tends to confound them with the phenomena of nature. We teach children the names of sensible existences, just as we teach them the names of the characters which compose the alphabet. The sight which we call moon, becomes to a child as much the sign of the word moon, as the sight of the character **A** becomes the sign of the sound which the character represents. The name and thing named become strangely confounded and identified. All our learning, from youth upwards, tends to confirm the confusion which exists between language and nature. Nothing is, however, more important to a correct understanding of language, than a subordination of it to natural existences; and this subordination cannot be effected till we discriminate between words and natural existences. Nothing is also more easy than to make the discrimination, provided you cease from speaking, both audibly in words, and inaudibly in thought." (A. B. Johnson, *Treatise on Language: or the Relation Which Words Bear to Things.* New York: Harper & Brothers, 1836, 43, 151-152.)

Do you find that this quotation helps to clarify the point about the necessity of achieving "silence on the objective levels"?

CHAPTER XI

THE FOUR "IS'ES"

>◇◇◇<

When the American exclaimed that he was not represented in the House of Commons, because he was not an elector, he was told that a very small part of the people of England were electors. As they could not call this an actual *representation, they invented a new name for it, and called it a* virtual *one. It imposed on the English nation, who could not object that others should be taxed rather than themselves; but with the Americans it was a sophism! and this* virtual *representation, instead of an* actual *one, terminated in our separation; "which," says Mr. Flood, "at the time appeared to have swept away most of our glory and our territory; forty thousand lives, and one hundred millions of treasure!"*

—Isaac Disraeli[1]

The common people will manie times give such bie names *as seemeth best liking to themselves.*

—Holingshed

What is the Sublime? Everything that is or will be so called by those who have employed or shall employ the name.

—Croce

Perhaps Judgment *was nothing else but the composition or joining of* two names of things, or modes *by the verb IS.*

—Thomas Hobbes

As one studies the history of taste one sees that works of art have many values, not one. The same picture may be highly esteemed for opposing reasons and highly condemned for opposing reasons. One of the best instances is that of Courbet. Courbet was championed by Zola because of his individual and personal manner. He showed Zola a "corner of the universe seen through a temperament." He was championed by Proudhon, the revolutionist, because he summed up the "spirit of his time." He showed Proudhon all the meanness of the bourgeoisie with its pettiness, its love of luxury, its individualism. One of Courbet's paintings which Proudhon particularly admired showed two fat nudes by a river. To Proudhon this painting was satire, to Zola it was realism. To the academic critics it had all the ugliness which Proudhon saw in it, but they could not see it as satire. Therefore they could not admire it.

—George Boas[2]

※※◇※※

The above statements epitomize some fundamental facts about the uses of the little word "is." Sometimes the "is" "means" something and sometimes something else. Can you see any of the possibilities?

[1] Isaac Disraeli, "Confusion of Words," *Curiosities of Literature, III,* 70-71.
[2] George Boas, "Accounting for Tastes," *Harper's Magazine,* July, 1937, 197. Reprinted by permission.

THE FOUR "IS'ES"

✕✕✕✕✕✕✕✕✕✕✕✕✕✕✕✕✕✕✕✕✕✕✕✕✕✕✕✕✕✕✕✕✕✕✕✕

What Is It Really?

The argument was by this time getting hot. "It's clear," said the older man, "that if you want to understand Mark Twain, you'll have to see him as he was, a humorist, probably America's greatest."

"Well, that may be. But the Mark Twain I read is a satirist, as sharp and biting in his outlook as they come. If you want to know the secret of his great influence you'll read almost everything he wrote as satire of American life and customs," was the retort of the younger man.

Throughout the debate the third man had listened quietly. He now broke in. "Mark Twain was a story teller. He was the master of the art of fiction. The novels that made him famous did so because they told stories that were exciting and original. Long after his biting pictures and sharp wit are forgotten his stories will still be read. Mark Twain, the novelist, is the man you ought to study."

What was Mark Twain *really*, humorist, satirist, or great novelist?

The two little boys were playing on a sand pile. One heaped the sand up and said, "It is a mountain." The other boy insisted, "No, it isn't. It's a house." They argued this way for a few minutes until their mother said, "You stop your fighting. Neither of you is right. That's really just a pile of sand."

Which was it *really*?

Most biologists say that bacteria are plants, but a recent decision of the Court of Customs and Patent Appeals said that bacteria are animals. The Supreme Court once decided that the tomato was a vegetable, although contesting scientists said it was a fruit.

227

What are the bacteria and the tomato *really*?

Have you ever sought to find what anything or anyone *really* was? Were you able to settle the question? Or did the discussion end in futility, with no answer the decisive one? That such a question cannot be answered finally one way or another, except by the intervention of some authority or by arbitrary agreement, will be clear once we have analyzed what is asked by the question. We shall locate the source of the difficulty in the forms of the verb *to be*. The assumptions underlying the uses of the little "is" and "was" will be found at the heart of the confusion.

The Four Uses of "Is"

Readers may have noted a general pattern in procedure in these pages which can be stated as a general rule. If at any time we face confusion, disagreement, or futility, before resorting to force or outside settlement we go back to the life facts, after which we see if the key terms (those which arise most often in the discussion) are structurally similar and whether they are being used in different senses by different people.

The ignorance of or failure to realize the varied uses of the "is" (or any form of the verb *to be*) may well stem from our too usual assumption that "given a term, it can be used only as we use it," with a consequent unwillingness to study the life-fact relationships represented by it.

At least two uses of the verb are fundamental and necessary in English.

1. As an auxiliary in the formation of tenses in English. Thus, "he *is* reading"; "we *are* studying"; "they *have been* fighting"; etc.

2. As a synonym for existence. When someone says, "I am here" or "There are ten people in the room" or "The Capitol of the U. S. is at Washington, D. C." the verb in each case acts as a substitute for "exist," which may in turn replace it, preserving (or even emphasizing) the original sense.

At least two other uses of the verb we find false-to-fact

and instrumental in making for confusions and misevaluation.

3. When the "is" leads to the *identification* of different levels of abstraction, implying in the utterance that one "thing" can exist as another. The use has this form: "Man *is* an animal"; "Joe *is* a radical"; "Having done that, she *is* a sinner." The "is" of identity serves to link two nouns, obscuring the differences between silent and verbal levels. This "is" serves as a synonym for "may be called or classified as."

4. When the "is" leads to the predication of "qualities." Here we make the assumption that characteristics exist in "things," whereas they are to be found only in the relation of an observer to what is observed. This "is" covers up the fact that impressions arise in *us*, although we project our impressions on the "things" whenever we say, "The sergeant *was* heroic to the last"; "The music *was* beautiful"; "He *is* most charitable." The "is" of predication brings together nouns with adjectives, implying that the "heroic," "beautiful," "charitable" are somehow *in* the sergeant, the music, and the man. This "is" serves as a synonym for "appears . . . to me, him, them, etc."

These two uses will be considered at more length.

The "Is" of Identity

The sentence, "Man is an animal," we can take as an example of the false-to-fact operations of the "is." Let us use some "uncommon common sense" in analyzing it.

Note first the four words. Perhaps the "is" can be translated by "exist." The sentence would then read, "The word 'man' exists as the word 'animal.'" Put this way, we have an obviously impossible situation. One word cannot exist as another word. One word can exist only as one word (in a context at a date). The statement expresses an identity of one name with another. If we read the sentence in terms of the words only, we get an identification of two different words. Such identity must be considered false-to-fact.

Note now that the word "man" can be taken as a map, a form of representation. What might it represent? Following the analysis in Chapter IX, we should say an abstraction of high order representing a class of non-verbal, unique individuals, George₁, George₂, etc., that we see moving around, eating, sleeping, working, etc. We use the word "man" to represent something which *is not* words. Suppose we say, "The non-verbal objects called 'man' exist as the word 'animal.'" Here, again, we have an impossible situation. How can something non-verbal exist as something verbal? How can one level of abstraction exist as another level? So that if we identify silent objects with words, we speak in a false-to-fact fashion.

Other combinations are possible. "The word 'man' exists as an object 'animal,'" and "The object 'man' exists as an object 'animal.'" But here, too, words and objects are said to exist as something else, which existence cannot be demonstrated.

The accompanying diagram may help clarify the matter. A is not B. The non-verbal level is not the verbal level. The non-verbal level, which can be pointed to, can also be spoken about. We may come upon some abstraction of first

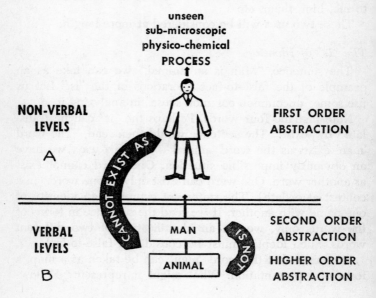

unseen
sub-microscopic
physico-chemical
PROCESS

**NON-VERBAL
LEVELS**

A

CANNOT EXIST AS

**FIRST ORDER
ABSTRACTION**

**VERBAL
LEVELS**

B

| MAN |
| ANIMAL |

IS NOT

**SECOND ORDER
ABSTRACTION**

**HIGHER ORDER
ABSTRACTION**

order and call it "a man," or we may call it "an animal" or whatever we choose. It matters little what names are given to whatever we may become acquainted with; but regardless, the names will not be the silent levels, the labels will not be the objects. The characteristics of a "man" are not "identical" with the characteristics of George₁ or George₂, even though we may say they appear so.

A thoroughgoing consciousness of abstracting reveals immediately the false-to-fact character of the "is" of identity pattern. In front of me I find what is called a "pencil." At deeper levels it is "known" as an electronic dance, a process. With my nervous system I abstract the object and I call it, leaving out many details, a "pencil." Leaving out more details, I move to higher levels, saying, "a very useful instrument." The abstracted object thus appeared at a level different from the verbal abstraction "pencil." If we would evaluate properly, these must be seen as different products of a human nervous system and not as one and the same.

We must conclude, then, with Korzybski, that "whatever you say something 'is,' it is not, because the 'something' *is not* words."[1] What is said belongs to verbal levels and not to silent levels.

The Classification of Objective Levels

In order to find a method by which the identification created by the "is" can be immediately recognized, it will be useful to follow the behavior of Mr. George through a morning. At 8 A.M. he eats breakfast with his family. At 8:50 he takes a train to the city. By 9:30 he is working in his office. At noon he lunches with friends at a club. Looking at these activities we could say, "Mr. George was successively a father, a commuter, an office manager, and a club man." To avoid the false-to-fact identity (because he does not exist as words) while preserving the sense of the statement, we should say, "Mr. George may be verbally classi-

---

[1] Alfred Korzybski, *Science and Sanity, an Introduction to Non-Aristotelian Systems and General Semantics*. Lancaster, Pa.: The Science Press Printing Co., 1933, 409.

fied successively as a father, etc.," in terms of the activities and details of his behavior which we choose to observe. To ask what he was *really* during the morning can only be answered in terms of the life facts as we observe what he does and describe him accordingly. If we classify Mr. George, it must be in terms of some specific way of looking at him. Abstracting the pattern of his day, we might call him "a member of the privileged class," "a prosperous man," or anything else; but whatever name is applied will grow out of the details we choose to abstract.

. . . [This] announcement [is] said to be taken from the *Moniteur* of France, in March, 1815, on the escape of Napoleon from Elba:

First announcement.—"The monster has escaped from the place of his banishment; and he has run away from Elba."

2nd. "The Corsican dragoon, (*l'ogre*) has landed at Cape Juan."

3rd. "The tiger has shown himself at Gap. The troops are advancing on all sides to arrest his progress. He will conclude his miserable adventure by becoming a wanderer among the mountains; he cannot possibly escape."

4th. "The monster has really advanced as far as Grenoble, we know not to what treachery to ascribe it."

5th. "The tyrant is actually at Lyons. Fear and terror seized all at his appearance."

6th. "The usurper has ventured to approach the capital to within sixty hours' march."

7th. "Bonaparte is advancing by forced marches; but it is impossible he can reach Paris."

8th. "Napoleon will arrive under the walls of Paris tomorrow."

9th. "The Emperor Napoleon is at Fontainebleau."

10th. "Yesterday evening his Majesty the Emperor made his public entry, and arrived at the Tuilleries—nothing can exceed the universal joy!"[2]

Suppose it is asked which of these names most adequately describes the man? Which is he *really*? It seems clear that with the man's approach to the city, new interests begin to

[2] Frederic Hudson, *Journalism in the United States*. New York: Harper & Brothers, 1873, 231.

operate, and with them new modes of naming. The courage suggested by the first five announcements was represented by classifications very much different from the last five, which seemingly represent "feelings" of fear and the necessity for ingratiation. The editor classified the man in terms of the way the editor looked at him at a date. At new dates, the basis for naming shifted—and so did the names.

In much the same way we might look at the child who has experiences with his teacher, nurse, playground director, and truant officer. His relationships with each of these will be named differently. In succession he might be classified as a pupil, a case of defective vision, a poor sport, a truant. What the child would *be* at any moment is determined only by the interests and purposes of those who deal with him. They classify him in terms of their ways of looking at him. With different intentions and purposes others would classify him differently.

There is a certain kind of popular word analysis which seeks to show the injection of economic and political prejudices in the reporting of news in the public press. From one point of view this is better studied as the making of inferences under the guise of straight description. The practice may also be understood as a matter of classification. In so far as the policy of one editor or publisher grows out of a certain set of interests, we should expect him to classify individuals and situations accordingly. Thus, George$_2$ is classified from one perspective as a radical, a labor agitator, an inquisitor, a C.I.O. dictator, or an alien; while from another perspective this George$_2$ is called a progressive, a labor organizer, an investigator, a C.I.O. chieftain, and a foreigner. Similar differences will be apparent in the classification involved in government witch-hunting and Senate investigation, regimentation and regulation, dole and home relief, farm dictatorship and crop control.[3]

A newspaper reader should not be unduly dismayed because editors' or publishers' prejudices are injected in the

[3] See S. S. Sargent, "Emotional Stereotypes in the *Chicago Tribune*," *Sociometry*, II (1939), 69-75.

news. It may be asking too much to seek their elimination. A reader would, however, be justified in asking or searching out the interests which lead to certain kinds of naming. Given knowledge of them, one is ready to go to the life facts with full realization that the naming does not completely cover them, that it came from someone's abstraction of some and not all the details. For the reader, then, the important question is not what are the men and actions called? but *what men and actions* are so called?

In order to become conscious that the "is" followed by a noun constitutes little more than a naming process, we should seek to eliminate this "is" from daily use, replacing it wherever possible with "may be verbally classified as." Failing this, however, it is enough if the absurdity of the question "What is he *really*?" is realized. All important, in any event, is not the mere elimination of the noun-is form from our speaking and writing habits. More important is the development of the consciousness that this "is" breeds false-to-fact evaluation. If that consciousness becomes a part of our daily living, a host of confusions will be on the way to dissolution even if we keep on using the "is."

When the "Identity" Is Unrecognized

When the "is" of identity is used without a consciousness of its false-to-fact character, attitudes of "allness" seem readily generated. When someone says that "Mr. A, the lawyer, is a racketeer," it is easy to assume that the totality of ways in which he can be classified is exhausted. Such a sentence makes for finality and completeness, with overtones of "That's what he is, and that's all there is to it." There comes a sense, too, that the speaker has in some way plumbed the ultimate details of this man, catching them all in the one term. As soon as one says, "Mr. A, classified as a lawyer, may be further classified as a racketeer," we see that he might be classifiable in other ways too. To call him a "racketeer" is to have focused on one set of details in looking at this non-verbal individual. With attention directed at other details in his life—for example, his family relationships—

Mr. A might be verbally classified as a good father. This, of course, does not deny the "racketeer" naming. It may well be to our interests to want to punish him or eliminate his racketeering. That we can do. Understanding of the process, however, may prevent our stopping on the easy assumption that "that is all there is to him."

When one philosopher asserts that "history is the history of class struggles," while another argues that "history is the history of great men," the necessary conditions for conflict are at hand. If each describes what history *is* once and for all, then clearly any other final statement must be the work of either a fool or an idiot. In any case, when either theory is affirmed or denied, the stage is set for conflict. However, suppose one develops the "is" so that the sentence now reads, "History (people, actions, etc.) may be verbally classified as the history of class struggles"; we should more readily see that the classification grew out of the interests which led to absorption in the details of class struggles. Further, if another student wished to center his concern on other aspects of life, books might be written to show that "history is the history of corn-raising, or the migration of rats and lice, or the development of gunpowder." In short, the dogmatism that so often results from the adoption of single ways of looking and single theories is abetted by the finalistic character of a sentence in which an "is" is preceded and followed by nouns.

Ben Hecht wrote of the two men, H. M. Thornton and John Doe, who

. . . had been ejected from the Palace Theater for hitting each other over the head with brief cases, Coca-Cola bottles and finally the ring posts. Blood had flown. Police had been summoned. A fine of $25 paid by each of the combatants had closed the case. . . . Mr. Thornton's story of what happened was curt and graphic. It had to do with Wendell Willkie, but very obliquely. Wendell had appeared in a newsreel shot exuding charm and a new patriotism whereupon a theater-goer abutting Mr. Thornton's seat had burst into applause. H. M. countered with a long hiss. This had led to a discussion as to whether

Wendell Willkie was a great American or a wanton publicity-seeking turncoat to the national weal. The rest was police history.[4]

It is interesting to speculate about whether or not there would have been open conflict if these belligerents had been aware that the controversy hinged on a matter of verbal classification. Of course, the political interests of each were markedly different. As a result, the way each classified Mr. Willkie was different. But given the "is" of identity form, how easy it became for each to assume the exhaustive character of his description. Whenever two people are led to "allness" positions, we should not be surprised if their behavior goes beyond the verbal.

On April 13, 1941, Harold L. Ickes gave a speech in which, among other things, he said that Hugh S. Johnson was

Hitler's unconscious tool . . . Nazi fellow traveler . . . Active supporter of America "Next" Committee . . . One of a collection of worst reactionaries . . . Labor-baiter . . . Aid lender to enemies of democracy. . . .

On April 16, 1941, Hugh S. Johnson, in his syndicated column, said, among other things, that Harold L. Ickes was

my more-or-less friendly enemy . . . Howling Harold, the lovable "old Ick" of the Interior Department . . . Horrendous Harold . . . This he-fishwife . . . Unofficial hatchet-man . . . A human wood-pussy congenitally so well equipped with offensive odorosity . . . A hen sitting on eggs . . .

We must be thoroughly clear on one point: in terms of his interests each could classify the other in those phrases. If their interests were different, we should find them expressed in different terms. An enormous danger arises, nevertheless, when the classification is unnoticed. We are led to believe that this is all that can be said about each. For example, for his handling of PWA expenditures, Mr. Ickes may be classi-

[4] By permission of PM and The Viking Press, Inc., publishers of "1001 Afternoons in New York" by Ben Hecht, *PM,* March 3, 1941, 19.

fied as an honest and able administrator. But if the "unofficial hatchet-man" designation remains in the minds of readers of the column, it is all too possible that controversy about Mr. Ickes will seize on one or the other, thus stimulating and even setting up the conditions for larger social conflict. If the multitudinous activities of Mr. Ickes can be looked at differently, we get nowhere by trying to insist that they can be looked at in only one way. No one name given to Mr. Ickes (to Mr. Johnson or anyone else) can bring to an end the vast number of ways he can be classified, depending upon what aspects of his life are abstracted. The label does not describe the "whole" man and his work, but only a corner of his doings.

Sometimes the naming process is taken seriously, with disastrous results.

Resentful of being called "Crocodile" at school and angered by a threat against his life, Glen A. Brough, Jr., 15 years old, slashed and beat John Kelly, 13, a neighboring farm boy, to death in the kitchen of the Brough home Saturday morning, he confessed to police in Lansing, Mich., tonight. . . .

According to Glen's confession, he was alone in their home Saturday when the Kelly boy called and asked him to help cut wood. Glen said he long had borne a grudge against Kelly because he had fastened the name "Crocodile" on him and induced other schoolboys to use it.

Glen said he refused to help Kelly, whereupon Kelly threatened to get a rifle and shoot him. Glen tried to prevent Kelly from leaving the kitchen and Kelly hit him with a coffee can.

Glen said he grabbed a hatchet and hit Kelly, then took a paring knife from a table and stabbed him in his throat. He said he struck the boy several times with the hatchet and stabbed him a second time before starting to drag his body out of the house.[5]

May we not suppose that Glen A. Brough, Jr., became angry because others concluded quite unconsciously that he *was* a "crocodile" and nothing else? They then reacted to the label and not to the boy. As soon as they identified him (a

[5] The Chicago *Daily Tribune,* March 25, 1941, 4. Reprinted by permission.

complex, first-order abstraction, existing at a date) with the word he didn't like, we can begin to understand how his rage would mount.

But it must not be thought that such behavior is limited to youngsters. Here is an example of grown-ups similarly confusing the orders of abstraction.

Representative Beverly M. Vincent of Brownsville, Ky., had a trying week. First short, grey, steely-eyed Congressman Vincent was besieged in his office by a harpy-like group of women who said they were from Kentucky . . . and grew so bitter in their denunciation of conscription that he had to throw them out. Then, with the rest of the House, Representative Vincent had to sit through an equally violent denunciation of conscription by small, red-faced Martin L. Sweeney of Ohio. A Coughlinite and Irish patrioteer, Martin Sweeney declaimed that conscription was a scheme to deliver the U. S. to the British devils. When Representative Sweeney finally ran out of gas, he sat down next to Representative Vincent. It was too much.

"I'd rather you would sit somewhere else," quietly said Beverly Vincent. When Sweeney bristled, Vincent added: "You are a traitor." Words passed. Vincent called Sweeney a --- -- - -----. Sweeney swung at him.

Taking careful aim and with obvious satisfaction, Beverly Vincent planted a good hard right, smack! It staggered, and silenced, Martin Sweeney. Though Congressmen not infrequently threaten one another and have been known to throw bound copies of the *Record* when vexed, ancient Doorkeeper Joseph Sinnot said it was the best blow he had heard in his 50 years in the House.[6]

Would the blows have been struck if each realized the classification character of the assertions?

In the *Twilight of Man*, Earnest A. Hooton has some things to say about the usefulness of language.

The naïve supposition that universal understanding and peace are promoted by linguistic intercommunication is so obviously contrary to fact that it requires no discussion. The spoken or written word is quite as potent an instrument for the fomentation of human discord and for the destruction of culture as for the

[6] *Time*, Sept. 16, 1940, 12. Reprinted by permission.

promotion or harmony and the upbuilding of civilization. Words are more easily and more frequently employed for the former maleficent than for the latter benevolent ends.[7]

He can become quite specific, too.

Such a device as the radio extends to the uttermost parts of the earth the range of one person's potentiality for misleading and befuddling his fellow men, either by taking advantage of their semantic difficulties or by broadcasting his own. I am a frequent radio listener, and it is my considered opinion that what comes over the air is mostly cacophony, lies, and imbecilic nonsense. I do not believe even the time signals. The dog listening to "his master's voice" is a singularly inappropriate trademark for the phonograph, and upon each radio receiving set should be engraved the warning: *Vox et praeterea nihil* ("noise and nothing more").[8]

But notice that Mr. Hooton does little to prevent the "fomentation of human discord." One can almost hear the roar of the apologists for the radio rising to battle. For, of course, they will counter with facts and figures showing how much time is given over to the opera, symphony concerts, public discussions, and presidential speeches, thus allowing them to classify the radio as "a great institution dedicated to the public welfare." For a moment suppose that Mr. Hooton had written the middle sentence of this last paragraph this way:

I am a frequent radio listener, and it is my considered opinion after listening to these soap-operas [with a list of titles], these advertising plugs [with samples written out], these music programs [with a list of titles], and these "adviseering" gentlemen [with names], etc., that these may be verbally classified as cacophony, lies, and imbecilic nonsense.

The "is" having been eliminated and the kinds of programs designated, Mr. Hooton is probably justified in making his classification. He then shows that his naming grew out of specific interests and ways of looking at indexed items at a

[7] Earnest A. Hooton, *Twilight of Man*. New York: G. P. Putnam's Sons, 1939; see pp. 46-48. Reprinted by permission.

[8] *Ibid.*

date. The original form of his statement, however, seemed to emphasize (in spite of the "mostly") an unlimited evaluation. Let Mr. Hooton classify in terms of what he hears and how he reacts. Let the radio apologists do likewise. But let both realize that the "is" covers up the limited character of both the hearing and the naming. Then we may achieve "the promotion of harmony" Hooton so devoutly hopes for.

Searching for a Definition

What is a Teacher? What is Poetry, Democracy, Patriotism, Personality, Honesty, Love, Duty, Law, etc.? You have probably heard such "what is" questions before. And you may have experienced difficulty in answering them. As a way of dealing with such a question, it might be wise to find out what the questioner wants to know. There are at least three possibilities.

1. He seeks some one-and-only-one definition. Our analysis of the Many-Uses principle in Chapter III has already revealed why time will be wasted in that quest.

2. He seeks some "essence," some ultimate characteristic, some seemingly intangible substance that is at the heart of what the term stands for. It may be just possible that he is searching the inside of "things" where the word exists as an attribute, a part of the "things themselves." We have already suggested why this will take our questioner to a never-never land far from life and living beings.

3. He seeks the indexed and dated objects, actions, situations, people, feelings, etc., which the word is being (or has been) used to represent. This, of course, brings the questions to earth. We can now look to some life facts which the nouns are intended to classify. Each of the terms (unless we merely intend to make noises) can do little more than stand for a variety of direct experiences, however vague and remote inside and outside of human skins. The purpose of the question, then, is to be understood as an effort to describe the specific experiences which have been so named. Thus, the question "What is Democracy?" should be translated "What actions, situations, etc., is the word Democracy

being used to classify or name?" We can go to life situations directly, or, failing that, we can make verbal answers. For example,

a. When men are allowed to vote without someone's forcing them to vote one way or another;

b. When decisions of government officers are subject to discussion and trial in the courts;

c. When opportunity for free public education is available for those who want it; etc.

There is nothing in the classification process which forces anyone to use the word Democracy to name these activities only. The choice remains, after all, a matter of agreement between men. When it is to our purpose in the interests of getting work done, or in organizing human affairs, or for any reason whatsoever, we proceed to classify so that those purposes become manifest. We can argue the usefulness or desirability of any one class label over another, but the choice and the judgment are with us. Thus, from the point of view of adequate language-fact relationships, we should urge the preservation of such "Democratic Ideals" as hinted at above. For in such a context we have, perhaps, the only opportunity not merely to talk about but also to achieve "good sense." It is doubtful if anti-democratic countries would even permit the analysis.

In many situations the role of interest may be submerged. We may simply be eager to know how another person is using a term. An interchange in the House of Representatives suggests this purpose:

Mr. Shannon. Mr. Speaker, in his speech yesterday the gentleman from Mississippi [Mr. Rankin] took occasion to refer to a candidate whom he called a mugwump. I would like to have the gentleman tell us what a mugwump is.

Mr. Rankin. Mr. Speaker, the voters have already told us that. There are so many definitions that are applicable that I would not want to burden the Record with them. At the same time I refer the gentleman from Missouri to an answer that came from Alabama some time ago. If he will look at the Record, he will find a mugwump described as a bird that sits on a political fence with the "mug" on one side and the "wump" on the other.[9]

Whether Mr. Shannon was sufficiently informed by the definition is a nice point. For us, it is pertinent to notice that Mr. Rankin's answer omitted the "is" by substituting the word "described," thus revealing the classification process. For more thorough analysis, the answer could go on to list verbally the kinds of actions by a candidate which could be so named, with nothing in the verbal process that must force the acceptance of such naming. For the practical work of daily speaking we are usually satisfied when we learn *what* is being represented by the term, whether or not we would use the term that way.

Whether we seek definitions or merely an understanding of how a term is being used, the "what is" question can still lead us to confuse the levels of abstracting. There remains the possibility that by trying to give answers we will treat one level as if it "were" another. To prevent this, Korzybski would emphasize again and again the necessity of becoming conscious that the "is" breeds identification and so misevaluation.

For thousands of years, millions upon millions of humans have used a great deal of their nervous energy in worrying about delusional questions, forced upon them by the pernicious "is" of identity, such as: "What *is* an object?", "What *is* life?", "What *is* hell?", "What *is* heaven?", "What *is* space?", "What *is* time?", and an endless array of such irritants. The answer, based on the human discrimination of orders of abstractions and so proper *human evaluation*, is definite, undeniable, simple, and *unique*: "Whatever one might say something *is*, *it is not*." Whatever we might *say* belongs to the verbal level and *not* to the unspeakable, objective levels.

Let me repeat once more that the "is" of identity forces us into semantic disturbances of wrong *evaluation*. We establish, for instance, the *identity* of the unspeakable objective level with words, which, once stated, becomes obviously false to facts. The "is" of identity, if used as indicating "identity" (struc-

[9] *Congressional Record,* Nov. 20, 1940, p. 21005.

turally *impossible* on the objective levels), says nothing. Thus, the question, "What *is* an object?" may be answered, "An object *is* an object"—a statement which says nothing. If used in definitions of classifications, such as "Smith *is* a man," a type of statement used even in the *Principia Mathematica*, or "A *is* B or not B," as in the formulation of the law of "excluded third" in the two-valued "logic," it always establishes an *identity*, false to facts. The first statement expresses the *identity* of a proper name with a class name which must lead to the confusion of classes (higher-order abstractions) with individuals (lower-order abstractions). This confusion leads automatically to disturbed evaluation in life, because the characteristics of a class are *not* the "same" as, nor identical with, the characteristics of the individual. I shall not analyze in detail the "A *is* B," because obviously, it *is not.*[10]

The "Is" of Predication

When a form of the verb "to be" connects a noun and an adjective, we invariably express a false-to-fact relationship. In its simplest and sharpest form this is to be seen in such sentences as "The leaf is green," "The picture is ugly," "The speech was trite," "He is most unkind," etc. Let us analyze the first of these.

As it stands, "The leaf is green" implies that the "green" stands for some kind of objective existence in our world. It suggests that the "green" represents something discoverable just as pencil$_1$ represents the non-verbal object on my desk. Suppose you look at a leaf. Can you isolate some "greenness"? Can you point to the non-verbal entity in the same way that you can point to the object pencil? You will find that you will be able to verbalize at length about the "green," but you will not get to it in the outside world no matter how diligent your search. As the sentence stands, it implies that "green" is something added to the leaf. Unfortunately the "something" remains ever illusory, the product of the assumption that the "is" can be translated by "exists."

What does the "green" represent? Your high school primer

[10] Alfred Korzybski, *Science and Sanity*, 408-409.

in general science may help. It should explain that light rays from the sun, a candle, or other source impinge on the leaf. Some of the rays are absorbed. In this case, some of the "packets of energy" which are reflected fall on or are picked up by the sensitive areas (retina) of the eye and pro-duce inside-the-skin sensations or feelings which we have learned to call "green." The impressions, in short, inter-preted by the nervous system arise within the observer and not outside in the object. The object merely serves as the origin or source of the stimulation.

If the phenomenon of color is here correctly described, it must be considered as a product of a *relation* between an observer and what is observed. It should be understood, then, that the "is" form of the sentence reverses the facts, in so far as the "color" is attributed to the leaf rather than to processes in the nervous system of the observer. Unaware-ness of the relation leads readily to the assumption that "colors" exist outside. Note the following paragraph:

There is a belief among many solitary woodsmen that every color or tint to which a tree is exposed during its life, glows in the fire when that tree is burned. Look deep into the coals and you can find the pinks and violets of dawn, the blueness of the sky, the burning brightness of the noonday sun, the angry black of a thunder-cloud, the crimson of the sunset, the silver radiance of the moonlight, the brilliant transparency of the stars.[11]

If Larry Foster would claim that the "pinks," "the angry black," "the silver radiance" exist outside of his skin, then we should expect him to be able to show them. Otherwise, another relationship must be found.

The next time you are moved to say that some "situation or joke was funny," you might perhaps remember with Shakespeare that

> A jest's prosperity lies in the ear
> Of him that hears it, never in the tongue
> Of him that makes it.

[11] Larimore Foster, *Larry.* New York: Association Press, 1930, 13-14. Reprinted by permission of The John Day Company.

We conclude, then, with Korzybski:

If we use a language of adjectives and subject-predicate forms pertaining to "sense" impressions, we are using a language which deals with entities *inside our skin* and characteristics entirely non-existent in the outside world. Thus the events outside our skin are neither cold nor warm, green nor red, sweet nor bitter, but these characteristics are manufactured by our nervous system inside our skins, as responses only to different energy manifestations, physico-chemical processes, etc. When we use such terms, we are dealing with characteristics which are absent in the external world, and build up an anthropomorphic and delusional world non-similar in structure to the world around us.[12]

We thus discover that our use of the "is" of predication tends to lead us into false-to-fact utterances. The mechanism involved has been well explained by Zilboorg.

A small boy, three years of age, sits with his parents in the rear seat of an automobile, obviously enthusiastic about the sensations caused by the motion of the car. The countryside is hilly and the road follows the curves of the landscape. Each time the car begins to climb or descend, the boy exclaims, "A hill!" A sudden rather steep descent, and the passengers, the boy included, instinctively throw themselves backward to counteract the downward pull. "It is a strong hill!" exclaims the boy. Just as the biologist learned to see many a mystery of life in the microscopic dots and filaments observed in a single living cell, so does the psychologist see in this amusing exclamation of a tot of three many a mystery of the human mind. By what singular twist of primitive imagination did the boy arrive at the conclusion that the hill was "strong"? He obviously measured the *strength* of the hill by the effort he was forced to make to keep his body balanced in a vertical sitting position; he had to use strength and objectivized this strength by endowing the hill with the property which he himself possessed; he *projected* his strength *into* the hill. We call this mental mechanism *projection*.[13]

It is by the working of this mechanism of projection, of

[12] Alfred Korzybski, *Science and Sanity*, 384.
[13] Gregory Zilboorg, "The Heritage of Ignorance," *The Atlantic Monthly*, June, 1937, 734-735. Reprinted by permission.

which we are often unconscious, that we believe the "green" is in the leaf.

Translating This "IS"

"Isn't that a cute hat?"

"Oh, yes," says a friend, "it's darling."

Such sentences, our analysis shows, imply qualities in the object. Unwittingly the judgment of "cuteness" is projected into the hat. What can be done to make the speakers aware of such delusional evaluation? The characterizing process with respect to "cuteness" parallels that of color. Stimuli from the object and judgments formed by prior experiences affect various nerve centers, producing various impressions which are indicated by the word "cute." Thus, it might be said, that a hat, looked at by a girl, led to impressions quickly summarized by the adjective. In shortened form, the hat *appeared* "cute" *to* the girl. Put this way, the source of the impression is located inside and not outside of the nervous system.

Such an explanation suggests that sentences in which an adjective follows an "is" will be made correct-to-fact if "appears . . . to me, him, her, you, or them" is substituted for the "is." If the adjective precedes the noun without the "is"—for example, "the cute hat"—the translation should still be made for proper evaluation.

It should be urged, if we would avoid improper placing of impressions, that the "appears . . . to" translation be adopted as a thoroughgoing everyday habit. The delusional effects will be eliminated even if we become conscious that our nervous system manufactures the characteristics indicated by the adjectives inside-the-skin and not in the outside world. Little harm is done if we use the "is" in connection with adjectives so long as we are conscious of the projection mechanism.

Some Consequences of Unconscious Projection

One of the first consequences of the failure to locate "qualities inside" comes in connection with the making of judgments about "things." Observers who do not know that the adjective "is" represents projection tend to rigid and inflexible behavior on the assumption that the "qualities" are in the object, and obviously "what is seen is seen." If other observers are unable to see the "same" as I do, then they must *be* perverse, blind, or simply dumb. That is, if "beauty" or "ugliness" or "hardness" or "difficulty" (or any other "quality") exists in "things," and if they are apparent to me, why do others not see and appraise them my way? Of course, the argument is phrased more subtly, but the effect is similar. And invariably, investigation of some of the assumptions of the speaker reveals that he or she ends with, "Well, it *is* beautiful," quite unmindful that the inside impressions only are being described. Given an understanding of the interpretation process, it should be all too clear how another observer might well have other impressions, and why we should agree with Pascal that "orthodoxy on one side of the Pyrenees may be heresy on the other." The habit of reacting to the "is" form is, however, deeply ingrained, and it is not easily changed.

A student of home-making in a Brooklyn high school set fire to her parents' furniture because, as she said, "It is ugly." Such behavior can be analyzed as a manifestation of unconscious projection. Because she had interiorized certain patterns of response and interpretation, the sight of the furniture gave rise to "feelings" inside-her-skin. When they were projected out on to the objects, the resulting violence seemed a "logical" conseqeunce.

When the movie *Tobacco Road* opened in New York City, three newspaper critics came to quite different conclusions.

Cecelia Ager, *PM:* It's an intact, consistent job, delivered up out of steady craftsmanship. No part of it is overdone. The comedy wells out of the inevitability of these *Tobacco Road* people's reacting exactly thus and so. It ain't pretty, but it's real and warm.

Bosley Crowther, New York *Times*: As a matter of fact, it barely resembles a believable slice of life, and just comes under the wire as an amusing but pointless film. . . .

Kate Cameron, New York *Daily News*: . . . the picture re-solves into a broad comedy. . . .[14]

Notice that in each case the heart of the criticism appears in the untranslated adjective-noun phrases, "steady crafts-manship," "pointless film," "a broad comedy." If the adjectives imply the existence of some objective entities, it is not easy to explain the differences in estimates of the movie. But if the assortment of stimuli from the movie makes for a variety of impressions inside-the-skins of the observers, then the adjectives which reveal the "inner states" will not be the same. If the critics got together for discussion, sharp dis-agreements might result if each were to insist that the "steadiness," "pointlessness," and "broadness" are to be found in the film. The bases of the conflict might be clarified as soon as each realized that the movie "appeared so to him or her."

How does it happen that stimuli from objects and situa-tions produce different adjectively described impressions in different people? Many are the explanations for this phe-nomenon of varying evaluation: the climate, glands, diet, physical condition, class or economic bias, the books and teachers to which one is exposed, the religious creeds and doctrines one has learned, the political party to which one belongs, the sensitivity of his receptors, etc. It is not neces-sary that we have *the* answer. For practical purposes we can accept all the theories. The facts remain, however, that stimuli do have varying effects on different observers and that we are misled when we misplace the effects.

When Impressions Differ

Suppose an issue arises between observers who have de-scribed a situation with quite different adjectives. Mr. A insists that "George is most unpleasant," while Mr. B argues that "George is a very pleasant sort of person." Discussions in which there is such marked difference of opinion often end in stalemate, mere " 'tis-'tain't" squabbling and open

[14] Excerpt from *PM*, Feb. 21, 1941, 22, copyrighted by The News-paper PM, Inc., N. Y. Reprinted by special permission of the copy-right owners.

conflict. When this happens, verbal interchange between people leads to little constructive, with no settlement of the question, and with opinions often more deeply ingrained than when the discussion began. If talk would be enlightening, some way must be found to prevent *impasses* from developing and disagreements from becoming solidified. The problem is not acute when George appears as the issue, but if the larger questions of economics, politics, and religion are talked about in similar fashion, wrangling and bitterness become inevitable consequences. Group discussions degenerate into sessions marked more by heat than light. And when rancor and ill will develop from talk, the usefulness of human interchange is lost. It therefore seems imperative that we use whatever means are available as safeguards against verbally induced conflicts.

We should here urge the adoption of the following two-part plan whenever differing adjectives appear in the course of different interpretations.

First, we must become conscious that the projection of "pleasantness" and "unpleasantness" is coached by the use of the "is" form, which should be translated into "appears . . . to . . ."

Second, instead of reasserting that "George is pleasant" in different ways with mounting fervor, students may find it most helpful to move the talk from the level of judgment-making to more descriptive levels. That is, let the student who recognizes the predication problem ask his friend or antagonist questions such as these: What actions of George lead you to the judgment of "pleasantness"? What did you see him do which I also might see? What extensional facts that you observed provide the basis for your adjective?

Much evidence gathered from individuals who have used such tactics makes abundantly clear one fact: that agreement is more readily achieved on descriptive levels than on higher orders of abstraction. When conversation can be brought to terms of actions and performances, the opposition is often resolved right there. The particular life facts which appeared "pleasant" to Mr. B are very often not the life facts which appeared "unpleasant" to Mr. A. Even if a

particular situation is witnessed by both with differing judgments, the statements reduced to descriptive levels give
further opportunity for the analysis of the ways each of the
men looked. If the participants can discover the "ways of
looking" which gave rise to the varied judgments expressed
in different adjectives, that, too, represents an achievement.
And no matter what else comes about, the very effort of
talking descriptively, we have found, frequently produces
two other effects. In the first place, it brings about a delay
in the reactions and a noticeable lessening of tension. Secondly, we frequently discover that the describing of the
situation by both parties brings to each the beginning of
a consciousness of abstracting. When these have been
achieved, the continuation of talk becomes possible, and
on some occasions there also results genuine understanding
that each has been interpreting in terms of different creeds,
doctrines, and patterns of evaluation. When that happens,
men can agree to disagree without disagreeable consequences.

Many kinds of verbal quarreling are resolved whenever
it is possible to measure some aspects of the objects and
situations which produce the impressions inside of observers' nervous systems. Suppose Mr. A and Mr. B had been
speaking about George's "intelligence." If one of them says
that "George is intelligent," the other can readily shunt the
discussion into ways of measuring that characteristic. "If
George appears intelligent to you, can you show me the
basis for your assertion and just how intelligent he appears
to you?" Agreement becomes possible if the judgments
grow out of tests and measurements which both may see
and study. The moment the two are able to abide by *public*
ways of checking, a major sources of disagreement has
been eliminated. To say that "George is pleasant" moves us
to more *private* ways of looking, not so susceptible to common observation. And in so far as Mr. A's impressions of
"things" remain private, they may stem from details quite
different from those abstracted by Mr. B, despite the fact
that both assume that they have abstracted similar details.

In some respects our era may be characterized by our increasing ability to measure and check phenomena by instruments which make possible the desired common observation. Through standardized techniques it is now possible to make sharp and precise statements about wide areas which formerly appeared subject only to vague "impressionistic" description. We no longer need be satisfied with our impressions represented by the adjectives *long, heavy, far, drunken, cold, hard, bright, late, durable, strong, fast, tall, wide, deep, elastic, smooth,* etc. Meters, yardsticks, and instruments enable us to say "how much." In these areas differing interpretations can be subject to further analysis and possible agreement. We have merely to look at the objects and situations and make the measurements.

Unfortunately, our technicians have not yet learned how to apply the same methods in those areas in which disagreements have been and continue to be most vigorous. We have not yet—and the difficulty of maintaining peace in our world bears evidence—found ways which make us "look together" while we decide about the inner interpretations represented by *beautiful, just, important, good, wrong, responsible, necessary, wise, interesting, moral,* etc. When these terms appear in discussion, we have no recourse to measurement which we can readily agree upon. We must fall back upon the descriptive levels and life facts about which the terms are used. And in the last analysis we must come to see that the creeds we have been nurtured on, and the inner experiences which we have learned to talk about exist in each of us, and that when we project them on the world we are misevaluating.

Here and there individuals have laid down "standards" which they expect others to follow. But so far, these "ways of looking" have been the products of individual nervous systems and not "ways" derived from any "outside" discoverable and verifiable sources. In this book, too, can be found perspectives derived from efforts to see how talk can be made to fit life facts. Our looking at human speech and action has led to the conclusion that when talk fits what it is intended to represent, when we do not confuse the orders of abstraction, when we realize that "identity" is not to be found, and that impressions arise inside-our-skins, we shall be more likely to make evaluations that have adequate and accurate relationship to the world we talk about. Then something will happen to lessen the strain and stress and disorder in the relationships that depend on what we say to one another. The survival, not the destruction, of the time-binding class of life becomes a significant "way" for us. And to it the reconstruction of language habits must look.

Projection and Other Language Habits

Readers who understand the mechanism of projection will find it profitable to analyze some of the previously discussed language habits for evidences of its operation.

It has appeared (though not explicitly) in at least three chapters. A few hints might help your study.

1. Whenever we assume that someone else is using a word as we do, or as we have been accustomed to, we project our interpretations on to his.

2. Whenever we ascribe two or few values to the infinitely varied, unique individual objects, situations, feelings, etc., we project prior evaluations which are inside-our-skin, instead of going to the life facts and describing what can be found.

3. Whenever we leap to inferences and judgments without survey of the extensional facts, we project our creeds and ways of looking on to situations which may be evaluated otherwise.

4. Signal reactions, responding without indexing to people and happenings, belief in the "magic of words," in these, too, is the mechanism of projection to be observed. Can you find others?

In Short

Something cannot exist as something else. An object is not a word. An object may be classified in as many ways, by as many terms as an observer wishes in terms of his interests at a date. When any form of the verb *to be* is followed by a noun the translation "may be classified as" should serve to prevent the assumption of "allness"—that there exist no other modes of classification. Sense impressions arise as a joint phenomenon of an observer with something observed. "Qualities" do not exist in "things," though projected there by the implications of any form of the verb *to be* preceded or followed by an adjective. The translation "appears . . . to me" reveals the existence of relations and helps dissolve the conflicts which come from ignorance of the projection mechanism.

Basic questions: not, What "is" it? but, How may it be classified? How does it appear to you?

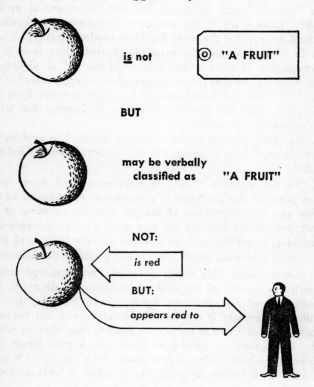

is not   ⊙ "A FRUIT"

BUT

may be verbally
classified as   "A FRUIT"

NOT:
is red

BUT:
appears red to

For Further Study

1. For more extended analysis, though quite different from ours, read these two essays on the "Is":
   1. I. A. Richards, *Interpretation in Teaching*. New York: Harcourt, Brace & Co., 1938, Ch. XVIII.
   2. George Santayana, *Obiter Scripta*, ed. by Justus Buchler and Benjamin Schwartz. New York: Charles Scribner's Sons, 1936, 189-212.

2. For further discussion of the nature of interests, see Kenneth Burke, *Permanence and Change*. (New York: The New Republic, 1935.) The mechanism of projection is analyzed by Bernard Hart in *The Psychology of Insanity*. (New York: The Macmillan Company, 1932.)

3. Take any word, say propaganda, which people have put after "what is" and, following the pattern suggested in this chapter, make a list of the actions and situations, or kinds of writings, etc., which the word has been used to classify.

4. In what way does the principle of abstracting lead to an understanding of what is involved when the "is" of identity is used? How do the two principles complement each other? What basic fact about the functioning of language emerges from the study of the two? Can you describe what an observer does when he *abstracts* and *classifies*?

5. Use your answers to the questions in No. 4 to explain the observations of John Burroughs in this paragraph from *Leaf and Tendril*:

> "To the scientist Nature is a storehouse of facts, laws, processes; to the artist she is a storehouse of pictures; to the poet she is a storehouse of images, fancies, a source of inspiration; to the moralist she is a storehouse of precepts and parables; to all she may be a source of knowledge and joy."

6. Put in your own words what is being said in the following:

> "Nevertheless, this world manifests for mankind distinguishable aspects of tremendous number and diversity. We perhaps need not champion Spinozism by insisting that 'an infinity of aspects' is a more suitable statement, but we must maintain that there is no known limit to the ways in which the world may be related to observers. A pine forest is a different body of preferred phenomena for a botanist, a hunter, a forester, a farmer, a geologist, an artist, a recluse, and a

lost child. Beyond question, the forest *is*—but *what* is it? Not only does it have differing aspects for botanists, A, B . . . *n*, for hunters A, B . . . *n*, and so on and on. Further, the forest may be viewed by men who combine several observer-capacities within themselves; there may be botanist-hunters, forester-farmers, recluse-artists, and the like, throughout a stupendous range of permutations and combinations. Running as a constant motif through these shifting patterns, moreover, is the persisting influence of the language in terms of which the observers take note of, arrange, and communicate their variously assorted 'facts.' Up to this point of our exposition, the tacit assumption has been made that they all speak the same tongue. When we introduce the additional factors of linguistic diversities—syntaxes, accidences, vocabularies, and all the paraphernalia familiar to the comparative philologist—we may begin to feel that Spinoza's 'infinity of aspects' comes discomfortingly close to the truth." (Howard Becker, "Supreme Values and the Sociologist," *American Sociological Review*, VI, 2 (April, 1941), 156-157. Reprinted by permission.)

7. "Primitive man, when conversing with his fellow-man, is not in the habit of discussing abstract ideas. His interests center around the occupations of his daily life; and where philosophic problems are touched upon, they appear either in relation to definite individuals or in the more or less anthropomorphic forms of religious beliefs. Discourses on qualities without connection with the object to which the qualities belong, or of activities or states disconnected from the idea or the subject being in a certain state, will hardly occur in primitive speech. Thus, the Indian will not speak of goodness as such, although he may very well speak of the goodness of a person. He will not speak of a state of bliss apart from the person who is in such a state. He will not refer to the power of seeing without designating an individual who has such power." (Franz Boas, "Introduction," *Handbook of American Indian Languages*, Bulletin 40, Part I, The Bureau of American Ethnology, Washington: Government Printing Office, 1910, 64-65.)

Describe the language habit of the Indian in terms of the "is" of predication. To what extent do you talk as he does? What are some consequences of such talking?

8. The phenomenon called *reification,* the assumption that some words stand for "things" or the response to words as if they necessarily represented observable life facts, may be profitably studied in connection with the "is" of identity. Reification is analyzed in the following:

1. Max Eastman, "A Significant Memory of Freud," *The New Republic,* May 19, 1941, 693-695.

2. Ellis Freeman, *Principles of General Psychology.* New York: Henry Holt & Co., 1939.

3. James W. Woodward, *Intellectual Realism and Culture Change, a Preliminary Study of Reification.* Hanover, N. H.: The Sociological Press, 1935.

9. What should be done about the use of the translations of the "is" in the writing of themes, stories, articles, speeches, etc.? Would not the use of "may be classified as" and "appears . . . to me" slow up and make the writing unwieldy? Is it enough if the writer remains conscious of the mechanisms?

10. For a demonstration of the existence of projection in political analysis, see Arnold Thompsen, "Psychological Projection and the Election: A Simple Class Experiment," *Journal of Psychology,* XI (Jan., 1941, First half), 115-118.

11. How would you account for the indignation of the writer of the following letter?

"The fellow who is continually trying to upset traditions and make history a liar is a bad gazabo, and we are against him. Some time ago a he-ape attempted to discredit George Washington and prove that George was a rounder. Think of what that meant—to shatter all the good things we had been taught about the father of our country. Then came some smart aleck and tried to make the world believe that Thomas Jefferson was a slick ear; that he lacked sincerity and really was just a cheap sort of politician.

"We might stand all that, but now we have before us an Eastern idiot who wants to tear down the memory of Betsy Ross. He says she did not make the American flag and had nothing to do with it. Kill him. He is not fit to live. Any man who will destroy the beautiful in thought and in tradition is worse than the man who burns down your house in the dead hour of night. To us Betsy Ross made the American flag; she designed it and she superintended the making of it, regardless of what any Eastern bohunk has to say regarding the matter." (*The American Mercury*, Sept., 1928, 31. Reprinted by permission.)

12. "What is the moon? If an infant were to ask me this question, I might tell him to go into the street, and on looking toward the sky, he would discover something that looks like a large round piece of silver. That is the moon. You may say that my designation will not enable the child to find the moon, and you may give him some better description. We probably shall not altercate, because we shall understand that our words are intended to merely point out to the child something that is different from the words. But suppose I were to ask a philosopher to tell me what the moon is; he might say that the moon is an opaque globe of land and water, like our earth. He is not attempting to designate an existence, as I did to the child; but he is defining the word moon. My words were not supposed to be the moon itself; but the philosopher's definition is the moon, verbally at least. You probably now understand what I mean by saying, that in all verbal discussions we should discriminate whether we are attempting to define a word, or to designate an existence. The discrimination is seldom made, and the want of it produces much contention and confusion." (A. B. Johnson, *Treatise on Language: or the Relation Which Words Bear to Things.* New York: Harper & Brothers, 1836, 156.)

Need anything more be said about the notion of identity aroused by the "is"?

CHAPTER XII

THE NECESSITY FOR APPLICATION

As the diagram is based on the denial of the "is" of identity, its use is practically indispensable; it has been made in relief and in printed forms, to be kept on the wall or the desk as a permanent visual structural and semantic reminder. Without actual handling, pointing the finger or waving the hand at it, seeing the order, and so on, it is practically impossible, or very difficult, to become trained, or to explain the present system to ourselves or others, because the foundation of all "knowing" is structural. . . .

One of the best ways for grown-up persons to train themselves in the present theory of sanity is to try to explain it to others, repeatedly pointing to the Structural Differential. In my experience, those who have disregarded this advice have always made very slow progress, and have never got the full semantic benefit of their efforts.

—ALFRED KORZYBSKI[1]

✕✕✕◇✕✕✕

Some "new" language habits have now been explained. How will you go about remembering and applying them?

[1] Alfred Korzybski, *Science and Sanity, and Introduction to Non-Aristotelian Systems and General Semantics*. Lancaster, Pa.: The Science Press Printing Co., 1933, 13. Reprinted by permission.

THE NECESSITY FOR APPLICATION

><><><><><><><><><><><><><><><><><><><><

Having analyzed some language habits which make for misevaluation, and having suggested methods for the achievement of a more extensional orientation, there remains an important problem which Korzybski has sharply emphasized.

Curiously enough, the principles involved are often childishly simple, often "generally known," to the point that on several occasions some older scientists felt "offended" that such "obvious" principles should be so emphasized. Yet my experience, without any exception, was that no matter how much these simple principles were approved of verbally, *in no case* were they *fully applied in practice*.[1]

How to motivate the application of these new language habits remains fundamentally a matter of personal realization that they do make our speech correct-to-fact, and that from that correctness tremendous benefits must result. When students come to understand the confusion, misinterpretation, and conflict, both personal and social, that have their origins in the failure to index, to date, to remember the ETC., to differentiate descriptions from inferences, etc., further urging by writers or teachers will be unnecessary. The first step in re-education, then, is clear—to establish the fact that identification plays a major role in human difficulties.

Frequently, however, students will agree with what has been said in these pages, insist that they have gained new insight into human affairs, and then proceed in the next few minutes to disregard in practice what they would in theory

[1] Alfred Korzybski, *Science and Sanity, an Introduction to Non-Aristotelian Systems and General Semantics*. Lancaster, Pa.: The Science Press Printing Co., 1933, 539. Reprinted by permission.

condemn immediately after. Lip service to the value of talking sense is unfortunately not necessarily accompanied by the more serious business of actually talking sense. Until the formulation of these simple and obvious principles and methods, there may have been some excuse (on the grounds of difficulty, philosophical complexity, etc.) for non-application of discrimination in our evaluations. But, given methods which five-year-olds have been able to apply, the excuse is now somewhat tenuous. In a larger context Norman Angell sees the failure to use existing knowledge as the tragedy of our times, and as a challenge to educationalists.

If the world has nearly destroyed itself, it is not from lack of knowledge in the sense that we lack the knowledge to cure cancer or release atomic energy (this last, incidentally, being a piece of knowledge which would probably finish off civilized mankind) but is due to the fact that the mass of men have not applied to public policy knowledge which they already possess, which is indeed of almost universal possession, deducible from the facts of everyday life.

If this is true—and it seems inescapable—then no education which consists mainly in the dissemination of "knowledge" can save us. If men can disregard in their policies the facts they already know, they can just as easily disregard new facts which they do not at present know. What is needed is the development in men of that particular type of skill which will enable them to make social use of knowledge already in their possession; enable them to apply simple, sometimes self-evident, truths to the guidance of their common life.[2]

Preliminary investigations in the teaching of language habits of accuracy and proper evaluation have repeatedly revealed what was at first a curious fact, that talking about the methods and devices was practically valueless. It was too easy for students to nod their heads, write essays, and pass examinations on the principles, while again and again manifesting confusion of the orders of abstracting in the very sentences in which they were writing about it. There

[2] Norman Angell, "Education and the Present Crisis," *News Bulletin of the Institute of International Education*, XVI, No. 5 (Feb. 1, 1941), 5. Reprinted by permission.

was, we discovered, an enormous difference between being able to talk about these notions and getting them deep down in the nervous system. If we stimulated only the ears of our students and became satisfied if they read words in articles, nothing much happened to affect their ways of reacting. They prattled glibly about extension but kept on in the old intensional patterns. Just as it is impossible to teach swimming or typewriting by verbal means alone, so we cannot expect to teach methods of evaluation which involve more than verbalizing without some techniques of participation.

Korzybski had come to the same conclusion by August, 1924, when he delivered a paper called *Time-Binding: The General Theory* before the International Mathematical Congress in Toronto, Canada. In this he attempted to present *visually* a diagrammatic structure by means of which he was able to explain many mechanisms of non-identity and significant discrimination. What can be shown is not what is said. Silent levels are not verbal levels. If we analyze only on verbal levels, the non-verbal levels escape attention, so that we go by words without concern for what they represent.

Furthermore, one usually remembers the rule *after* instead of during the talk, whereas we must remember the rule so as to forestall and prevent confusion. What students seemed to need was some reminder of the governing patterns of language-fact relationships which could be resorted to quickly, even during the course of discussion. There were, in short, three needs to be met: (1) a way of affecting deeper comprehension, of getting to channels in the nervous system other than the ear (i.e., the eyes, the senses of touch and pressure, etc.); (2) a way of showing, as well as talking about, the silent levels; and (3) a way of jogging the memory so that the principles are remembered whenever talk occurs.

These needs had been met for us by the construction of a relief diagram, with detachable parts, which could be seen, pointed to, and handled. Korzybski calls it the Structural Differential.[3]

(A) Event Level (Silent)

(1) The deeper process level, "a mad dance of electrons, something acted upon by everything else and reacting upon

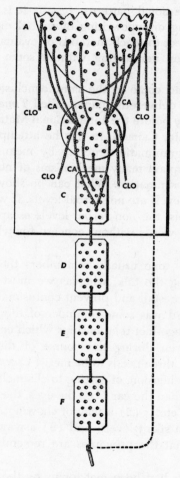

THE STRUCTURAL DIFFERENTIAL

[3] This adaptation of the Structural Differential is reproduced by the kind permission of Alfred Korzybski, the copyright owner.

everything else"; (2) a variable *different* all the time; (3) "something" which we do not recognize directly; (4) given as result of tested inferences by the Science of 1941; (5) the broken-off line indicates that the parabola could be extended to infinity; the holes represent characteristics, infinite in number.

(B) Objective Level (Silent)

(1) What a nervous system abstracts from the *event*, fairly permanent, which we recognize directly; (2) finite size, with large, yet definite number of characteristics, fewer than the event; (3) a first-order abstraction indicated by lines CA, characteristics left out indicated by lines CLO; (4) our life facts, extensional facts (including "feelings" inside-our-skin); (5) each "object" unique, a relative variable different for every observer, and in process (sometimes slow); (6) the level of ordinary sense impressions.

(C) Descriptive Level

(1) Labels and statements (second-order abstractions), which are used to represent the above first-order abstraction; (2) words standing for *some* characteristics of the object, the "meaning" of the term here being fixed by definition, any term being used in many ways subject only to explanation by example; (3) for predictability these statements must be similar in structure to the event and object levels.

(D) Inferential Level

(1) Labels and statements (third-order abstractions) which are used to represent the second-order verbal abstractions; (2) come from speaking about descriptive statements; (3) more general statements applying more widely than (C); (4) since more tentative and less probable they are to be tested by going back to lower-order abstractions; (5) inferences made by human nervous systems must not be projected out on to (A) and (B); inferential terms must not be objectified and made to stand for "things" (A and B) when they arise as statements about other statements.

(E) Inferential Level

Higher-order abstractions, statements about statements, etc.

(F) Inferential Level

Higher-order abstractions, statements about statements about statements, etc.

The explanatory comments should be sufficient to suggest that on the diagram we can organize the major principles covered in this book. In the relationship of the parts we can show the basic facts that have been unearthed in the effort to find functionally useful language habits. How this may be applied we can show by a series of summary statements.

1. The sense of process is encouraged by the broken line and infinity of details given at the event level.

2. The holes representing characteristics should remind the observer of the great quantities that can be found in the unspeakable levels.

3. The loose-hanging strings help to develop the memory of characteristics left out, the first step in emphasizing that we cannot say "all" about anything.

4. The absolute individuality of the silent objective level (object, person, situation, feeling, etc.) can be pointed to for purposes of indexing and also to emphasize how from it different observers can abstract different characteristics about which to verbalize.

5. The stratification and visualization of the levels helps to make clear that a map is not the territory, that two worlds are discoverable—the verbal and non-verbal—so that we can differentiate what too often we identify.

6. Revelation of the difference between the silent and the verbal renders quickly intelligible the denial of the "is" of identity, that whatever one says something *is*, it *is not*. We can point to the two levels, showing that "this *is not* this." By pointing or handling we can remain silent ourselves, thus reaching a level that cannot be reached by words alone. The diagram thus conveys what we cannot when we burst into speech.

7. On the diagram the process of abstracting in different orders is visualized. We can show the abstracting from the event to the object, the giving of labels, the making of descriptive statements and the making of statements about statements, bringing us to different levels. We can take any

statement and place it, thus illustrating the level of the statement.

8. By seeing the objective level as coming *before* and different from the descriptive level, we should learn to observe life facts which would free us from "preconceived ideas" founded on similarities, etc., thus making our orientation basically extensional. This process, when habituated, makes inevitable a delay in reaction with time for further looking and questioning, thus eliminating harmful, animalistic, signal responses.

9. Going by the levels, we can fairly easily check to find whether our talk represents discoverable life facts, life facts conjured up by our "imaginations," "impressions" inside-our-skins, or lower-order verbal abstractions, etc.

10. We can trace our *daily experiences* by the aid of the Structural Differential.

We find ourselves on at least five levels. The first represents the un-speakable event, or the scientific object, or the unseen physico-chemical processes on the submicroscopic levels which constitute stimuli registered by our nervous system as objects. The second consists of the external, objective, also un-speakable, levels on which we see with our eyes, etc. On this level, we could make a moving picture, including actions, etc. (Writing a book is also behaviour). The third level represents the equally un-speakable psychological "pictures" and evaluations. On the fourth level of abstractions we describe verbally our facts, that humans (a) eat, sleep, etc.; (b) cheat, murder, etc.; (c) moralize, philosophize, legislate, etc.; (d) scientize, mathematize, etc. Finally, in the present context, our inferences belong to the fourth level.

Unfortunately, we usually abstract facts (a), identify the levels, and form a conclusion "man is an animal," etc. From this *conclusion* we confuse the levels again and colour the description of the facts (b), (c), (d), etc.; jump again to higher levels and build conclusions from descriptions (a) and from *distorted*, coloured descriptions (b), (c), (d), and so obtain the prevailing doctrines in all fields. These again lead us, in the field of action, to the mess we all find ourselves in. In this dervish dance between the levels we entirely *disregarded un-coloured facts* (d).

The ideal observer would observe *all* forms of human be-haviour at a given date, *not leaving out facts* (d); then, without confusing his levels, and also without confusing descriptions with inferences, he would reach his higher order of abstractions properly, with very different resultant doctrines, which would produce entirely different semantic evaluation, and motivate equally different action.[4]

Many matters of "good sense" can be shown without much effort when once the student gets the "feel" of the diagram. One example may be sufficient. Thus, we may say glibly with William James that "whatever individual excep-tions might be cited, these are of the sort that prove the rule"; but translate "prove" by the word "test" and it should be obvious that a *new* fact or case forces us to modify the generalization so as to include it or else admit that the rule merely covers those cases not directly excepted. An excep-tion must, of course, show the generalization not "proved" but limited in character. Thus, given the following data, we can no longer preserve our old notion intact; the new facts are not to be waved aside and avoided, but to be studied and included in new and broader generalizations.

Colds and Acids—Contrary to popular belief, a person with a head cold or allergy of the nose should acidify rather than alkalinize. For this discovery the Casselberry award for the most outstanding and original American nose and throat research investigation of the past year was presented to Dr. Noah D. Fabricant, associate in otolaryngology at the University of Illinois College of Medicine in Chicago by the American Laryngological Association. Dr. Fabricant has shown that every type of nose drop should be slightly acid. Alkaline drops may prolong colds. It took Dr. Fabricant two years to make this discovery.[5]

[4] Alfred Korzybski, *Science and Sanity*, 447-448.
[5] In "Reported from the Field of Research," the New York *Times,* June 1, 1941, D5. Reprinted by permission.

We conclude, then, with Bridgman,

A general principle by definition is a correct description of *any* case; if I can find a single case in which it is not correct, then by definition it is not a general principle, and I have proved that the principle is not true.[6]

On the diagram these notions can be grasped by looking at a loose-hanging string on the objective level and carrying it to the descriptive level. The statement thus constructed is not the same as before, showing the influence of the added factor.

When you have been able to visualize the basic principles on the diagram, and after time for review and application, you should begin to "feel" the relationship between the principles. One correct-to-fact language habit will presuppose others. Examples of false-to-fact reactions will tend to have evidences of misevaluation which can be explained in a variety of ways. The systematic listing of the forms of structural dissimilarity leads to formulations which, though not necessarily overlapping, have common factors. These in turn fall into recognizable classifications. Having found them, Korzybski was able to summarize the principles into three premises which describe the elementary conditions governing the use of language for proper evaluation.

1. A statement is not the life facts which it represents.
2. Statements do not cover all the life facts.
3. Statements are self-reflexive; i.e., statements may be made about statements, which may be made about statements, etc., without end. A statement is not the same as the statement it is about.

What is the next step in the acquisition of these new language habits?

The methods of training are obvious. First of all the student ought to understand the general principles. Then he should keep the Structural Differential before his eyes; look at it; handle the labels and strings, and thus become thoroughly acquainted

[6] P. W. Bridgman, *The Nature of Physical Theory*. Princeton, N. J.: Princeton University Press, 1936, 39. Reprinted by permission.

with it; tentatively explain it to friends and so slowly acquire the habit of it, thus keeping the labels in his pocket, so to say. In this way the consciousness that we abstract, which is the main issue, will become a permanent acquisition. Whenever he hears an argument of any kind, or reads one in the papers, some political speech for example, he should try to apply the diagram, which means to trace the confusion of orders of abstractions and the underlying assumptions. Of the confusion of orders of abstractions two at present are the most important; first, the objectification of higher abstractions; second, the reading of inferences into descriptions. If this is done, the student will find abundant material, some of it astonishing enough for further inquiry. . . .

Literature, the speeches of politicians, lawyers, reformers, propagandists of every description, and family quarrels usually give the best examples of improper evaluation.[7]

Should the student expect to learn these habits quickly?

It might appear at first glance that all being said here is simple and easy. On the contrary it is not. In all my studies and experience I have never found anything more difficult. It involves the uprooting of old habits, taboos, philosophies and private doctrines, the worst being our primitive-made . . . language, all of which is deeply rooted in us, working unconsciously. Therefore rationalisation, lip-service to the "understanding" of it, will not do whatsoever. Patient and persistent *training* is the only way to acquire this *special sense*, the habit for sensing the mixing of orders of abstractions. This *sense* is difficult to acquire, as difficult perhaps as learning to spell correctly, but when acquired we can never miss the continuous jumping of levels of abstractions, and so utilise it *consciously* and become immune to its dangers. . . . It seems needless to repeat that all said here applies in the fullest extent to our social, political, economical and international problems. Before any sanity can be brought into these problems, before they can be rationally analysed at all, the very investigators would have to be trained first to avoid these verbal pitfalls, without which training and re-education older verbalistic debates on all sides are a waste of time and effort. I say "waste of time" simply because there

[7] Alfred Korzybski, *Time-Binding: The General Theory,* second paper. Washington, D. C.: Jas. C. Wood, 1926, 48-49.

is no end to the paradoxes which, with a little cleverness, we can build up when we begin to gamble with the jumping of levels. Any doctrine, no matter how true and beneficial, can be defeated, confused or delayed with the help of such methods. As a fact all of us do this continuously but at present the enormous majority are entirely innocent of this danger with the net result that usually we only sneer at each other. At present I have no doctrines to offer; what I offer and suggest is a method for the beginning of the revision of doctrines, which after years to come might lead to some feasible revisions.[8]

In Short

"One of the best ways for grown-up persons to train themselves in the present theory of sanity is to try to explain it to others, repeatedly pointing to the Structural Differential. In my experience, those who have disregarded this advice have always made very slow progress, and have never got the full semantic benefit of their efforts."[9]

For Further Study

In addition to the materials listed by titles on pages 9-11, for a more thorough comprehension of the scope of General Semantics, students ought to know as many as possible of these writings of Alfred Korzybski *before* going on to the various references suggested throughout the book. See especially the following:

1. Alfred Korzybski, *General Semantics,* Mimeographed stenographic report of lectures at Olivet College. Olivet, Michigan: Olivet College Bookstore, 1937.

2. —————, *General Semantics, Psychiatry, Psychotherapy, and Prevention.* Chicago, Illinois: Institute of General Semantics, 1940.

3. —————, "Neuro-Semantic and Neuro-Linguistic Mechanisms of Extensionalization. General Semantics as a Natural Experimental Science," *American Journal of Psychiatry,* XCIII (July, 1936), 29-38.

4. —————, "Outline of General Semantics," *General*

[8] *Ibid.,* 46-47.
[9] Alfred Korzybski, *Science and Sanity,* 13.

Semantics, compiled by Hansell Baugh. New York: Arrow Editions, 1938, 1-28.

5. ————, *Science and Sanity, an Introduction to Non-Aristotelian Systems and General Semantics.* Lancaster, Pa.: The Science Press Printing Co., 1933.

6. ————, "The Science of Man," *American Journal of Psychiatry,* XCIII (May, 1937), 1343-1351.

7. ————, *Time-binding: The General Theory,* first paper. New York: E. P. Dutton & Co., 1924.

8. ————, *Time-binding: The General Theory,* second paper. Washington, D. C.: Jas. C. Wood, 1926.

INDEX